HISTORY'S
BIGGEST
BLUNDERS

HISTORY'S BIGGEST BLUNDERS

AND THE PEOPLE WHO MADE THEM

Ian Whitelaw

METRO BOOKS
NEW YORK

METRO BOOKS
New York

An Imprint of Sterling Publishing
387 Park Avenue South
New York, NY 10016

Conceived, designed, and produced by
Quid Publishing
Level 4 Sheridan House
114 Western Road
Hove BN3 1DD
England

www.quidpublishing.com

Cover illustration: Matt Pagett

ISBN: 978-1-4351-3987-9

For information about custom editions, special sales, and premium and corporate purchases,
please contact Sterling Special Sales at 800-805-5489 or specialsales@sterlingpublishing.com.

Manufactured in Singapore

1 3 5 7 9 10 8 6 4 2

www.sterlingpublishing.com

I would like to dedicate this book to our two wonderful children, Amelia and Gabriel, who bring us so much pleasure.

CONTENTS

INTRODUCTION

Blunders, mistakes, bad decisions—we've all made them, but for most of us the consequences are slight and affect only ourselves and those close to us. Very few of us wield such power that our mistakes affect thousands of others, or are so well known that our blunders become world news. Some, however, are in that position. *History's Biggest Blunders* is, for the most part, about powerful and prominent individuals and the negative effects—intended or accidental—that their decisions and actions have had upon the world and/or themselves.

Define Negative

The pros and cons of a historical event depend very much upon your point of view—one man's victory is another's defeat (or death)—and there are very few major events that don't have a downside from someone's perspective. Sadly, there are far too many that have no upside whatsoever; acts of greed, stupidity, selfishness, and savagery that gain nothing for anyone and cause untold suffering to many. You will find plenty of those between the covers of this book. In other instances, a decision has been labeled as negative because it achieved the opposite of what was intended. Pope Leo X, for example, tried to silence Martin Luther to prevent the Roman Catholic Church from losing its religious monopoly over Western Europe. Santa Anna attacked the Alamo to maintain Mexican control over Texas. Japan bombed Pearl Harbor to keep the US out of the war. Causing environmental damage also counts as a negative, although, in the cases of the Deepwater Horizon blowout and the Fukushima nuclear power plant, one could argue that to find the bad decision one has to go further back than the failure to take the necessary safety precautions and look at the whole issue of risky energy sources. Bringing about one's own embarrassment or downfall, as in the cases of President Clinton and Anthony Weiner, is perhaps negative on a smaller scale, although Napoleon's Waterloo cost the lives of a great many soldiers, and President Nixon's behavior throughout the Watergate affair displayed utter contempt for democracy, the legal system, and the American people.

What's the Motivation?

It's often hard to give a clear-cut answer to what drives people to issue commands or take decisions or actions that are almost bound to result in disaster in one form or another, but as a form of shorthand we have identified one or more of the seven deadly sins and the cardinal virtues as the motivating force or forces in each case. Greed and pride come up a good deal, charity less so. That having been said, if we had to choose one word to describe the cause of most of the worst outcomes in this book, it would be "ideology," ways of thinking that convince people that their belief—be it religion, politics, nationalism, or ethnic fervor—is not just right but is so utterly right that it justifies imposing it on others even if that means killing them.

Who Are the Culprits?

If the measures of a blunder are the number of people affected and the severity of the impact, then clearly the more power a person has the bigger the blunders they can commit. What is evident from the events covered in this book, however, is that big mistakes require cooperation—and therefore shared motives—on a grand scale. Hitler could not have done that much harm without the support of millions. Stalin and Mao Zedong relied upon the participation of the secret police, the army, the Red Guard, even the average citizen, to shatter the lives of millions of their compatriots. In situations such as the conflict that accompanied the partition of India, or the genocides in Rwanda and Bosnia, the violence didn't even need any real leadership. On a less dramatic level, there are plenty of bad decisions that can't really be pinned on any individual. No one person deregulated the financial system in the US, allowed dozens of oil rigs to drill in deep water in the Gulf of Mexico, or said it was OK to place nuclear reactors on a tsunami-prone coast. Interest groups, corporations, governments, and whole societies make these kinds of blunders possible. To misquote a well-known phrase, for big mistakes to happen, it only requires sensible people to do nothing.

MOTIVATION

Anger

Charity

Envy

Faith

Gluttony

Greed

Hope

Lust

Pride

Sloth

HUMANKIND DOMESTICATES PLANTS AND ANIMALS

ca. 10000 BCE

Main Culprits: Our ancestors some 12,000 years ago

Damage Done: Laid the foundations for all the ills of civilized society

Why: It just seemed like a good idea at the time

In such condition [i.e. in the absence of civilization], there is no place for industry; because the fruit thereof is uncertain: and consequently no culture of the earth; no navigation, nor use of the commodities that may be imported by sea; no commodious building; no instruments of moving, and removing, such things as require much force; no knowledge of the face of the earth; no account of time; no arts; no letters; no society; and which is worst of all, continual fear, and danger of violent death; and the life of man, solitary, poor, nasty, brutish, and short.

**Thomas Hobbes, *The English Works*,
Vol. III (Leviathan), 1651**

Throughout this book we will be examining and explaining a wide range of blunders, mistakes, and bad decisions, and the effects they have had throughout the ages on individuals or groups of people—sometimes millions of people. Almost without exception, the perpetrators are people in positions of power—kings and queens, military leaders, politicians, captains of industry—who are looking to maintain or extend their authority over people, land, or resources. However, none of their bad decisions would have been possible had it not been for one mega-blunder a long, long time ago. Curiously, it is something that has, until recently, been hailed as one of the best decisions in human history.

If we go back more than 15,000 years and watch one of our ancestors, we see someone who feeds himself and his family primarily by gathering wild plants, fruits, and roots, and occasionally hunting down a wild animal. Of course the plants and animals are wild. There isn't anything else. If the family, or group of families that hang out together, needs shelter then temporary structures are put up, only to be abandoned when the group has used up the local food sources and moves on. Hunting and gathering is the way it's been for a very long time, and it works just fine.

SOWING THE SEEDS OF CIVILIZATION

Over the next 5,000 years, however, humankind's means of feeding itself undergoes a gradual, but fundamental and radical, change. We begin to catch and tend some of our food animals, such as sheep, goats, and pigs. They're scrawny and they're feisty, but if you just breed the fatter and less rambunctious ones then over hundreds of generations they get easier to manage and there's a lot more meat on those bones. And you don't have to go running through the hills with a spear every time you want dinner.

Something similar applies to the plants, especially cereals and pulses. Plant the seeds from the best ones and they just keep getting bigger and more productive. And it gets even better if you dig the earth over, throw the goat droppings on it, pull up the weeds, and add some water. The domestication of plants and animals, and the development of agriculture, look like a really good idea.

There are a host of consequences that flow from adopting an agricultural way of life. If you're going to plant things and help them grow, then it makes sense to stick around and harvest them, so the mobile lifestyle of the hunter-gatherer gave way to a more sedentary way of life. Shelters were built to last and settlements were created. Hunter-gatherers, who were always on the move, tended not to have (or keep) another child until the first one could walk, but if you're staying in one place you can raise more children at the same time, so the population began to grow more quickly. That was OK because the agricultural way of life produced more food. In fact, it produced enough to create a surplus, which meant that not everyone had to work. Society could now stratify, with some people telling other people what to do, organizing the food-growing operations, and even interceding with the incomprehensible power that can ruin the harvest in return for some of that surplus. Some even convinced the rest that they were the incomprehensible power and that all the harvest was theirs, to be shared only with those who did exactly what they were told.

© Drewcorser | Creative Commons

NEOLITHIC FARMING
The inhabitants of this Neolithic stone house, the Knap of Howar farmstead in the Scottish Orkney Islands, were raising cattle, sheep, and pigs, and growing wheat and barley, more than 5,000 years ago, but maybe they should have stuck to fishing.

Some settlements became really big, and built up a really big surplus, but then settlements that weren't doing so well, or that just wanted to do better, tried to steal it. Then the people gave their own tough guys food in return for defending the settlement, but they soon realized that an army could be used to take over other settlements and make those people grow the food and generally do what they were told. There are quite a few examples of that kind of thing throughout this book.

OK, so there are some downsides to civilization, but at least it's better than being a hunter-gatherer. Just look around the world. There are very few hunter-gatherers now, and they look as though they lead a fairly tough life. There's no doubt that we live longer, have a better diet, and have a great deal more leisure time, which is why we've been able to develop art and music and architecture and cities and science and . . . .

We need to be a bit careful about making comparisons between ourselves and modern hunter-gatherers. After all, since the rest of the world is made up of societies that depend on agriculture—and that have developed occupational specialization and armies and governing classes and urbanism—the hunter-gatherers have long since been pushed off the most fertile land. Back in the day they had the run of the whole planet, and finding dinner wasn't that hard. If local supplies ran short, they would simply move to a more fruitful area, whereas settled societies that suffer a drought, a flood, or a plague that kills the crops are more likely to starve. The diet of a hunter-gatherer is also much more varied and contains a wider spectrum of nutrients than that of an agriculturalist who lives on a narrow range of sugars and carbohydrates. Hunter-gatherers, living in small, widely dispersed and mobile groups are also much less prone to the infectious diseases that thrive in large communities. Recent paleoanthropological studies of teeth and bones from pre- and post-agricultural peoples indicate that hunter-gatherers were actually healthier, longer-lived, and taller than people in early agricultural societies. The leisure time argument doesn't hold water either. Studies of contemporary hunter-gatherers show they spend less than 20 hours a week finding all they need to survive, and that's a good deal less than the average working week in the civilized world.

THE FURROW'S CURSE
This 3,000-year-old Egyptian painting shows the land being plowed. The civilization of Ancient Egypt was based on the production of food in the fertile flood plains of the Nile.

The 17th-century philosopher Thomas Hobbes believed that the natural condition of humankind is to be at war, and that only the "civil state" can prevent this. The evidence suggests that pre-agricultural people had less to fight about, and a cursory examination of the last two millennia shows that "civilized" people find plenty of reasons to go to war. Perhaps trapping that goat and planting those grass seeds wasn't such a great decision after all.

MOTIVATION

Anger

Charity

Envy

Faith

Gluttony

Greed

Hope

Lust

Pride

Sloth

FAILING TO LET GOD'S PEOPLE GO

ca. 700 BCE

Main Culprit: The Egyptian pharaoh

Damage Done: The land of Egypt and its people suffered terrible plagues and misfortunes, and many died

Why: The pharaoh just wouldn't accept that the God of the Israelites was the true God, and he wouldn't free the Israelites from slavery and let them leave Egypt

*And the Lord spake unto Moses, Go unto Pharaoh,
and say unto him, Thus saith the Lord, Let my people go,
that they may serve me.*

Exodus 8:1, *King James Bible*

Some time in the first millennium BCE, the Egyptian pharaoh at the time was given the option of doing the right thing again and again, and every time he chose not to. As a result, ever greater suffering was heaped upon him, his people, and his country, but still he persisted. According to the scriptures, God Himself was leading the pharaoh to make these bad decisions, but is that a good enough excuse?

The story began when famine forced Jacob, his twelve sons, and their families to leave the land of Canaan (modern-day Israel, the Palestinian Territories, and parts of Jordan and Lebanon) and travel west to Egypt, where they were welcomed by the pharaoh and settled in the fertile province of Goshen. (Jacob, the grandson of Abraham, was renamed Israel by an angel, and his descendants are known as the Israelites, each of his sons founding one of the 12 tribes of Israel.) In Egypt their number grew over the generations, and the Egyptians, worried that the Israelites might take power, enslaved them, and gave them a very hard time. The Israelites had taskmasters placed over them and were forced to make bricks and build cities and work in the fields, but still their numbers increased. Eventually the pharaoh insisted that all male Israelite children must be thrown in the river as soon as they were born, but one woman couldn't bear to kill her baby son and so hid him in the reeds beside the river. He was found by the pharaoh's daughter, who named him Moses, and he was raised as her son. When he reached adulthood, he saw an Egyptian beating a Hebrew worker and, believing no one was watching, he killed the Egyptian, but the pharaoh got to hear about it and Moses had to flee for his life. He went to live in Midian, where he married and had children.

THE FINDING OF MOSES
Sir Lawrence Alma-Tadema's painting depicts the pharaoh's daughter returning from the Nile with the child that would one day lead the Jewish people out of Egypt.

Meanwhile, conditions for the Israelites had become even worse, and God, remembering the agreement he had made with Abraham to give him and his descendants the land of Canaan forever, visited Moses and told him to go to the pharaoh and lead the children of Israel out of Egypt. Moses doubted whether the Israelites would believe that he had been visited by God, or that the pharaoh would let the Israelites go, but God assured him that Aaron, the elder brother of Moses, would be his spokesman and showed him that he would be able to turn his staff into a snake, demonstrating that God was with him. However, He agreed that the pharaoh would take a lot of convincing because God would harden his heart against the Israelites. Well, the Israelites did indeed believe Aaron and Moses, but when they asked the pharaoh to let the Hebrew people go, just for a few days to sacrifice to their God in the desert, the pharaoh not only refused but increased the amount of work that the Israelites had to do. Acting on God's instructions, Moses and Aaron returned to the pharaoh, threw the staff on the ground, and it turned into a snake. When the pharaoh's magicians did the same thing with their staffs, Aaron's staff/serpent ate those of the magicians, but the pharaoh still refused.

According to the book of Exodus, through Moses and Aaron, God then heaped ever greater ills upon the Egyptians. To begin with, Moses waved his staff over the water in Egypt and turned it all to blood—rivers, streams, ponds, lakes, even the water in pots and barrels. The fish in the lakes and rivers died, everything stank, and there was no water to drink in the whole kingdom. This lasted for seven days, but the pharaoh didn't give in.

Then Moses warned him that unless he released the Israelites then God would send such a plague of frogs that they would be in every field, and every home, and every room. He still refused and, sure enough, there were so many frogs and their noise was so maddening that the pharaoh had to give in, saying that the Israelites could go. The following morning the plague was over, but the pharaoh's heart hardened, just as God had said it would, and he went back on his word.

Next came a plague of lice that infested all the people and all the animals. Even the pharaoh's magicians had to admit that the hand of God was behind this, but the pharaoh remained obdurate. On God's instructions, Moses and Aaron warned the pharaoh that a plague of flies would be next, but that it would not affect the Israelites—and that's exactly what happened. There were swarms of flies everywhere throughout Egypt, even in the pharaoh's palace, but the province of Goshen remained free of them. The pharaoh called for Moses and Aaron and told them to take their people into the desert and to carry out their sacrifices, but to ask their God to get rid of the flies. Once again, no sooner was

ACTING ON GOD'S INSTRUCTIONS, MOSES AND AARON RETURNED TO THE PHARAOH, THREW THE STAFF ON THE GROUND, AND IT TURNED INTO A SNAKE.

the plague over than the pharaoh changed his mind and forbade the Israelites to leave. God then sent a terrible illness that infected all the animals that belonged to the Egyptians—cattle, horses, asses, camels, oxen, everything—but the animals belonging to the children of Israel were unaffected. Still the pharaoh wouldn't give in.

Doing as God instructed, Moses then took a handful of ashes and threw it into the air, and all the people and all the animals in Egypt were afflicted with terrible boils. The boils were so bad that the pharaoh's magicians couldn't even stand to face Moses, they were in such pain. Nonetheless, the pharaoh remained steadfast in his refusal to let the children of Israel depart.

God then told Moses to warn the pharaoh and the people of Egypt that there was going to be a hailstorm of unprecedented ferocity, and that any person or animal left outside would be killed by the hailstones. Those Egyptians who had understood that all these terrible ills really were being brought upon them by the God of the Israelites brought their animals in and hid indoors. Moses stretched his hand toward the sky and the granddaddy of all hailstorms was unleashed, killing animals, smashing down every plant in the fields, and breaking the trees to pieces throughout Egypt—except in the province of Goshen. This time the pharaoh was genuinely frightened, and he called Moses and Aaron to him and told them that he believed their God was the true God and he would let them go. Moses doubted whether the pharaoh really did believe, but he raised his hands again and the storm abated. And, sure enough, the pharaoh's heart hardened once again and he went back on his word.

STORM WARNING

God explained to Moses that He was deliberately hardening the heart of the pharaoh so that He could show him all these signs, and so that future generations would remember how powerful God is. Moses and Aaron asked the pharaoh, once again, to let the children of Israel leave Egypt, and the pharaoh asked who they intended to take with them, to which Moses replied that they would all go, men, women, children, and all the flocks. The pharaoh said that only the men could leave, which wasn't good enough for Moses and Aaron, so God sent a plague of locusts. The wind blew from the east and brought such clouds of locusts that no green plant was left in the whole of Egypt. At this, the pharaoh capitulated, saying that he had sinned against God and would let the Israelites leave, so God sent a westerly wind and the locusts were blown away into the Red Sea. And yet again God hardened the pharaoh's heart and the Israelites were not allowed to leave.

Now God told Moses to stretch out his hand and bring darkness to the land of Egypt, and for three days it was pitch black. Finally the pharaoh said they could go, but they had to leave their flocks behind. That was unacceptable, so God told Moses that he would send one last plague upon Egypt—He would kill all the firstborn children in the whole country. So that the Israelites would be spared, every family must sacrifice a lamb and daub its blood on the lintel and doorposts of the house so that when God came to kill the firstborn he would see this sign and pass over the houses of the Israelites. This is the origin of the Passover, or Pesach.

DEATH OF THE FIRSTBORN

"And all the firstborn in the land of Egypt shall die, from the firstborn of Pharaoh that sitteth upon his throne, even unto the firstborn of the maidservant that is behind the mill. . . ."

Moses warned the pharaoh what would happen unless he freed the Israelites, but he wouldn't listen, and at midnight on the appointed day the firstborn in every Egyptian household, from the pharaoh's to the lowliest servant's, was killed. And now the pharaoh did free the children of Israel from slavery and let them leave, and the Egyptians gave them silver and gold and jewels and fine clothes to take with them.

The pharaoh's bad decisions had brought the kingdom to its knees, depleted of crops, trees, livestock, water, and even the firstborn of every family. You would think that by now he would have been convinced of the wisdom of letting the Israelites go but, no, he had one more really bad decision to make. Even now he regretted allowing the Hebrews to leave, so he decided to follow them with his army, finally catching up with them on the shores of the Red Sea. God instructed Moses to hold up his rod and stretch out his hand over the water. The sea parted so that the Israelites could walk across on dry ground with a wall of water on either side. The Egyptian army followed but Moses raised his hand again and the waters returned, drowning every single Egyptian.

PERSIA INVADES GREECE

490–449 BCE

MOTIVATION

Anger

Charity

Envy

Faith

Gluttony

Greed

Hope

Lust

Pride

Sloth

Main Culprits: The Persian Emperor Darius I and his son Xerxes

Damage Done: Tens of thousands of Persian soldiers died and the Persian fleet was destroyed

Why: The only thing better than a large empire is a huge empire

Now when tidings of the battle that had been fought at Marathon reached the ears of King Darius, the son of Hystaspes, his anger against the Athenians ... waxed still fiercer, and he became more than ever eager to lead an army against Greece. Instantly he sent off messengers to make proclamation through the several states that fresh levies were to be raised, and these at an increased rate; while ships, horses, provisions, and transports were likewise to be furnished.

Herodotus, writing in 440 BCE (translated by George Rawlinson)

The first Persian invasion of Greece took place in 492 BCE, but its seeds were sown ten years earlier by the Ionian Revolt. The Persian Empire at the time was vast, extending from India in the east to the Bosphorus and Egypt in the west. This included Ionia, in what is now southwest Turkey, where the Greeks had established several city states that had fallen under Persian control. When, in 499 BCE, these rebelled against the harshness of the rules imposed by the Persians, Athens and Eretria (a city on the island of Euboea, close to the Greek mainland) sent military aid. By 493 BCE, the forces of the Persian Emperor Darius I had quelled the Ionian Revolt and regained control, but the rebellion prompted him to extend his dominion throughout the islands of the eastern Aegean and to set his sights on mainland Greece, where he intended to punish Athens and Eritrea for helping the Ionians.

NUMERICAL ADVANTAGE

Taking mainland Greece looked like a straightforward proposition for the greatest empire there had even been—the Persian army and its fleet of ships could easily outnumber those of the Greeks—and, under the leadership of Mardonius, the Persians quickly took the northern regions of Thrace and Macedonia. The fleet was then caught in a fierce storm and some 20,000 soldiers lost their lives at sea. Mardonius was replaced by the generals Datis and Artaphernes, and in 490 BCE they led a naval task force across the Aegean, taking several islands on their way, to the island of Euboea and the city of Eretria, which they looted and burned.

From there it was a short crossing to the Greek mainland, and the Persians chose a bay close to the town of Marathon, some 25 miles northeast of Athens, as their landing site. At least 25,000 Persian soldiers and 1,000 cavalrymen were sent ashore, and many more may have remained on the ships. Athens mustered an army of men from the ten Athenian tribes as well as soldiers from the city state of Plataea. The army, composed of some 10,000 hoplites (armored infantrymen bearing swords, spears, and shields) marched to the plain of Marathon and prevented the Persians from moving inland. The two armies faced each other in a stalemate for several days, during which time the Greeks' fastest runner, a man by the name of Pheidippides, was sent to Sparta, southwest of Athens, requesting the Spartans to send military aid to defend Athens, which was now undefended (the marathon race takes its name from this event). The Spartans, however, replied that they would be unable to help for at least ten days as they were celebrating a festival during which peace was sacred.

On the fifth day the Greek army attacked the superior Persian forces, either because they had received news that the cavalry had returned to the ships to launch a direct attack on Athens or because there were signs that the Persian army was about to attack. The Battle of Marathon should have been a walkover for the Persians, who outnumbered the Athenians by at least 2:1, but the Greek army shocked the Persians by forming themselves into phalanxes—rectangular formations of men that each moved as a unit—across a battle line as wide as that of their enemy, rushing forward and then, with their shields at the fore, pushing steadily into the opposition. The more heavily armored Greeks overcame the Persian flanks and then enclosed the center, inflicting terrible damage with their swords and spears and finally forcing the Persians to flee to their ships. The Persians then sailed south to round the peninsula and attack Athens directly, but the Greek army was able to get there before them and prevent a landing. The Persians gave up the attempt and sailed for home.

BATTLE OF MARATHON
The defeat of the Persians by the much smaller Athenian army proved to be a turning point in Greek history.

The Athenian victory has been seen as a turning point in European history and the beginning of the rise of Classical Greece. Up until this point, subjugation by the Persians had looked more or less inevitable, but now, through cooperation between the tribes, the Greeks had shown the Persians—and themselves—that they could resist. Even the Spartans, to whom war was a way of life, were impressed when they arrived a few days later and inspected the battlefield at Marathon. History recounts that more than 6,000 Persians lay dead, while the Greeks had lost less than 200 men.

Darius I was, unsurprisingly, unwilling to let the matter drop there. He began planning for another campaign against the Greeks and raised a new and gigantic army for the purpose, but he died in 486 BCE while preparing to put down a rebellion in Egypt. That task was completed by Darius's son Xerxes, who then led the second Persian invasion of Greece beginning in 480 BCE. Versions of the size of the invasion force vary widely, but 250,000 troops, 1,200 triremes (warships more than 100 feet (30 m) long and with three banks of oars on each side), and 3,000 supply ships are plausible figures. This time the Persians were taking no chances.

PREPARATION FOR WAR

In preparation for the inevitable return of the Persians, Athens and Sparta had been building their own fleet of triremes but could not compete when it came to manpower. They did, however, canvass support from other city states and were able to form a coalition of allies, some of whom had previously been at war with each other but were now willing to cooperate in the face of a greater enemy.

By the summer of 480 BCE the Persian army had crossed the Hellespont between Asia and Europe and was marching southward through the Greek mainland. The Greeks sent a force of 7,000 men under the leadership of the Spartan king Leonidas to block their path at the pass of Thermopylae, between the mountains and the sea. They were able to hold Xerxes and his army back for several days, despite two attempts to break through during which they inflicted heavy losses on the invaders, but the Persians were then made aware of a path through the mountains and sent infantrymen to outflank the Greeks. Leonidas had been aware of the path and had positioned guards there. When they informed Leonidas of what was happening he instructed the majority of his troops to depart while he and 1,500 soldiers fought what was to become a famous last stand, and one that gave rise to the legendary bravery of the Spartans. Every last Greek in this rearguard was killed, and the Persians continued their advance, but it is thought that they paid with the lives of some 20,000 men at Thermopylae. More importantly, Thermopylae stood as an example of free men choosing to defend their country against what was, in effect, an army of slaves.

LEONIDAS'S LAST STAND
The bravery of Leonidas and his men at Thermopylae, delaying the advance of the Persians and paying with their lives, has gone down in history.

During the Battle of Thermopylae, the Greeks had also used their naval force to prevent the Persians from making their way south by sea. In the confrontation, both fleets suffered serious losses, and once news of the fall of Thermopylae reached the Greeks they sailed for the island of Salamis to the west of Athens. As the Persians approached Athens, the citizenry were largely evacuated to the island, and the city was soon taken and burned. The Persians were now in control of the whole of mainland Greece, but still the Greeks resisted, their fleet remaining just off the coast in the hope of engaging the Persian ships. The Persians finally did attack, but their large numbers proved to be their undoing in the narrow waters between the island and the coast, where the great triremes had difficulty maneuvering. The Greeks won a decisive victory and effectively put an end to Persian naval superiority.

The following year, the Persian general Mardonius offered peace terms to the Athenians, hoping to break up the coalition of city states, which was already showing signs of instability. Athens refused them, but demanded support from Sparta for a march northward to attack the Persians, only to find that the Spartans were already on their way. When Mardonius learned of this, he and his troops retreated northward. The Greek and Persian forces met near to Plataea and once again the outnumbered hoplites achieved a remarkable—and, this time, final—victory over the Persian troops. At sea, possibly buoyed up by news of the Persian defeat, the Athenian and allied navies combined to attack the Persian fleet that had now been drawn up on the beach on the island of Samos and was being guarded by some 60,000 soldiers. The Greeks sent troops ashore, overcame the much larger Persian force, and torched the beached fleet, putting an end to the second—and last—Persian invasion of Greece.

Over the next few years an even stronger alliance of Greek city states, under the leadership of Athens, succeeded in pushing the Persians back to the north and the east until, by 449 BCE, they had retreated from Macedonia, Thrace, and the islands of Ionia and the Aegean. It would soon be the turn of the Greek civilization to overrun the Persian Empire.

THE PERSIANS FINALLY DID ATTACK, BUT THEIR LARGE NUMBERS PROVED TO BE THEIR UNDOING IN THE NARROW WATERS BETWEEN THE ISLAND AND THE COAST.

MOTIVATION

Anger

Charity

Envy

Faith

Gluttony

Greed

Hope

Lust

Pride

Sloth

ALEXANDER THE GREAT PUSHES TOO FAR

334–323 BCE

Main Culprit: Alexander the Great

Damage Done: Pushed his army to the point of mutiny, and many thousands died on the journey home

Why: The only thing better than ruling a huge empire is ruling the whole world

Alexander was born . . . the same day that the temple of Diana at Ephesus was burnt; which Hegesias of Magnesia makes the occasion of a conceit, frigid enough to have stopped the conflagration. The temple, he says, took fire and was burnt while its mistress was absent, assisting at the birth of Alexander. And all the Eastern soothsayers who happened to be then at Ephesus, looking upon the ruin of this temple to be the forerunner of some other calamity, ran about the town, beating their faces, and crying that this day had brought forth something that would prove fatal and destructive to all Asia.

Plutarch, writing in 75 CE (translated by John Dryden)

Athens emerged from the Greco-Persian Wars as top dog, but over the next 100 years power on the Greek mainland passed from Athens to Sparta, then to Thebes, and ultimately to Macedonia in the north. The Macedonian king, Philip II, had ascended to the throne in 359 BCE at the age of 21 and had quickly unified Macedonia, taking back territory that had been lost to neighboring tribes using a new and highly efficient army organization. Having seen the Greek army in action as a teenager, he introduced two innovations. Improving on the Greek concept of the phalanx, he armed the soldiers with exceptionally long spears, up to 20 feet (6 m) in length, which meant they could impale their enemies long before they themselves could be reached by enemy weapons, and secondly, he turned the army into a full-time, well-paid, professional organization that was always training and always ready.

Over the next 20 years, through a combination of military force and diplomacy, he extended Macedonian control to the east and west and then southward through Greece, culminating in the Battle of Chaeronea in 338 BCE, which put an end to Greek independence. Indeed, after the battle, thousands of Greeks fled for the Ionian shores of the Mediterranean, preferring to place themselves under Persian rule rather than that of the Macedonians.

Philip now began preparations to extend his conquests into the Persian Empire. In the spring of 336 BCE he sent an advance force of some 10,000 Macedonian soldiers into Asia Minor, but before he could join them he was assassinated while attending his daughter's wedding celebrations.

This, then, was the situation that his son, Alexander III, inherited as Philip's successor—an extensive and diverse empire of his own, a large and highly efficient army, and the preliminaries for an invasion of the world's largest empire already in place. Alexander "the Great" soon proved himself to be more than equal to the task. He had certainly been well prepared. As a child he had watched his father achieve military victory after victory. As a young teenager he had been tutored by the great Aristotle, and Alexander was well versed in literature, rhetoric, science, and philosophy. At the age of 16 he was considered so capable

© Andrew Dunn | Creative Commons

ALEXANDER THE GREAT
As a young man, Alexander displayed remarkable skill and courage, and throughout his life he had a driving ambition to rule the world.

that his father left him in charge of Macedonia while he invaded Thrace, and in his absence the young Alexander assembled and led an army to quell a rebellion that threatened his country's border. Two years later he was at the Battle of Chaeronea, where he displayed remarkable bravery and tactical wisdom.

RUTHLESS STREAK

In fact, Alexander had to put the invasion of the Persian Empire on hold for two years, as news of Philip's death had sparked revolts in many parts of his own territory. Moving his army with remarkable speed to all points of the compass, these revolts were put down quickly and mercilessly. In the storming of the rebellious Greek city of Thebes, for example, some 6,000 men, women, and children were slaughtered, and 30,000 more were sold into slavery. The city was then looted and demolished.

In the spring of 334 BCE, leaving a force of more than 10,000 soldiers under the leadership of Antipater (one of his father's top two generals) to maintain control in the territories surrounding Macedonia, Alexander

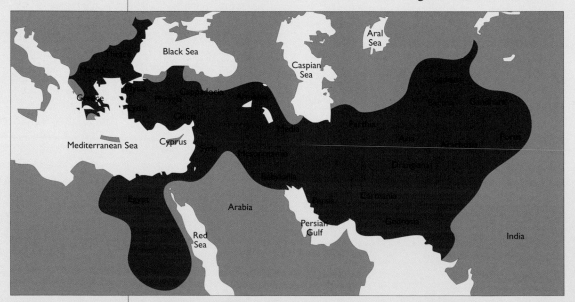

EMPIRE
At its peak, the Macedonian empire of Alexander the Great covered an area from the Balkan Peninsula, through Mesopotamia, to the Indian subcontinent.

crossed the Hellespont into Asia with at least 50,000 soldiers, as many as one sixth of whom were Greeks. The other great general, Parmenion, was his second in command. The fact that Greeks occupied many key positions, that Greek was the common language used throughout the campaign, and that the army brought a "Hellenizing" influence to bear throughout the growing empire has led to it being referred to as the Greek army, despite the fact that in many instances it was pitched against Greeks fighting for the Persians.

In the first of many battle victories, Alexander's army (which remained unvanquished throughout the whole of its ten-year campaign) met the Persians at Granicus and received the surrender of the Persian governorship of what is now northwest Turkey. They then headed south down the eastern Mediterranean coast and met the army of Darius III in the Battle of Issus, which took place close to the modern Turkish city of Iskenderun (originally Alexandria ad Issum). Despite being outnumbered by more than 2:1, and being taken by surprise, Alexander's army got the better of the Persians and King Darius fled, leaving both his army (which was butchered) and his family (whom Alexander spared). This decisive routing, the first time that their army had been vanquished with their king at its head, was a shock to the Persians, and Darius sued for peace, offering some of the Persian territory as well as a large sum of money as a ransom for his mother, wife, and two daughters. Alexander refused the offer, saying that he would take the whole of the Persian Empire and would not have terms dictated to him.

Over the next nine years he proceeded to do precisely that. Continuing down through Syria, Alexander took city after city. When Tyre held out, it was besieged until it surrendered, and then the men were slain and the women and children taken as slaves. In 332 BCE Alexander entered Egypt, where he was welcomed as a liberator and hailed as the son of Ammon Ra, the Egyptian sun god and counterpart to the Greek god Zeus. From this point on Alexander appears to have become increasingly convinced that he was indeed divine, a delusion that was later to sour his relations with the army.

Having captured Egypt (where he founded the city of Alexandria), Alexander was now in control of all the coastal cities and ports in the eastern Mediterranean, denying the Persians (and their Greek subjects) any means of launching a campaign of liberation against the Macedonians occupying mainland Greece.

DESPITE BEING OUTNUMBERED BY MORE THAN 2:1, AND BEING TAKEN BY SURPRISE, ALEXANDER'S ARMY GOT THE BETTER OF THE PERSIANS AND KING DARIUS FLED.

ALEXANDER GOES PERSIAN

His route now took him through Mesopotamia, where he vanquished Darius's army yet again in the Battle of Gaugamela, and once again Darius fled. Alexander then took Babylon, followed by Susa, an important center in the Persian Empire, and then Persepolis, the ceremonial capital of Persia. Darius was taken captive by one of his own provincial governors, a man called Bessus, who had Darius killed and then proclaimed himself Dariuxzs successor. Alexander pursued Bessus throughout Afghanistan and Tajikistan until the usurper was finally executed. The Persian Empire was now, to all intents and purposes, Alexander's. He adopted the title "King of Kings," and began to wear Persian clothing and adopt Persian customs in his court. As part of this he insisted that his subjects prostrate themselves before him in the manner of the Persians, but the Greeks and Macedonians, for whom such obeisance was only granted to the gods, balked at this. Alexander was forced to back down, but his actions, which suggested he did indeed think he was a god, attracted some animosity. This was intensified when he got wind of a plot against him and discovered that the son of his general, Parmenion, had known and not informed him. Not only did he have the young officer executed, but the father too, a man who had been his faithful ally and a brilliant commander throughout the campaign. Alexander also earned the contempt of many when, hurling a javelin in a fit of drunken anger, he killed a young officer who had saved his life at the Battle of Granicus but who was now criticizing him.

After further campaigns in what are now Afghanistan and Pakistan, and several bloody and brutal battles that established his control, Alexander reached the Indus River. He had now conquered the whole of the Persian Empire, and was the ruler of more than 2 million square miles (5.2 million km^2) of Europe and Asia, but it wasn't enough. The son of Zeus wanted to expand the empire yet further and fulfill his aim of becoming the ruler of the world, and so he led his army across the Indus and on to the Hydaspes, where, in the summer of 326 BCE, they crossed the river and defeated the forces of the Indian ruler Porus. Continuing eastward they reached the Beas River, which ultimately flows into the Indus, and here the army mutinied. They had been away from home for eight years, they had heard tales of the mighty enemies they might meet if they were to go further, and they had had enough.

Unwillingly Alexander conceded. After building a huge fleet of ships, the army sailed downstream to the confluence with the Indus and then further south. The fleet halted some 200 miles (320 km) from the Indian Ocean and Alexander sent part of the army northwest to return overland. A hundred miles later he and some 80,000 soldiers disembarked while the remaining 2,000 continued their journey by river and sea. Alexander's plan was to march west through the Gedrosian desert in what is now southwestern Pakistan. It was now August, the height of summer; there was very little water available en route; there were many women and children with the troops; transport was limited and unsuitable for the harsh, rocky, and barren terrain. It was a really bad plan. By the time the army reached Susa the following spring, thousands of men, women, and children, not to mention horses and donkeys, were dead in the desert sand. Ironically, a large number of women and children had died when their camp, next to a stream bed, had been washed away by a flash flood fed by rain in the distant mountains.

At Susa, Alexander hosted great celebrations before continuing on to Babylon, where he began planning an invasion of the Arabian Peninsula, to the south, but it was not to be. In the second week of June 323 BCE Alexander died of a severe fever. The cause of his illness is not known, but he had been unwell since drinking wine some two weeks earlier, and there was speculation that he had been poisoned, possibly at the instigation of Antipater, who had been called to Babylon and may have feared meeting the same end as his fellow general, Parmenion.

After his death, Alexander's generals divided up his empire, but the spread of Greek language, learning, and culture throughout the Near Eastern and Western worlds continued, and the death of Alexander ushered in the dawn of the "Hellenistic period," which lasted until the rise of the Roman Empire.

THE BATTLE OF HYDASPES
Alexander's army defeated the forces of King Porus at the Hydaspes, despite the Indian ruler's war elephants, but his men refused to go further and meet even greater armies.

MOTIVATION

Anger

Charity

Envy

Faith

Gluttony

Greed

Hope

Lust

Pride

Sloth

PYRRHUS OF EPIRUS ACHIEVES COSTLY VICTORIES

280 and 279 BCE

Main Culprit: Pyrrhus of Epirus

Damage Done: He achieved his aims and beat the Romans, but lost many soldiers, commanders, and friends

Why: The Romans could recruit reinforcements, but he was too far from home to do so

At last, the elephants more particularly began to distress the Romans, whose horses, before they came near, not enduring them, went back with their riders; and upon this, he [Pyrrhus] commanded the Thessalian cavalry to charge them in their disorder, and routed them with great loss. Dionysius affirms near fifteen thousand of the Romans fell; Hieronymus, no more than seven thousand. On Pyrrhus's side, the same Dionysius makes thirteen thousand slain, the other under four thousand; but they were the flower of his men, and amongst them his particular friends as well as officers whom he most trusted and made use of.

Plutarch, writing in 75 CE (translated by John Dryden)

Pyrrhus, a Greek of the 4th century BCE, was by all accounts a great military commander. Hannibal, who was no slouch when it came to battlefield tactics, rated him second only to Alexander the Great. It is therefore unfortunate that his name lives on only in the phrase "Pyrrhic victory," meaning a victory that has been achieved at too high a cost.

Born in 319 BCE, Pyrrhus was the son of Aeacides, who ruled the region of Epirus on the northwest coast of the Greek mainland, but his father was deposed when the boy was just two years old and he was raised by Glaucias, the king of the Illyrians, as part of his own family. Glaucias refused to hand Pyrrhus over to Cassander, the son of Antipater (Alexander the Great's general), even when he was offered a considerable amount of money, and when Pyrrhus was 12 years old Glaucias sent him to Epirus with an army to take back the throne. However, when he was 17, Pyrrhus left Epirus to attend the wedding of one of Glaucias's sons, and while he was away there was a coup in which he lost everything.

Since the death of Alexander the Great, his generals and friends, known collectively as the Diadochi, had been fighting each other for control of parts of his empire. One of Pyrrhus's sisters was married to Demetrius, the son of Antigonus, one of the Diadochi, and in 301 BCE Pyrrhus fought alongside his brother-in-law in the Battle of Ipsus, in what is now Turkey, against a coalition that included Cassander. Pyrrhus made a name for himself for his bravery and skill in the battle, but Antigonus was killed, the army was beaten, and Demetrius fled back to Greece while Pyrrhus was sent to Egypt to try to negotiate a settlement between Demetrius and King Ptolemy of Egypt.

Pyrrhus clearly impressed the Egyptian court, because he was offered the hand of Ptolemy's step-daughter, Antigone, in marriage. With her help he raised the funds to recruit an army, and in 297 BCE he returned to Epirus where he negotiated an agreement to rule jointly with the unpopular Neoptolemus II, a nephew of Alexander the Great. When Pyrrhus got wind of a plot to poison him, he killed Neoptolemus and ruled Epirus on his own.

BRAVE AND IMPETUOUS
In his lifetime, Pyrrhus was hailed as one of the great military leaders, but he was ambitious and was forever looking for new challenges.

When his former brother-in-law Demetrius (Pyrrhus's sister was no longer alive), who was now king of Macedonia, invaded Epirus in 291, Pyrrhus defeated one of his armies and then invaded Macedonia, where many Macedonian soldiers, fed up with Demetrius's decadence and high-handed attitude, defected to his side and he almost succeeded in taking control of the whole kingdom before returning to Epirus. Profiting from his own reputation and the ill will that the Macedonian troops bore Demetrius, Pyrrhus then entered Macedonia as a liberator and took over the kingdom without even raising his sword, ruling from 286 until 283 BCE, when he was ousted and returned to being just King of Epirus.

His next adventure took him to Italy, where Tarentum, one of the many Greek colonies in that country, was being threatened by Rome. In 280 BCE, at the invitation of the Tarentines, Pyrrhus sailed across the Adriatic with an army of some 25,000 soldiers, cavalrymen, archers, and "slingers." He also brought 20 elephants. Despite a storm that scattered the fleet along the Italian coast, the army was able to regroup at Tarentum and Pyrrhus set about turning the citizenry into soldiers, somewhat against their will. Several other Greek cities also offered to send troops as reinforcements.

ROAD TO RUIN When Pyrrhus learned that a large Roman army was on its way he decided not to wait for the reinforcements but to advance on the Romans before they could approach the city. The two armies met on the plain of Heraclea, and when Pyrrhus saw the size and level of organization of the Roman camp he reconsidered waiting for the additional troops, but it was too late. The Romans had no intention of waiting.

The battle was a long one and, having killed several well-known Roman warriors, Pyrrhus realized that sooner or later his highly recognizable armor and helmet (which was adorned with the horns of a goat) would attract challengers anxious to kill him, so he swapped his for those of a friend. This had two disastrous consequences. Not only was his friend soon slain (who needs friends like Pyrrhus?), but when the Roman victor displayed the distinctive helmet as a trophy, the Greek and Tarentine soldiers believed they had lost their leader and began to give up hope. Pyrrhus had to ride through the battlefield bareheaded to show them he was still alive and rally them.

The two armies were very evenly matched, but Pyrrhus's forces finally broke through by using the elephants, which terrified the horses of the Roman cavalry, and he was able to take the Roman camp and advance on Rome itself. Aware that his army was not large enough to take Rome, Pyrrhus suggested a peace treaty, to which the Romans agreed provided that Pyrrhus and his men leave Italy. Pyrrhus would not accept this, and the following year the two armies—that of Pyrrhus being supplemented by soldiers from other Greek colonies in Italy—met again in battle, this time at Asculum. Once again the battle was long, with each side alternately advancing and retreating, but once again the elephants carried the day and the Romans were beaten back. Nonetheless, Pyrrhus gave a wry response when he was congratulated on the victory. In both battles, the Romans had lost more men than the Greeks (approximately 13,000 Romans to 7,000 Greeks), but Pyrrhus understood the reality. The

© Private Collection | The Bridgeman Art Library

army he had brought from Epirus was severely depleted, he had lost most of his faithful commanders and good friends, his Greek allies in Italy could not be relied upon as a fighting force, and there was no way he could replenish his troops. Rome on the other hand could draw on a vast resource of capable militia and soon replace their losses. Yes, he had won both battles, but the cost was too great. "One more victory against the Romans," he said, "and we'll be ruined."

REJECTING THE PEACE OFFER

This painting by Cesare Maccari shows Appius Claudius persuading the Roman Senate not to accept Pyrrhus's offer of peace unless he leaves the country.

MOTIVATION

Anger

Charity

Envy

Faith

Gluttony

Greed

Hope

Lust

Pride

Sloth

CONSPIRATORS MURDER JULIUS CAESAR
44 BCE

Main Culprits: The Liberatores, a group of Roman senators

Damage Done: Removed a benign dictator from power and opened the door to the tyrannical rule of the Roman emperors

Why: In order to retain or regain their personal privileges and influence over matters of state in the Roman Republic

ANTONY
...The noble Brutus
Hath told you Caesar was ambitious:
If it were so, it was a grievous fault,
And grievously hath Caesar answer'd it.

From *Julius Caesar*, Act 3, Scene II

It can easily be argued that murdering someone is always bad but, putting the moral issues aside, we can judge the wisdom of the conspirators' decision to do away with Julius Caesar by asking whether the consequences of his assassination were those they had hoped for. Although he ultimately paid the price for accumulating enormous personal power, he was certainly an extremely talented man, and his life story is quite remarkable.

Gaius Julius Caesar was born in about 100 BCE into a noble, though not particularly wealthy or influential, family. In terms of the two major divisions in the political life of Rome, his family had ties with the Populares, aristocratic leaders whose political power was founded on the people's assemblies and the tribunals and who drew support from the plebs (land-owning citizens), as opposed to the more conservative Optimates, whose power derived from the senate and the nobility. At the age of 16, upon the death of his father, he became head of the family, and at 18 he married the daughter of a leading member of the Populares, who bore him a daughter called Julia. He obtained the post of high priest of Jupiter, but was forced into hiding by the Optimate dictator Sulla, who carried out a purge of his political enemies. Deprived of his priestly position (as well as his wealth and inheritance), Caesar then spent several years in the army, where he quickly distinguished himself both in battle and in diplomatic roles.

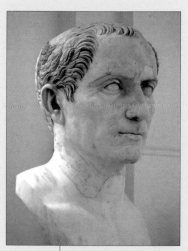

JULIUS CAESAR
He distinguished himself in the army, as a governor, and most of all as a politician, but Caesar's success won him the enmity of the Roman nobility.

Caesar was able to return to Rome in 78 BCE, when Sulla died, setting himself up as a lawyer and proving himself to be an eloquent orator with a talent for self promotion. At the age of 28 he took his first step on the political ladder when he was elected as a tribune (an official of the republic), followed shortly by positions as *quaestor* (an elected treasury official), as the high priest of the Roman religion, and then as a member of the senate. As one of the city's *aediles*, he organized the Roman games in 65 BCE, at great personal cost but gaining considerable popularity. As consul, in 59 BCE he introduced legislation, against the wishes of the senate but with the backing of the public assembly, that granted land to retired soldiers, and this brought him the support of the army.

He was then appointed governor of Spain, but he was still deeply in debt and therefore turned to the wealthy Crassus for financial help, which he gave in return for Caesar's political support against his rival Pompey. On Caesar's return from Spain and his election as a consul, Caesar brought Crassus and Pompey, both Populares, together and the three men formed an informal coalition, aggressively pushing through legislation in the senate with help from Caesar's armed henchmen.

INCREASING INFLUENCE

With the support of powerful allies, Caesar was then given the governorship of three further provinces—northern Italy, southern Europe, and southern France, which meant that he was now in control of four legions of the army. He proceeded to extend Roman control northward as far as the Rhine, conquering tribe after tribe, and using his position to amass considerable personal wealth by looting towns sacked by the army. In 55 BCE he crossed the English Channel and brought the Roman army into Britain for the first time, although he was unable to establish a permanent presence there. Over the next five years he brought Gaul under complete Roman control with a number of outstanding military victories that were widely reported back home, largely through Caesar's own writings, but by 50 BCE, Caesar's growing popularity and power were ringing alarm bells at the senate in Rome. Pompey, who had been appointed sole consul, ordered Caesar to return to Rome without his army, but Caesar, aware that he would no longer be immune to prosecution as his governorship had ended, crossed the Rubicon River into Italy with a legion of his army, an act tantamount to declaring civil war. Pompey, with his legions, fled the country, as did the majority of the senate who had expressed opposition. Over the next few years Caesar defeated Pompey's forces and then followed Pompey to Egypt, where the pharaoh, King Ptolemy XIII, presented him with his rival's head, hoping to ingratiate himself with Rome. The plan backfired, however. Caesar, enraged at the murder of a noble Roman, took control of Egypt, sided with the 21-year-old Cleopatra in a civil war against the pharaoh (her brother, husband, and co-ruler) and installed her as queen, for which she was extremely grateful. She bore Caesar's only son, Caesarion, in the summer of 47 BCE.

After military triumphs in the Middle East and Africa (where he defeated the last of the opposing senators), Caesar was given the position of dictator for the next ten years by the Romans, as well as being made sole consul. He then introduced a new constitution that not only consolidated his power but sought to bring peace and cohesion to the Roman Empire, and he set about a host of reforms affecting everything from state policing and subsidized grain to the legal system, taxation, land allocation, and personal debt. He also introduced the solar year to replace the former lunar calendar. He had great plans, too, for major construction and engineering works, including temples, ports, and canals, but they were never to reach fruition.

Looked at in the kindest light, those members of the senate who felt that Caesar was overstepping the mark may have been lamenting the demise of the virtues and ideals of the Roman Republic. Although Caesar had publicly refused to accept the crown of kingship, the nature of his rule had reduced the public Assemblies and the senate to the role of rubber-stamping bodies with no choice but to accede to Caesar's wishes. Although he had expanded the senate, he had filled it with his own appointees, as well giving himself the right to appoint the magistrates and the consuls, so that they were effectively his own representatives. This was a far cry from the principles of a republic, which, although by no means democratic, did give at least some of the people a voice in the running of the affairs of state. Seen in a harsher light, the heads of the noble families of Rome—who had once constituted the senate—had seen their power, wealth, and privileges dramatically reduced and were desperately seeking a return to their former status and positions of influence. In either case, removing Caesar appeared to be the solution to the problem.

ROMAN SENATE
In the last years of his life, Caesar appointed many of his own allies as senators and effectively robbed the senate of its power and its independence.

In February 44 BCE Caesar was appointed dictator for life, and this step toward tyranny was the final straw for a large group of disaffected senators, calling themselves *Liberatores*, or liberators. Caesar was to leave for Parthia on a military campaign on March 18, and the conspirators set the date for his assassination for March 15, the Ides of March, when Caesar would be present at a meeting of the senate in the Theater of Pompey and the conspirators could smuggle in daggers beneath their togas.

On the 14th, Marcus Antonius (Mark Antony), Caesar's faithful friend and second in command, got wind of the plot and the following day he attempted to warn Caesar but was prevented by a group of senators. Caesar's wife, too, had fears for his safety and implored him not to attend the senate, but Decimus Brutus (the brother of Marcus Brutus, one of the leading conspirators) successfully persuaded Caesar not to disappoint the senators. The details of what then occurred were subsequently recorded by several Roman historians, and Shakespeare's play *Julius Caesar* is fairly faithful to these accounts.

When he entered the Theater of Pompey, Caesar was approached by Tillius Cimber on the pretext of presenting him with a petition for the return of his brother from exile, and the conspirators closed in around him. When Caesar waved him away, Cimber grabbed Caesar by the shoulders and pulled down his toga. A senator by the name of Casca then struck at Caesar's neck with a dagger, but Caesar grasped his arm. Casca called out for help, and the group of conspirators then drew their daggers and stabbed Caesar who, realizing what was happening and understanding that resistance was futile, wrapped his toga about his head. According to one historian, his last words, directed at Marcus Brutus, were "You too, child?" spoken in Greek, although another recorded that he said nothing. Shakespeare's phrase *Et tu, Brute?*—"You too, Brutus?" spoken in Latin—is a literary rather than historical version. With a total of 23 wounds to his body, Caesar then fell lifeless to the floor at the feet of a statue of his great rival Pompey. (He was to lie there for several hours until three slaves placed the body on a litter and brought it to his home.)

CASCA CALLED OUT FOR HELP, AND THE GROUP OF CONSPIRATORS THEN DREW THEIR DAGGERS.

While the rest of the senators fled the building, the conspirators made their way to the capital, shouting to the citizens of Rome that they were once again free, but most people were hiding in their homes, having heard what had happened and fearing what might follow.

If the Liberatores thought their deed would either restore their power or save the Roman Republic, they were sorely mistaken. Mark Antony's eulogy at Caesar's funeral artfully highlighted all the good that the late leader had done for his people and painted the conspirators' act of "liberation" as treasonous murder, turning the Roman people against them and causing them to flee the country for their lives. With the populace on his side, Mark Antony may have hoped to become ruler, but Caesar had made his grandnephew Octavian his heir and adopted son, and Octavian was quickly able to consolidate political power. There followed many years of brutal civil wars, initially involving the partnership of Octavian and Mark Antony against the leading conspirators and their armies, but finally pitting Octavian against Mark Antony and his former master's lover, Cleopatra. Octavian's troops triumphed over the Egyptians in 31 BCE (both Mark Antony and Cleopatra committing suicide as a result), and Rome claimed Egypt. In 27 BCE he became not only the first emperor of the Roman Empire (Imperator Gaius Julius Caesar Augustus) but also supreme spiritual leader of the Roman people. Although some of the trappings of people's representation remained, the head of the Roman Empire from then on was, to all intents and purposes, an autocratic tyrant. The assassination of Caesar had put paid to any personal ambitions the conspirators may have had, and ended any hopes of a return to the ideals of the Roman Republic.

CAESAR'S GHOST
In Shakespeare's play, the dead Caesar appears to Brutus and warns him of his imminent defeat at the Battle of Philippi, at which both Cassius and Brutus committed suicide.

MOTIVATION

Anger

Charity

Envy

Faith

Gluttony

Greed

Hope

Lust

Pride

Sloth

CHOOSING CALIGULA AS EMPEROR

37–41 CE

Main Culprit: When Emperor Tiberius chose Caligula as his successor, he had no reason to suspect that his adopted grandson would prove to be as mad as a box of frogs

Damage Done: Bankrupted the state and led to the deaths of many innocent Romans

Why: Caligula was a megalomaniac with delusions of divinity

Nature seemed to have brought him forth to show what mischief could be effected by the greatest vices supported by the greatest authority.

Seneca, writing shortly after the death of Caligula

With the transformation of the Roman Republic into an empire, the emperor became leader for life and was able to designate who should succeed him. The first emperor, Augustus, passed the throne to his stepson and adopted son Tiberius, who proved capable but somewhat brutal in dealing with any opposition. He in turn nominated Gaius Julius Caesar Germanicus (better known as Caligula), the son of his nephew and adopted son Germanicus, as his joint heir, together with Tiberius's grandson Tiberius Gemellus. When Tiberius died in ca. 37 CE (possibly with a little help from Caligula and the Praetorian prefect Macro), Rome celebrated the arrival of the young new emperor, who benefited from the popularity of his father, the highly successful and much-loved general Germanicus, which also guaranteed him the backing of the army.

Apart from immediately having the young Tiberius Gemellus put to death, Caligula began his reign well, repealing some unpopular laws, putting an end to the bloody treason trials instigated by Tiberius and recalling exiled victims, and spending a small fortune on gladiatorial games, but the honeymoon was to be short-lived. After a few months, Caligula was taken ill, and when he returned to public life he was a different person—self important, power mad, sadistic, irrational, deluded, and depraved.

© De Agostini | Getty Images

EMPEROR CALIGULA
Tiberius is reported to have said of his heir, "I am nursing a viper in Rome's bosom. I am educating a Phaethon who will mishandle the fiery sun-chariot and scorch the whole world."

Believing himself to be divine, and insisting on being treated as such, he demanded that his sisters be honored by the people and the army, and it is said that he committed incest with all three of them and may have prostituted them to other men. He treated the senate with utter disrespect and even tried to have his favorite horse, Incitatus (which lived in the palace and had dinner parties held in its name), elevated to the position of consul.

Although accounts of his behavior may have been exaggerated, there is little doubt that Caligula indulged in the pleasures of the senses to an extreme degree, openly sleeping with other men's wives, hosting orgiastic parties, practicing a range of sexual perversions, and enjoying killing for its own sake. Caligula spent money like water, not only on public entertainment and construction projects such as harbor improvements, aqueducts, and canals that benefited the people but also on buildings and monuments to his own glory. In one particularly wasteful stunt he oversaw the construction of a two-and-a-half-mile floating bridge across the Bay of Baiae, to the west of Naples, so that he could ride his horse from one side to the other. This act was intended to pour scorn on a soothsayer's earlier prophecy that Caligula had as much chance of becoming emperor as he had of riding a horse across the bay. He also commissioned a luxurious floating palace in which to entertain his guests on Lake Nemi, a volcanic crater sacred to Diana.

MAKING ENEMIES

Within two years of his investiture the treasury coffers began to run dry, and he instituted treason trials in the style of Tiberius in order to get his hands on the estates of the wealthy citizens, exiling and even killing his chosen victims. As the rumblings from an increasingly hostile senate grew louder, he turned his attention upon them, opening investigations into the loyalty of some senators and having some of them executed. Plots were undoubtedly being hatched against him, and in 39 CE one was uncovered involving Lepidus (the husband of Caligula's favorite sister, who had died the previous year) and Caligula's other two sisters. Lepidus was executed and the sisters were sent into exile.

Possibly feeling the need to follow in the illustrious footsteps of his father Germanicus and his predecessor Tiberius, Caligula embarked on a military campaign northward through Gaul with the intention of adding Britain to the empire, but it is reported that when he reached the English Channel he instructed his soldiers to collect seashells from the shore, and the campaign ended there.

By 40 CE Caligula seems to have been fully convinced that he was a god, turning his palace into a temple, presenting himself to the people dressed as various divinities and demanding that he be treated as one. He even commanded that a statue of himself be erected in the Temple of Jerusalem, which would probably have led to civil war had the order been carried out.

Although the populace remained largely in favor of Caligula despite his excesses, which included having a section of the crowd thrown to wild animals when the games ran out of gladiators, antagonism toward him among the senators, the nobility, and the army finally resulted in a successful conspiracy against him. In January 41 CE, officers of the

Praetorian Guard came upon him in a corridor beneath the Imperial Palace and he was stabbed repeatedly, very much in the manner of Julius Caesar's death. Caligula's wife and daughter were murdered soon afterward, the senate hoping to eliminate the imperial family and reinstate the republic, but support for the position of emperor was greater than they realized. Another section of the Praetorian Guard found and protected the last male member of the family—Caligula's uncle, Claudius—and he was soon hailed as Caligula's successor.

SECURING POWER
With the help of the Praetorian Guard, Claudius succeeded Caligula as emperor, restoring order to the Roman Empire.

Caligula's deluded reign of murder and debauchery had lasted for less than four years, but during that time he had virtually bankrupted the state. It fell upon Claudius to bring order and probity back to the empire, a task to which he was to prove equal.

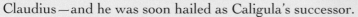

MOTIVATION

Anger

Charity

Envy

Faith

Gluttony

Greed

Hope

Lust

Pride

Sloth

JULIAN "THE APOSTATE" REJECTS CHRISTIANITY

362 CE

Main Culprit: Roman emperor Flavius Claudius Julianus (Julian)

Damage Done: Persecuted Christians and disrupted the nascent Christian Church

Why: Believed in the earlier Roman gods and wished to make paganism the ordering principle of the empire

Men should be taught and won over by reason, not by blows, insults, and corporal punishments. I therefore most earnestly admonish the adherents of the true religion not to injure or insult the Galilaeans in any way. Those who are in the wrong in matters of supreme importance are objects of pity rather than of hate.

Flavius Claudius Julianus

By all accounts (and his life and deeds are well documented), Emperor Julian, who only ruled from 361 to 363 CE, was a remarkable man, intellectually, administratively, and militarily. Unfortunately for him, and for many throughout the Roman Empire, he elected to swim against the current of religious change that was already flowing through his realm.

Flavius Claudius Julianus was born into the imperial family in 331 CE, the son of Julius Constantinus, half-brother of the Emperor Constantine I, also known as Constantine the Great, and it is with that emperor that this story begins. It was Constantine who extended the great city of Byzantium, or Constantinople as it was renamed, and made it the capital of the Roman Empire, and it was here that Julian was born. Constantine was also the first Christian emperor, committing himself to the religion after experiencing a vision before a great battle in 312 CE. In 313 he legalized Christian worship, and during his reign Christianity became the dominant religion throughout the empire. Although he was not baptized until shortly before his death, Constantine the Great became deeply involved in matters of the Christian Church, convening councils of the bishops and attempting to heal the deep theological rifts that were appearing, as well as entrusting certain government functions to the clergy, effectively making the Church an organ of the state. He also took steps to suppress pagan worship of the old gods by ordering temples to be closed or confiscated, removing temple treasures, and banning animal sacrifice.

BEARDED THINKER
With his "old-fashioned" philosopher's beard, Emperor Julian was considered by many to be inappropriately scruffy for his position as ruler.

Constantine the Great (who had conferred honors on Julian's father and made him a consul) died when Julian was six years old, to be succeeded by his three sons—the confusingly named Constans, Constantius II, and Constantine II. The three emperors immediately eliminated possible rivals with a bloody purge of the families of their father's half-brothers. Julian and his younger half-brother, Gallus, were the only male members to survive, probably because they were considered too young to pose a threat. Julian was sent to Nicomedia, the former capital of the eastern Roman Empire, where he was given a strict Christian education under the guardianship of Bishop Eusebius.

When Julian was 13, he and Gallus were exiled to Cappadocia, where their Christian education continued. Julian became very knowledgeable about the Bible and Christianity, but he also began to study classical Greek teachings, lent to him by Bishop George of Cappadocia.

In 351, after the death of his two brothers, Constantius II made Gallus a consul and Julian returned to Nicomedia, where he became deeply interested in the Greek religious philosophy of Neoplatonism, a form of pagan mysticism. He studied under some of the greatest Neoplatonist philosophers and was introduced to the Eleusinian Mysteries, an ancient system of beliefs and ceremonies dating back more than 1,000 years.

POPULAR TOUCH

In 354 Gallus was executed for treason and Julian was brought back to Italy, where he was placed under house arrest on suspicion of conspiracy, but he was released the following year and was able to return to Greece and continue his studies—although not for long. Realizing that the empire was too extensive for him to make his presence felt throughout it, Constantius II recalled Julian, appointed him as Caesar (or sub-emperor), and sent him to Gaul, but if he had expected Julian to be merely his representative, he was mistaken. The bearded scholar proved to be both an able administrator and a skilled military tactician. Over the next five years he conquered and/or negotiated peace with many of the tribes of the region, as well as winning over the people through just rule and fair taxation. He also won the approval and admiration of his troops, many of whom were natives of the area, and by 360 CE his popularity and success had aroused the jealousy of the emperor. Constantius II began by depriving Julian of some of his legions on the pretext of requiring them for a campaign against the Persians, but when the Petulantes, an infantry unit composed largely of Germanic men, were ordered to march east, they rebelled against the orders of Constantius II, unwilling to leave their families. Instead they hailed Julian as emperor. Despite his refusal to accept the honor, the troops insisted, carrying him on a shield and placing a chain about his head to symbolize a royal crown. Julian remained reluctant and was later to say that he only accepted after receiving guidance from the god Zeus. He was also to recount that he then led the troops in sacrifices to the gods, who had commanded him to return to the ancient rituals.

Julian wrote to Constantius II, explaining that receiving the title of emperor was not his wish but that of the soldiers, who had been put in an invidious position by being asked to leave their loved ones. The situation remained unresolved for a year, but then Julian decided to settle the matter and headed east with his army to meet Constantius II in battle. Julian probably felt little loyalty to the emperor, having suffered exile at his hands and having seen his family murdered on the orders of Constantius and his brothers.

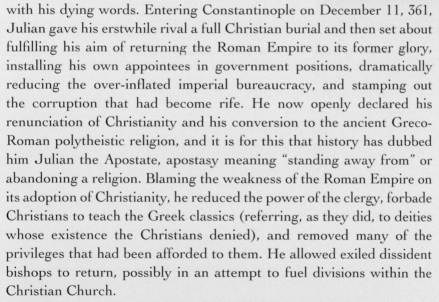

Civil war was looming, but as the armies drew closer the danger was averted by the sudden death, from natural causes, of the emperor, who is said to have named Julian as his successor with his dying words. Entering Constantinople on December 11, 361, Julian gave his erstwhile rival a full Christian burial and then set about fulfilling his aim of returning the Roman Empire to its former glory, installing his own appointees in government positions, dramatically reducing the over-inflated imperial bureaucracy, and stamping out the corruption that had become rife. He now openly declared his renunciation of Christianity and his conversion to the ancient Greco-Roman polytheistic religion, and it is for this that history has dubbed him Julian the Apostate, apostasy meaning "standing away from" or abandoning a religion. Blaming the weakness of the Roman Empire on its adoption of Christianity, he reduced the power of the clergy, forbade Christians to teach the Greek classics (referring, as they did, to deities whose existence the Christians denied), and removed many of the privileges that had been afforded to them. He allowed exiled dissident bishops to return, possibly in an attempt to fuel divisions within the Christian Church.

DIVIDE AND CONQUER
Julian the Apostate encouraged the many sects within Christianity, with the intention of creating splits within the Church.

If Rome was to be great again he needed the help of the gods. He took steps to resurrect the ancient Roman religion by reopening the temples, encouraging and even demanding the performance of animal sacrifices to the Roman deities, and appointing provincial high priests to oversee their subordinates in a structured pagan church that emulated that of the Christians. While launching a philosophical attack on Christian beliefs (from Julian's perspective it was the Christians who had apostatized

© Edward A. Armitage

from the religion of their forefathers), he showed greater tolerance for Judaism, possibly in the hope of striking a blow against Christianity. He went so far as to instigate the reconstruction of the Temple of Jerusalem, destroyed by the Romans in 70 CE, but the project was abandoned, reputedly because balls of fire kept erupting from beneath the foundations, preventing the workers from carrying out their task.

Although he largely succeeded in disenfranchising a powerful Christian elite—and in some parts of the empire the Christians suffered real persecution—his attempt to return Rome to its former religion failed, largely because the populace did not follow his lead. His own particular mix of paganism and philosophy was highly intellectual and had little popular appeal, and by its very nature paganism was, unlike Christianity, a private rather than public religion, one that comprised a wide range of different beliefs and resisted serving as an organizing principle for the empire. In any case, the experiment was a short-lived one. Julian ruled for less than two years, dying in June 363 from an arrow wound while leading a military campaign against the Persians. Although his reign had succeeded in doing enormous harm to the organized Christian Church and its relationship with the state, Christianity was there to stay, and it was paganism that soon came to be outlawed by the emperors of Rome.

MONOPHYSITISM IS DECLARED HERETICAL

451 CE

MOTIVATION

Anger

Charity

Envy

Faith

Gluttony

Greed

Hope

Lust

Pride

Sloth

Main Culprits: Intransigent theologians and an authoritarian church

Damage Done: Led to a major split in the Christian community

Why: The Catholic Church (with state backing) assumed the right to determine what was acceptable doctrine, and tolerated no deviation from orthodoxy ("straight belief")

According to the apostolic teaching and the doctrine of the Gospel, let us believe in the one deity of the Father, the Son and the Holy Spirit, in equal majesty and in a holy Trinity. We authorize the followers of this law to assume the title of Catholic Christians; but as for the others, since, in our judgment they are foolish madmen, we decree that they shall be branded with the ignominious name of heretics, and shall not presume to give to their conventicles the name of churches. They will suffer in the first place the chastisement of the divine condemnation and in the second the punishment of our authority which in accordance with the will of Heaven we shall decide to inflict.

From the *Edict of Thessalonica*, delivered by the Roman emperors Theodosius I, Gratian, and Valentinian II in 380 CE

Conflict between religions has been at the root of some of the world's worst and most protracted wars, but don't let that lead you to thinking that all is sweetness and light *within* religions. In its first few centuries, Christianity was riven with deep divisions, and one that tore the community apart permanently arose from disagreements about something that many would consider unknowable—the relation between the divine and human natures of Christ.

The doctrine of the Trinity—that God exists in three persons: the Father, the Son, and the Holy Spirit—has been central to Christianity since its beginning, but according to the scriptures Jesus Christ is both God and man, so what, then, is the relation of Jesus Christ to God the Father, and how can He be both divine and human? This philosophically difficult problem led to many different attempts at understanding, and they proved to be extremely divisive.

© Wayfarer | Dreamstime.com

CO-EQUAL, CO-ETERNAL
The nature of Christ, and his relation to the two other elements of the Trinity, proved to be highly divisive issues in the early Christian Church.

The orthodox line was, and is, that the three elements of the Trinity are co-equal, co-existent, and co-eternal. None is greater than the others, and they exist at the same time and forever. The first attempt at upsetting the apple cart came during the reign of Constantine the Great, when the very learned Alexandrian scholar Arius declared that Christ was neither co-equal nor co-eternal with God the Father. Citing a range of Bible verses, Arius taught that whereas God the Father had always existed, Christ was created by God the Father as the means of bringing salvation to the world, and Christ was not only subordinate to God the Father but was not of the same substance and was in fact human, and not divine. This went directly against the mainstream Trinitarian doctrine. The Church immediately pronounced his views to be heretical and Arius was excommunicated, but not before his teachings had gained significant influence throughout the eastern Mediterranean. In order to put an end to this flourishing heresy, which was threatening to divide the Church, in 325 CE, Emperor Constantine convened the first Council of Bishops, in Nicaea (now the Turkish town of Iznik), at which an assembly of bishops from throughout Christendom debated the issue for several weeks. Their discussions centered around definitions, in many languages, of such terms as "existence," "substance," "essence," "begotten," and "created," and arguments such as, if God the Father is eternal and has always had the attribute of being the Father, then the Son must also be eternal. The outcome of the debate was a declaration by the First Council of Nicaea that God the Father and God the Son are of one substance and are co-eternal, and this element of doctrine was incorporated into the Nicene Creed, a profession of faith that is still proclaimed (in an amended form) today. The bishops at Nicaea also determined that Christ is one substance but is both fully human and fully divine, one person in whom two natures—one divine and one human—are united. This is known as the hypostatic union—one person, two natures. Modern-day Christian denominations with non-Trinitarian beliefs akin to Arianism include the Unitarian Church and the Jehovah's Witnesses.

The term hypostasis was first used to refer to the concrete existence of Christ by the Syrian bishop Apollinaris, but when it came to Christ's nature, he was diametrically opposed to the views of Arius, maintaining that although Christ had a human body, the divine word had taken over His human soul and that therefore Christ had only one nature—a divine nature. This, too, was rejected by the Church, as it denied that Christ was fully human, and was declared heretical by the next Council of Bishops, held in Constantinople in 381. The belief that Christ has only one nature became known as Monophysitism (one-nature-ism), and it was later to lead to a fundamental split in the Church and ultimately to the weakening of its influence.

Nestorius, appointed Bishop of Constantinople in 427, went to the opposite extreme. Unwilling to accept that the Son of God could have a solely human form, he taught that Christ had two natures but that he was also two persons, one divine and one human. He maintained that Mary the Virgin should be called not the Mother of God (since God had always existed), but the Mother of Christ, since she gave birth only to the human person of Christ who was later imbued with a divine nature. Nestorius was a great speaker, and his teachings quickly became popular, but there were also many who thought his views were heretical. His strongest opponent was Cyril, the Bishop of Alexandria, and the argument between them became so heated that Emperor Theodosius II had to convene another council, this time at

HERETICAL BELIEFS

Ephesus, in 431. Here Cyril, who had already ensured that the majority of the bishops would be on his side, leveled the charge of heresy against Nestorius and the council condemned him. He was sent into exile in the Libyan desert, but his followers remained true to his teachings, leading to the formation of the Nestorian Church, or the Church of the East, mainly in Persia and later throughout parts of Asia. This church still exists, and it rejects the declarations of the First Council of Ephesus.

Present at the First Council of Ephesus, and vociferously opposed to Nestorius, was an elder of the Church in Constantinople called Eutyches. He later propounded the belief that in their union in Christ, human nature and divine nature were combined into a single nature, as though the first were dissolved in the second. Although he was careful to say that this did not diminish Christ's humanity, he put his views forward with such force that they were regarded as monophysite heresy, and he was excommunicated in 448. The following year, the Second Council of Ephesus reversed this decision, but this in turn was overruled by the Council of Chalcedon in 451, which declared that although the divine nature and the human nature were united in Christ, they each remained distinct and unaltered, and that Christ is "in two natures."

© Corbis

CYRIL
The Bishop of Alexandria crushed the "Nestorian heresy" and created the first major split. The Nestorian Church still exists today.

Eutyches was sent into exile, but the patriarch of Alexandria, in Egypt, and his bishops refused to accept the declarations of the Council of Chalcedon, believing that the formulation "in two natures" smacked of Nestorian heresy. In the late 5th century this led to a permanent schism between the "non-Chalcedonian" Oriental Orthodox Church, as it became known, and the rest of the Church, which declared the Alexandrian position to be monophysite and therefore heretical.

The Oriental Orthodox Church flourished in northeast Africa and the Levant, and its ostracization by the rest of Eastern Christianity was to have major historical consequences. In the 7th century, when the armies of Islam set out from Arabia to the north and the west, the Oriental Orthodox Christians of Egypt, Syria, and Palestine, already alienated from the rest of Christendom and oppressed by Byzantium, offered little resistance. This was in part because they practiced greater tolerance than the rest of the Christian Church. As a result these areas soon fell under Arab rule, being taken from the Byzantine Empire and becoming part of the growing Islamic Empire—a high price for Christendom to pay for a disagreement over the unprovable.

Fourteen hundred years later, the Oriental Orthodox Church (as distinct from the Eastern Orthodox Church) today comprises the Coptic Orthodox, the Syriac Orthodox (or "Jacobite"), the Armenian Apostolic, the Ethiopian Orthodox, the Eritrean Orthodox, and the Malankara (Indian) Orthodox Churches. These churches reject the accusation of being monophysite, since their position is not the same as that of Eutyches, and characterize their position as miaphysite ("joined-nature"), maintaining that Christ has one nature in which the divine and the human are combined but with the character of each fully retained.

MOTIVATION

Anger

Charity

Envy

Faith

Gluttony

Greed

Hope

Lust

Pride

Sloth

THE GREAT EAST–WEST SCHISM

1054 CE

Main Culprit: The autocratic leadership of the Roman Catholic Church

Damage Done: Led to a major split between the Western and Eastern Churches

Why: Rome claimed the right to rule the Christian Church, and unilaterally introduced changes in doctrine and practice

We believe in the Holy Spirit, the Lord, the giver of life,
who proceeds from the Father [and the Son],
who with the Father and the Son is worshiped and glorified,
who has spoken through the prophets.
We believe in one holy Catholic and Apostolic Church.
We acknowledge one baptism for the forgiveness of sins.
We look for the resurrection of the dead,
and the life of the world to come. Amen.

From the Nicene Creed

After several centuries of growing disagreement between the Church in Rome and the Church in the East, relations between the two reached breaking point in the middle of the 11th century. Although there were many sources of dispute between them, the clincher was, once again, the relations between the members of the Holy Trinity. A thousand years later, the rift that this caused (or, perhaps, revealed) has not yet been healed.

After Constantine moved the capital of the Roman Empire from Rome to Constantinople in the 4th century, the Church was divided into five "patriarchates," each administered by a patriarch, or archbishop. These patriarchates were those of Rome, Constantinople, Antioch, Jerusalem, and Alexandria, and in terms of authority on issues of doctrine and theology they considered themselves to be equal while acknowledging that the Holy Father in Rome was the "first among equals." Following the fall of Rome in the 5th century, which left something of a political vacuum, the head of the Church in Rome began to assume secular power as well as greater ecclesiastical authority, to the growing annoyance of the other patriarchates, where the relationships between emperor and archbishop were very different. Other factors, too, distanced them from Rome. In the first place, while the language of the Church in Rome was Latin, that of the rest of the Church was Greek, and while the Western Church imposed its teachings on a largely illiterate populace, literacy was more common in the east, where the Bible was translated into the language of the people, and wide-ranging theological discussion was encouraged. This resulted in philosophical and liturgical differences between the two, but the first major bone of contention combined both the increasingly dictatorial power of the Pope and a matter of doctrine.

In Spain in the first half of the 6th century, an addition was incorporated into the local version of the Nicene Creed. At the end of the sentence, "And I believe in the Holy Ghost, the Lord and Giver of Life; who proceeds from the Father," the words "and the Son," or, in Latin, *filioque*, were added. This was done in order to counter a claim by Spanish Arianists that if the Holy Spirit proceeds from the Father but not from the Son because the Father alone is the source of divinity, then the Son

COUNCIL OF NICAEA
The original wording of the Nicene Creed dates from the First Council of Nicaea, held in 325 CE under the Emperor Constantine.

FILIOQUE

cannot be fully God, in which case the persons of the Trinity are not co-equal. This would imply that we cannot experience God directly in the Son or the Holy Spirit.

Despite the fact that it had been agreed in the 4th century that no changes could be made to the Nicene Creed without the agreement of the Council of Bishops, this change was accepted throughout the sphere of influence of the Western Church, but it was not accepted by the other four patriarchates. They maintained, firstly, that to say that the Holy Spirit proceeds from the Son is to suggest that the Son is also a source of divinity, which undermines the fundamental monotheism of the Christian Church. Secondly, they questioned the right of the Pope to make such a change to the creed without consulting them.

The dispute notched up a gear in the 9th century when the papacy disputed the appointment of Photius as the patriarch of Constantinople, and also insisted that the *filioque* be included in the creed in Bulgaria, a region that Constantinople regarded as within its diocese and over which the Church in Rome had no jurisdiction. Photius responded by not only denying the authority of Pope Nicholas I to interfere with matters of the patriarchate of Constantinople, but also excommunicating him on the basis of a list of "errors" that included insisting upon celibacy for priests and adding the *filioque* to the creed. Known as the Photian Schism, the event drove the wedge deeper between Rome and the rest of the Church.

THE FINAL STRAW In the early 11th century, in what became known as the Petrine Doctrine, the Roman Church claimed that St. Peter was given special authority over the Church by Jesus Christ, that the bishop of the Church in Rome is the successor of St. Peter and as such is the vicar of Christ, and that therefore the Pope has spiritual supremacy over the whole Church and all the bishops. This doctrine, which had been expressly rejected by earlier Church Councils, was perceived by the more democratic Eastern Church as a usurpation of power, and in 1054 the patriarch of Constantinople, Michael Cerularius, wrote a letter to Bishop John of Trani in Italy. In it he outlined the many unilateral changes that had been introduced by the Roman Church, condemning some of them as sinful, and he asked the bishop to make known the contents of the letter as widely as possible.

In response, Pope Leo IX sent a delegation to Constantinople to depose the patriarch and to demand that Constantinople recognize the Church of Rome as the head of the Church. The patriarch refused to see the legates and finally they departed, but not before placing on the altar of the great Hagia Sophia church a papal bull excommunicating Patriarch Michael Cerularius. He in turn excommunicated them, and the Great Schism between the Roman Catholic Church and the Greek (or Eastern) Orthodox Church was complete, each claiming to be the true church. It has also proved, thus far, to be permanent, and certain events that have taken place since have served to deepen the rift. In 1204, the soldiers of the Fourth Crusade, sent by Pope Innocent II to take Egypt from the Muslims, instead sacked Constantinople and, in addition to carrying out horrendous atrocities, looted hundreds of churches and cathedrals in the majestic city, stealing priceless treasures and relics belonging to the Greek Orthodox Church. These were taken back to the cities of Western Europe, and most notably to the Vatican in Rome.

In 1870, the Pope's claim to supremacy was augmented by the declaration by the Vatican Council that, when acting in his capacity as Pope, he cannot be wrong on matters of faith or morals. This did not help to bring the two Churches closer together. Over the years, attempts have been made to heal the breach but, although the mutual excommunications were rescinded in 1965 and the Roman Catholic and Greek Orthodox Churches are now at least in dialogue, their list of disputed elements of doctrine and practice is a long one.

EAST VS WEST
In the 21st century, Pope John Paul II apologized for the siege of Constantinople and the damage done to relations between the Latin and Greek Churches.

MOTIVATION

Anger

Charity

Envy

Faith

Gluttony

Greed

Hope

Lust

Pride

Sloth

HAROLD HURRIES TO MEET WILLIAM AT HASTINGS

1066

Main Culprit: King Harold II of England

Damage Done: The throne of England passed to Duke William of Normandy, who shared the country out among his pals

Why: Harold's army was weary and depleted, but he was too impatient to wait for reinforcements

The victory being secured, the duke returned to the field of battle, where he viewed the dreadful carnage, which could not be seen without commiseration. There the flower of the youth and nobility of England covered the ground far and near stained with blood.

Orderic Vitalis (1075–1142), from *The Ecclesiastical History of England and Normandy*, translated by Thomas Forrester

The Battle of Hastings, which took place in the south of England in 1066, is one of history's most famous battles, seen as marking the point at which Anglo-Saxon Britain became Norman Britain, but to those of us with a Saxon soul who lament the sudden intrusion of the French it's important to note, firstly, that the Normans were not French, and secondly that the causes of William's invasion had their roots in a longstanding connection between the English monarchy and the Norman nobility. Harold's failure to defeat the Normans certainly led to a sea change in British history, but the fault lay not with his army nor his strategy. He may just have been in too much of a hurry to engage the enemy.

The story behind the conflict between Harold and William begins a century and a half earlier, in 911, when the king of France gave Rollo the Viking the northwest portion of France in return for an end to Viking predation. The area became known as Normandy, the land of the Northmen, and the Normans adopted the French language and customs. In 1002, the English king Ethelred II married Emma, the sister of Richard II, Duke of Normandy, and she introduced many of her Norman friends to the English court. Ethelred and Emma had three children, Alfred, Edward, and a girl named Goda, and when the Danish king Sweyn Forkbeard invaded England in 1013 the family fled to Normandy. Sweyn's son Canute became King of England, and when Ethelred died, Emma married Canute, possibly to save the lives of her sons, who had a claim to the throne. This created yet another bond between Normandy and England.

When Canute died in 1035, the two boys, Alfred and Edward, returned to England, but Edward had to flee again to Normandy when Alfred was taken captive by Godwin, Earl of Wessex, one of England's most powerful lords, who handed him over to Canute's son Harold. Alfred was intentionally blinded and he died of his wounds shortly afterward. Edward was brought back in 1041 at the invitation of Canute's son King Harthacnut, who made him his heir, and Edward "the Confessor" ascended to the throne the following year.

Although Edward was undisputed king, Godwin, Earl of Wessex, held as much power as he did, and Godwin and his family were fiercely opposed to the increasing influence of the Normans in English political

SO WHAT WAS THE BEEF?

NORMAN LANDINGS
This 19th-century lithograph by the French artist Alphonse de Neuville depicts the landing of William's forces on the south coast of England.

life that continued under Edward's rule. Although Edward was married to his daughter, Edith, the two men fell out and Godwin chose to take his family into exile in 1051. He returned the following year, but during that time King Edward (who had no children) had invited William, Duke of Normandy, to England and named him as heir to the English throne. William was the illegitimate grandson of Richard II of Normandy, the brother of Edward's mother Emma.

Godwin and Edward remained at loggerheads as Godwin did his best to remove Normans from positions of power in England, including deposing the Archbishop of Canterbury, and when Godwin died in 1053, his son, Harold Godwinson, became the rallying point for anti-Norman feeling in England. At the end of 1065, Edward became gravely ill and he died on January 5, 1066, but not before commending his wife (Harold's sister) and his kingdom to Harold's care. At a meeting of the Witenagamot (the king's assembly of noblemen) it was decided that Edward's words made Harold the rightful king and he was crowned the following day. This outcome did not suit William of Normandy, who immediately set about preparing a fleet of ships and an army. Harold's reign was to be a short one.

Unfortunately for Harold, William wasn't the only one with his eye on the English throne. Harold's brother Tostig had joined forces with King Harald Hardrada of Norway to invade England, and in September 1066 they arrived off the east coast of England with a fleet of some 300 vessels and 15,000 men. After sacking the town of Scarborough, they sailed as far up the River Humber as they could and then marched on York. Harold was relying on the armies of the Earls of Mercia and Northumberland to repel them, but the Vikings beat them hands down at the Battle of Fulford, York surrendered, and the victorious army camped beside the river where their ships were moored.

When Harold, who was in the south of England preparing for the invasion of the Normans, heard what had happened, he force-marched his army 200 miles (320 km) north in just five days and took the Vikings by surprise as they assembled to receive hostages at Stamford Bridge. Having left their armor aboard the ships, the Norsemen suffered huge losses as the Saxon army overran them. Both Tostig and Harald Hardrada (who received an arrow through the throat) were killed, and the invaders finally surrendered. The survivors were allowed to gather up their injured and sail home, having pledged not to attack Britain again, but their numbers were so depleted that they needed only 24 of their original 300 ships.

Although it had been victorious, Harold's army, too, had suffered considerable losses, as had the armies of Mercia and Northumberland, on whose help against William of Normandy Harold had been counting. Now came news that William's fleet had landed on the south coast of England. Battle weary, Harold's soldiers headed south with as much speed as they could muster.

For William's part, he had been ready to set sail from Normandy with a fleet of more than 500 long ships and possibly as many as 20,000 men since the middle of August, but bad weather had prevented him. In September he moved the fleet along the French coast, shortening the crossing, and was finally able to put to sea on September 27. After a night crossing, William made a first muddy landing at Pevensey Bay and set up camp there, but soon decided to move the fleet and the army eastward along the coast to a better location at Hastings. Here they built a wooden castle with a palisaded ditch, and for the next two weeks the soldiers pillaged the surrounding countryside, killing villagers and taking what they wished. As well as providing the army with meat and grain, this was a deliberate ploy to goad Harold into an early battle— and it worked.

Harold's tired army marched south, pausing for a few days in London, and it was here that a groundswell of opinion began to favor delaying before going into battle. The army was extremely tired and unprepared, and it was felt that Harold should wait a while to rest the soldiers and drum up more reinforcements before going into battle. For the moment, William's men were well rested, well provisioned, and ready for battle, but if they were to have to remain at Hastings throughout the winter they would soon run short of food and morale. Harold's brother also gave him some good advice, suggesting that he, Earl Gyrth, should lead the army against William. Harold had sworn an oath to William of Normandy in 1064, promising to support his accession to the throne,

WILLIAM MADE A FIRST MUDDY LANDING AT PEVENSEY BAY AND SET UP CAMP THERE, BUT SOON DECIDED TO MOVE THE FLEET AND THE ARMY EASTWARD ALONG THE COAST TO A BETTER LOCATION AT HASTINGS.

whereas Earl Gyrth owed him no such loyalty. What was more, should the Normans win, Harold would be able to raise a second army against William or, if the worst came to the worst, operate a scorched earth policy ahead of the advancing Normans and starve them into abandoning their attempt on the throne.

Harold, however, who had a reputation for being impetuous, chose to ignore the advice and to go into battle as soon as possible. After a few days, Harold and his army continued their journey south. They reached Caldbec Hill, a few miles north of Hastings, on the evening of October 13 and here they set up camp, but Norman scouts had seen them arriving and they knew that they no longer had the element of surprise.

When the battle began at about nine o'clock the following morning, Harold had the tactical advantage, his army occupying a high ridge with their flanks protected by streams and uneven ground, and soft ground in front of them. The Norman archers began the attack, but the English front ranks used their shields to form an effective wall. An attack by the Norman infantry was successfully rebuffed, and then William sent in the cavalry but they were rendered less effective by the uphill slope and had to pull back. At this the English front lines followed them and almost broke through the Norman lines. Some of the Normans fled and William had to remove his helmet and show his face to quell a rumor that he had been killed. The English had come close to routing the Normans, but it was as close as they were to come. William once again sent in the archers and this time, by aiming higher and overshooting the wall of shields, they did considerably more damage. It may have been at this point that Harold received an arrow in the eye. William's troops kept up a relentless assault, and the tiredness of the English troops began to tell. The Normans finally broke through the English defensive lines, Harold's brothers Gyrth and Leofwine were killed and, despite a brave rearguard action by the fleeing soldiers, the Normans, as we all know, won the day. The impatient Harold, fielding a weary and under-strength army, had lost the battle and his life, and October 14, 1066, marked the start of a new chapter in English history.

THE FRENCH UNDERESTIMATE THE ENGLISH ARCHERS AT AGINCOURT

1415

MOTIVATION

Anger

Charity

Envy

Faith

Gluttony

Greed

Hope

Lust

Pride

Sloth

Main Culprit: The weak leadership of the French army

Damage Done: Brought about the wholesale destruction of a large part of the army and most of the French nobility

Why: Too much misplaced confidence and not enough planning and organization

This story shall the good man teach his son;
And Crispin Crispian shall ne'er go by,
From this day to the ending of the world,
But we in it shall be remember'd;
We few, we happy few, we band of brothers;
For he to-day that sheds his blood with me
Shall be my brother; be he ne'er so vile,
This day shall gentle his condition:

Henry V, Act IV, Scene 3

HENRY V
After his success at Agincourt, Henry returned on two more campaigns, but he died in France (probably of dysentery) before he could be crowned King of France.

In 1415, almost 350 years after the Battle of Hastings, which won for William Duke of Normandy the crown of England, an English army led by King Henry V was on French soil. The Plantagenet kings, of which Henry was one, laid claim to the throne of France and had been engaged in a series of wars (known jointly as the Hundred Years' War) against the French House of Valois since 1337. The Plantagenet claim was based on their descent from Edward III, the son of Isabella of France, wife of Edward II. The Valois kings only recognized the male line and denied the legitimacy of a claim based on descent through a female.

Since his accession to the throne in 1413, Henry had been in negotiations with the French, but his demands had proved unacceptable. Henry had declared himself willing to give up his claim to the throne of France in return for the payment of an outstanding ransom of 1.6 million crowns owed to the English crown, the hand of Charles VI's daughter Princess Catherine in marriage, with a dowry of 2 million crowns, and acknowledgment of the English claim to Aquitaine and certain other French lands. The best French counter-offer was marriage to Princess Catherine, a dowry of 600,000 crowns, and Aquitaine, which Henry refused. Meanwhile, the preparation of an army of English and Welsh soldiers had been underway, ships had been commandeered, and now Henry was coming to press his claim in battle.

The English fleet, carrying a force of some 8,000 men (6,000 archers and 2,000 men-at-arms), landed on the French coast in the mouth of the River Seine on August 13. The plan was to take the French seaport of Harfleur, which would provide a base through which his army could be resupplied, and then to march on Paris, some 125 miles (200 km) away, but two things went wrong. Firstly, Harfleur was not the pushover that Henry expected. The French managed to reinforce the small garrison of 100 with 300 more soldiers, and the siege lasted for just over a month. Secondly, his soldiers were struck by an outbreak of dysentery that killed some and weakened many. By the time the army was ready to set off, on October 8, with around 5,000 men, the weather was worsening and it was too late in the year to contemplate attacking Paris. Henry decided instead to head for Calais, further up the coast, and to make a show of strength as his army marched through the countryside. His advisers counseled against this risky plan, as a powerful French force was on its way, but he persisted. His advisers were right.

When the army reached the River Somme, the presence of a French contingent forced Henry to take a wide detour, and when they were within 30 miles (50 km) of Calais one of the army scouts reported that the valley along which they were marching was blocked by the French army, which had overtaken them and headed them off at the pass. Unless Henry was willing to renounce his claim to the throne, he and his army would have to do battle. Estimates of the French numbers vary, but they outnumbered the English by at least two to one, and possibly by as many as six to one. The English and Welsh soldiers made camp and spent a somber night contemplating their imminent defeat. The French, on the other hand, were brimming with confidence and spent the night partying. Not only were they numerically far stronger, but they had great confidence in the knights, wearing armor of thick steel plate, mounted and on foot, that made up a large proportion of the army, and the cream of the French nobility who led them. The rest of the army was made up of peasants conscripted for the occasion.

Henry's army, by contrast, was a professional outfit of permanent soldiers, well paid and disciplined, a large proportion of whom were archers armed with the very latest in lethal weaponry—powerful longbows and armor-piercing arrows. The match was less uneven than it looked. The French had chosen a very poor field on which to do battle, and the weather was helping.

On the morning of October 25 (St. Crispin's Day), the two armies faced each other along a valley floor that had been plowed and on which the rain had been falling, with dense woodland on either side. The valley was less than three-quarters of a mile wide at the French end and narrowed toward the English. Henry arranged his army with the men-at-arms in the center and the bowmen forming a wing on each side. The French formed three tightly packed lines, one in front of the other.

Tired of waiting for the French to attack, at 11am Henry ordered his men to advance, stopping some 300 yards from the French front line. Here the archers placed a row of sharpened staves in the ground, sloping forward

THE ARMIES MEET

THE BATTLE OF AGINCOURT

to check any cavalry advance, and then loosed a volley of arrows. The French charged, the front rows of heavily armored knights running forward over the thick, wet earth that turned to mud as thousands of feet churned it up. Under a hail of arrows (each archer was capable of loosing an arrow every ten seconds), pressed shoulder to shoulder by the narrowing valley and unable to even swing their two-handed swords, the French knights fell and were trampled by the rows behind them. Unaware of what was happening ahead of them, the French cavalry then swept forward and added to the pandemonium. Horses, pierced by arrows, threw their riders and bolted away from the danger, crashing through the rows behind them.

The lightly clad English and Welsh archers now threw down their longbows and ran into the fray wielding their swords. The carnage was terrible, and some 1,700 of the most ransomable knights and nobles were captured. At this point word reached Henry that a further wave of French forces was attacking from the rear, and at this he ordered his men to kill all their prisoners so that they could not escape and rejoin the battle. Unwilling to lose potential ransom money, Henry's men had to be threatened by a group of his archers before they would put their charges to death, and hundreds were killed before it was learned that the "attack from the rear" was in fact local villagers looting the English camp. Virtually an entire generation of the French nobility had been massacred.

By now the rest of the French army was in flight, and the valley was littered with the dead. It is thought that while Henry's army lost less than 200 men, the French losses may have topped 10,000. The English, laden with booty from the battlefield, continued their march to Calais and King Henry V returned to England victorious. There were those, especially among the French, who felt that Henry had acted dishonorably in having the prisoners put to death, but he was received as the conquering hero, although he himself gave credit for the success of his army to God.

In fact, by underestimating the threat posed by the English longbows, and by choosing to do battle in a location that prevented them from using their cavalry, weapons, and skills to the full, it was the French who had snatched defeat from the jaws of victory.

THE MING DYNASTY TURNS ITS BACK ON THE WORLD

1435

MOTIVATION

Anger

Charity

Envy

Faith

Gluttony

Greed

Hope

Lust

Pride

Sloth

Main Culprits: The emperors of the Ming Dynasty

Damage Done: China's lead in so many aspects of culture and technology was lost

Why: Chinese civilization became focused inward, believing that the country could be economically and intellectually self-sufficient

We, Zheng He and his companions, at the beginning of Zhu Di's reign received the Imperial Commission as envoys to the barbarians. Up until now seven voyages have taken place and, each time, we have commanded several tens of thousands of government soldiers and more than a hundred oceangoing vessels. We have . . . reached countries of the Eastern Regions, more than thirty countries in all. We have . . . beheld in the ocean huge waves like mountains rising sky-high, and we have set eyes on barbarian regions far away, hidden in a blue transparency of light vapors, whilst our sails, loftily unfurled like clouds, day and night continued their course, rapid like that of a star, traversing those savage waves.

Zhou Man, Chinese admiral, 1431

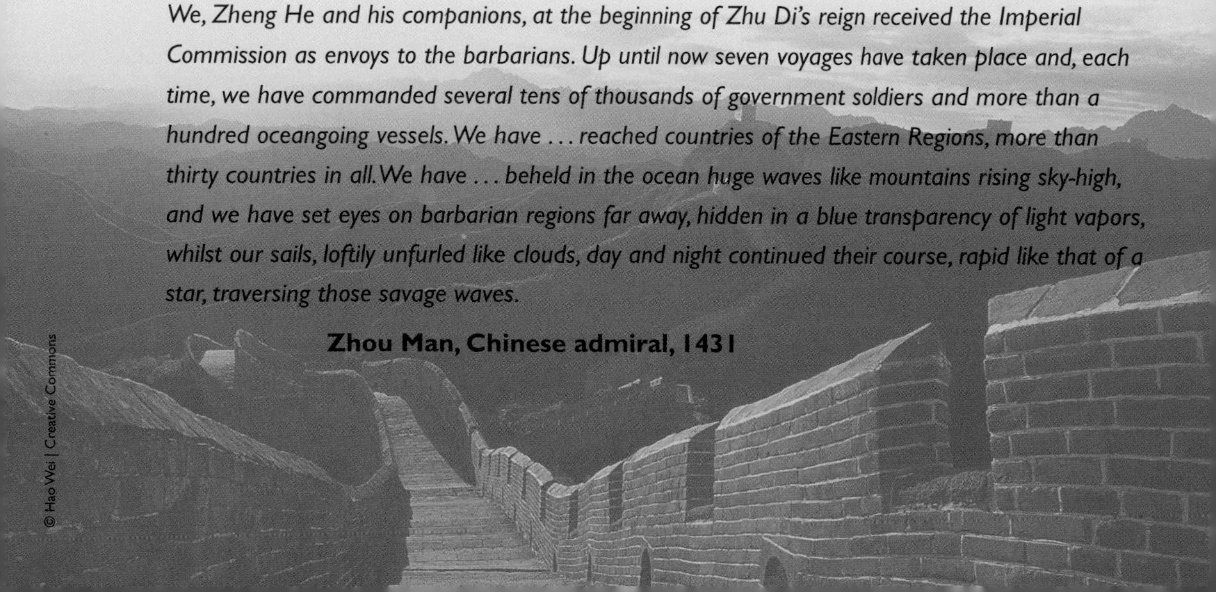

In the early 15th century, after dominating the world in terms of technology, culture, agriculture, infrastructure, and social organization for more than 1,000 years, China went through a period of exceptional exploration and self-promotion. It was on the verge of becoming a dominant power when the ruling Ming Dynasty suddenly and deliberately closed the door on the wider world. It was a decision that plunged China into centuries of isolation from commercial and intellectual exchange, making it a minor player on the international stage.

KUBLAI KHAN
The Yuan Dynasty, which preceded that of the Ming, was established in 1271 by the Mongolian leader Kublai Khan, the grandson of Genghis Khan.

The Middle Ages in Europe, from approximately the decline of the Roman Empire to the Italian Renaissance (the 5th to the 14th centuries), have been described as the Dark Ages, denoting a period during which there was little in the way of fine literature, great architecture, or intellectual and scientific progress. The characterization is an unfair one—unless one compares what was happening in Europe with events taking place in China. Throughout that same 1,000 years, China became the world's most advanced civilization, due in large part to technological inventions. The celebrated "Four Great Inventions"—paper, printing, gunpowder, and the magnetic compass—were all in common use in China long before they finally reached the West.

Paper was first invented in China at the beginning of the 2nd century, and in the 8th century printing was developed, first using wood blocks and later, in the 11th century, using moveable type. Literature—and literacy—flourished, along with dictionaries, histories, civil records, and even newspapers. In 10th-century China, gunpowder was being used in early guns and grenades, and later in landmines, cannons, and rockets. By the 12th century the magnetic compass was being used for navigation.

These famous four are just the tip of the iceberg. Cast iron, for example, was first used in the West in the 14th century. The Chinese had been using the material in a host of ways—in agriculture, weaponry, even building construction—for 1,700 years. Porcelain, the abacus, the mechanical clock, water pumps—the list of Chinese inventions is endless. Scientific learning, too, reached a remarkable level in fields such as mathematics, astronomy, biology, and medicine.

Under successive emperors, and a well-organized government bureaucracy, the country's agriculture production was developed using methods that were far ahead of those of Europe at the time. Well-maintained roads connected large urban centers, allowing for easy movement of goods, troops, and government officials. The Great Canal of China, a major transport highway running more than 1,000 miles (1,600 km) from Beijing to Hangzhou, was completed in the 7th century, and it is still the world's longest canal. A series of defensive walls, with a total length of almost 4,000 miles (6,500 km), was built and maintained to protect China's northern border.

After a period of deep social unrest under the Mongol-led Yuan Dynasty (1271–1368), order and stability within the country were restored under the Ming (meaning "Bright") Dynasty. The third Ming emperor, the Yongle Emperor (born Zhu Di), made Beijing his capital and oversaw the building of the Forbidden City there as the seat of government and the imperial family. Using military might, he extended China's influence over Mongolia and Tibet in the north, and over Korea and Vietnam in the south. The Yongle Emperor also looked farther afield, and in 1405 he sponsored the first in a series of voyages, the most remarkable seafaring expeditions the world has ever known in terms of their scale and duration.

Overall command for the voyages was entrusted to the eunuch Zheng He, an experienced mariner and the commander of the Imperial navy. The fleet that set off in 1405 is said to have consisted of more than 250 vessels, 60 of them being gigantic "treasure ships," more than 400 feet (120 m) long (more than five times the length of Columbus's *Santa Maria*), with four decks and up to nine masts, and each accommodating 500 passengers. Supporting ships carried troops, horses, food and supplies, and water. When one considers the size and scale of the fleets of such explorers as Columbus in 1492 (three ships and 90 men), Vasco da Gama in 1498 (four ships and 150 men), or Magellan in 1521 (five ships and less than 300 men), this was exploration on an epic scale.

The purpose of the voyages—of which there were seven altogether between 1405 and 1433—was to demonstrate to the world the might and splendor of the Ming Dynasty, as well as to collect tribute for the emperor from "the barbarians." It was essentially a diplomatic public

NATIONAL ORGANIZATION

ADMIRAL ZHENG HE
The exploits of the admiral, who died during a voyage in 1433, were suppressed by the authorities, but they lived on in popular writings and are now celebrated by the Chinese.

relations exercise, and no doubt it succeeded. The sight of such a fleet must have inspired terror and admiration everywhere it went. Although the fleet carried its own army, force was rarely used, and Zheng He and his floating community peacefully visited the coasts of some 30 countries throughout the Indian Ocean, from Thailand, Java, and India to the Arabian Peninsula and East Africa. They may even have rounded the Cape of Good Hope and traveled some distance up the Atlantic coast of Africa. To each country they brought gifts of precious metals, porcelain, and silk, and they returned to China with exotic tributes for the emperor (including the first giraffe ever seen in China), and even envoys sent by the countries they had visited.

Although the voyages were not intended as a trading mission, the contacts and information that were gathered by Zheng He and his entourage would have enabled China to dominate the region economically and politically, but it was not to be. After the end of the Zheng He's final voyage in 1435, the Ming rulers placed a ban on maritime trading, partly because government funds were needed to improve fortifications in the north and to repel the invading Mongols, but also because of a fundamental return to an inward-looking national philosophy that regarded China as complete in itself, with no need to look beyond its borders.

The greatest civilization on earth, poised on the brink of becoming a world-class maritime power, returned to self-imposed isolation. While the pace of change in Europe accelerated, especially through the Industrial Revolution, technological innovation in China ground to a halt, and although a certain amount of trade continued, it was the up-and-coming trading nations—Portugal, Japan, Spain, the Netherlands, Britain, and later the US—that came to dominate the eastern seas and even the Chinese coast.

THE POPE EXCOMMUNICATES MARTIN LUTHER

1521

MOTIVATION
Anger
Charity
Envy
Faith
Gluttony
Greed
Hope
Lust
Pride
Sloth

Main Culprit: Pope Leo X

Damage Done: Led to the Protestant Reformation, and half of Europe rejected the Roman Catholic Church

Why: The Pope refused to listen or respond to criticisms directed at the papacy or the Roman Catholic Church

Since your majesty and your lordships desire a simple reply, I will answer without horns or teeth. Unless I am convinced by Scripture and by plain reason (I do not believe in the authority of either popes or councils by themselves, for it is plain that they have often erred and contradicted each other) in those Scriptures that I have presented, for my conscience is captive to the Word of God, I cannot and I will not recant anything, for to go against conscience is neither right nor safe. Here I stand; I can do no other. God help me. Amen.

Martin Luther, replying to the Diet of Worms

In 15th-century Europe, as the Roman Catholic Church assumed ever greater political power and accrued ever more wealth, sometimes by questionable means, voices were increasingly raised in dissent. For his writings against the corruption of the papacy, the English theologian John Wycliffe, whose followers were known as Lollards, was posthumously declared a heretic, and his remains were dug up and burned 44 years after his death. In Prague, the Czech reformer Jan Hus was burned at the stake in 1415 for his criticisms of the Catholic Church, but the vast majority of the Czech people followed his teachings and broke away from Roman Catholicism. When, a century later, Martin Luther published his list of criticisms of the Church's doctrines and practices, and questioned papal authority, the Pope refused to discuss the issues and ultimately excommunicated him. The result was the Protestant Reformation, a series of religious wars, a second major schism in the Church, and the loss of Papal authority over half of Europe.

MARTIN LUTHER
The German priest raised important issues of doctrine and authority, believing that knowledge of God was a matter of direct and personal experience.

Born in Germany in 1483 and baptized a Catholic the following day, Martin Luther attended several schools where he was educated in the Latin staples of grammar, rhetoric, and logic, as his father wanted him to become a lawyer. After receiving his Bachelor's and Master's degrees from the University of Erfurt, he enrolled in the school of law there but became more interested in philosophy and then theology. Already the young Luther had a strong conviction that knowledge of God could only be achieved through divine revelation, and not through logic, philosophy, or reason. He soon left the university and joined a closed Augustinian order (much to his father's disappointment), where he devoted himself to reading the scriptures, praying, fasting, confessing his sins, and becoming increasingly introspective. After being advised by his superior at the friary that he should become a teacher, in 1507 he was ordained as a priest and the following year he joined the University of Wittenberg as a lecturer in theology. Here he continued his own Bible studies, receiving a doctorate in 1512. His studies of the scriptures were increasingly leading him to the conclusion that many of the doctrines and practices of the Roman Catholic Church, as well as the way it was structured and operated, were inconsistent with the teachings of the Bible, if not actually sinful. High on his list of criticisms was the selling of indulgences.

THE ISSUE OF INDULGENCES

Since the 11th century, the Catholic Church had developed the practice of selling indulgences, complete or partial remission of the temporal (as opposed to eternal) punishment for sins that have already been confessed and absolved. The Church was able to do this as the sole custodian of the Treasury of Merit that had accrued from the actions of Jesus Christ and the saints, from which the indulgences were drawn. Over the centuries, the practice became increasingly common and increasingly abused, coming to represent an important revenue stream both for the papacy, to whom much of the money was remitted, and for the local Church authorities, which shared the income. Indulgences were neither pardons for sinning nor remissions of punishment for the dead, but they came to be portrayed and understood in this way. For Martin Luther, the matter reached a head in 1516 during the visit to Germany of one Johann Tetzel, sent by Pope Leo X to raise money—through the sale of indulgences—for the rebuilding of St. Peter's Basilica in Rome. Luther took exception to the practice as a whole (questioning the idea of the Pope, one of the richest men in the world, raising money for his projects from the poor), but particularly to Tetzel's sales pitch, which claimed that the purchase of an indulgence could release a deceased person from purgatory. Even more fundamentally, Martin Luther questioned the moral right of the Church to sell something that only God could dispense. He believed that justification (or being made righteous) was not a reward for good works (such as donating money to Church coffers) but was freely given by God to all who have faith. Indulgences had come under attack from reformers in the past, but Luther was basing his objections on theological arguments.

At the end of October 1517, Luther put all his criticisms of this practice down on paper in the form of a discussion document entitled "Disputation of Martin Luther on the Power and Efficacy of Indulgences," which he sent to Archbishop Albrecht of Magdeburg and Mainz. (History has it that he nailed this document, which became known as the 95 Theses, to the door of the Castle Church, but there is little evidence to support this.)

The archbishop was not kindly disposed toward the criticisms. It was he who had initially invited Tetzel to Germany on a sales trip, and he was benefiting directly from the monies raised, which he was using to pay the Pope for a special dispensation that allowed him to be archbishop of two bishoprics at the same time. Rather than opening a debate on the matter with Luther, Archbishop Albrecht forwarded the document to the Pope, the subject of much of the criticism.

POPE LEO X
The Pope brought considerable pressure to bear on Luther in order to bring him into line, but excommunicating him only fueled popular protest against the power of the Catholic Church.

Over a period of years, Pope Leo X pitted theologians against Luther, brought a case for heresy against him, and tried to force him to recant his views, but Luther only became more outspoken, refusing to recognize the authority of the Pope and writing further essays attacking the Church. Finally, in 1520, the Pope had a papal edict made public in the city of Wittenberg threatening Luther with excommunication unless he recanted many of the 95 Theses. Luther responded by burning the papal edict, and in early January 1521 he was excommunicated. He was then called before a Church diet, or assembly, held in the city of Worms, at which he confirmed that he stood by what he had written and took the opportunity to have a further dig at the errors and contradictions committed by the Pope and the Church. The conclusion of the Diet of Worms was that his writings be banned and he himself be declared an outlaw and a heretic. If the Holy Roman Church thought that this would put an end to the matter, it was sorely mistaken.

This was no local fracas between the Church and one upstart theologian. In 1518, a friend and supporter of Luther had translated his 95 Theses from Latin into German and within weeks, benefiting from the recently developed printing press, his tract had been distributed throughout Germany. Within a year his criticisms were to be found throughout Europe, and they met with a broad popular response. As various reformers threw their weight behind Luther's central aims, differences between their views of Christian doctrine began to surface and several different Protestant ("protesting" Roman Catholic orthodoxy) denominations came into being, in many cases supported by state leaders and institutions anxious to be free of papal political power. These denominations included the Lutheran Church in Germany and

Scandinavia, and the Calvinist Reformed Church in Switzerland and France, as well as more radical variations. Despite a concerted Counter-Reformation by the Roman Catholic Church, which was successful in Spain and Italy, Protestantism dominated northern and eastern Europe by the middle of the 17th century, and the Peace of Westphalia, which ended the bloody Thirty Years' War, asserted the rights of European leaders to determine the state religion (choosing between Catholicism, Lutheranism, and Calvinism). Protestantism represented a permanent theological and organizational break from the Catholic Church, rejecting the doctrine that it is the one true church. Christians of all denominations were free to practice their chosen religion, and papal hegemony over Europe was at an end. Pope Innocent X responded by declaring the Westphalia treaty null and void, not to mention damnable and inane, but that didn't change the facts.

DESPITE A CONCERTED COUNTER-REFORMATION BY THE ROMAN CATHOLIC CHURCH, PROTESTANTISM DOMINATED NORTHERN AND EASTERN EUROPE BY THE MIDDLE OF THE 17TH CENTURY.

MOTIVATION

Anger

Charity

Envy

Faith

Gluttony

Greed

Hope

Lust

Pride

Sloth

THE INCA ATAHUALPA MEETS PIZARRO THE CONQUISTADOR

November 15, 1532

Main Culprit: Francisco Pizarro

Damage Done: The total destruction of an entire civilization

Why: To convert pagans to the true religion and garner unimagined wealth for king and country

Though rude nations are frequently cunning and false, yet, if a scheme of deception and treachery must be imputed either to a monarch that had no great reason to be alarmed at a visit from strangers who solicited admission into his presence as friends, or to an adventurer so daring and so little scrupulous as Pizarro, one cannot hesitate in determining where to fix the presumption of guilt.

William Robertson, *A General History of North and South America,* **1834**

When a small expeditionary Spanish force, led by Francisco Pizarro, made its way from the Pacific coast into the interior of what is now Peru, in 1532, they found a complex and highly organized society. In the course of the previous century, through conquests and political alliances, successive generations of the ruling Inca dynasty had brought under their control an empire that extended from Colombia in the north to Chile in the south—a distance of almost 3,000 miles (4,800 km)—and encompassed Ecuador, Peru, and parts of what are now Bolivia and Argentina. The terrain was enormously varied, from the jungle of the west, through the Andean highlands to the coastal plains and the desert of the south. Cities built from huge blocks of meticulously cut rock displayed a high level of architectural and engineering skill. A form of civil service regulated community life, and agriculture thrived under a feudal system that exacted labor and taxes from the work force. Along a system of well-maintained footpaths, messengers carried imperial instructions quickly throughout the territory, and pack animals transported food and goods between settlements. A rich material culture included beautiful textiles, ornate pottery, precious stones and—of particular interest to the Spaniards—finely worked objects of gold and silver.

FRANCISCO PIZARRO
Hailed by the Spanish as a great explorer and conquering hero, Pizarro is regarded by many Peruvians as the destroyer of their native culture, language, and religion.

Given that the Spanish force was small—less than 170 men and some 27 horses—and that their goal was nothing less than to take over the Inca Empire in the name of King Charles I of Spain, the timing of their arrival was fortuitous. Upon the death of the former ruling Inca, Huayna Capac, some five years earlier, control of the empire had been divided between his two sons—Atahualpa in the north and Huáscar in the south—and the result had been civil war. The majority of Atahualpa's troops, and two of his finest generals, were still in the region of Cuzco, a long way to the south. Furthermore, some of the tribes on the fringes of the empire had begun to rebel against the central power, and the first effects of a smallpox epidemic in the far north may have begun to be felt by the Incas. Atahualpa had just defeated his brother and he was camped with some of his army close to the town of Cajamarca, not far from the coast. Upon learning that a party of foreigners was making its way inland, Atahualpa sent one of his noblemen to meet them and to invite them to meet him in Cajamarca. The nobleman stayed with the Spaniards for two days, no doubt impressed by the Spaniards' armor, weapons, and horses, never before seen in South America, and reported back to Atahualpa.

Pizarro and his band accepted the invitation and entered the city, which was largely empty, on November 15. Sending an envoy to Atahualpa asking him to come to the town square the following day, Pizarro set about formulating a plan to capture the Inca, by force if necessary.

Before the appointed time, Pizarro deployed his men in three long buildings around the main plaza so that they, the horses, and the artillery were out of sight. Atahualpa duly arrived, borne upon a litter carried by 80 of his men and accompanied by several thousand of his soldiers, probably unarmed. There is little doubt that he felt in command of the situation—not surprisingly, given that he had lured the Spanish into the heart of his territory and had 80,000 of his troops positioned on the high ground around the city. Indeed, there is evidence that he intended to capture or even destroy the small Spanish force—but that's not the way it panned out.

Within the confines of the square, he was met by a small group of Spaniards, including Pizarro, or even, according to some accounts, by just the Spanish missionary Vincente de Valverde, who explained the truth of Christianity and ordered the Inca to convert to Catholicism. The friar then gave him a Bible or a prayer book, which Atahualpa (probably confused, certainly unable to read, and possibly anxious to maintain his dignity) dropped on the ground. Pizarro immediately took this perceived slight against the Church as an excuse to order his army to attack, and they promptly opened fire with muskets and four small cannons on the mass of Inca soldiers. Many of the Incas were killed or injured by gunfire or cut down by the charging Spanish cavalry—it is thought that as many as 2,000 died—and the remainder fled from the square in shock and panic. It is said that Atahualpa's litter bearers continued to protect and support their leader even when their hands had been cut off by Spanish swords. When the litter was finally dropped, others barred the way and allowed themselves to be killed by the Spanish soldiers, but eventually Pizarro himself reached the litter. He seized Atahualpa just as one of his own soldiers attempted to kill the

MANY OF THE INCAS WERE KILLED OR INJURED BY GUNFIRE OR CUT DOWN BY THE CHARGING SPANISH CAVALRY.

Inca with his sword, and Pizarro was wounded warding off the blow with his hand—he needed a captive ruler, not a dead one.

Atahualpa was held prisoner and treated well, and through him Pizarro effectively had control of the Inca Empire. Within days the abandoned army camp outside the city was ransacked and the Spanish took large quantities of gold and silver, but they now knew that this land held considerable treasure. Atahualpa bargained with them and agreed to half fill a specific room in Cajamarca with gold and to fill it twice over with silver in return for his freedom or, more probably, for his life. On his orders, gold and silver works of art and religious objects were brought from temples and palaces all across the empire, and by May of 1533 he had fulfilled his part of the bargain. Estimates put the weight of the gold at more than 11 tons, and the weight of silver at more than twice that. These precious artifacts were then melted down and cast into ingots, and the wealth was shared out, with one fifth being sent to the king of Spain and the rest being divided among the soldiers.

In the meantime, fearing that his brother might fall into the hands of the Spanish and replace him as puppet emperor, Atahualpa had arranged to have Huáscar killed. When Pizarro decided that Atahualpa had become more of a liability than an asset, this was one of the crimes of which he was accused, along with polygamy, idolatry, and plotting against the Spanish. To no one's surprise, the Inca emperor was found guilty and he was sentenced to be burned at the stake. This means of execution ran counter to the Incan belief in the afterlife, when he would need his body to be intact, and Atahualpa therefore agreed to be baptized into the Christian faith if he could be garroted instead. On August 29, 1533, after being given the name of Francisco, he was strangled as per his wishes and was buried as a Christian. His death sealed the fate of the Inca Empire.

CAPTURED INCA
This 18th-century engraving shows Pizarro and his men arresting the Inca emperor Atahualpa in the town of Cajamarca. He was later strangled.

Although there were several Inca uprisings against the Spanish in the years that followed, within 60 years the Conquistadors had subdued and Christianized the people of this vast portion of South America. Following the destruction of the Aztec and Mayan cultures by the Spanish in Central America, the demise of the Incas marked the end of several millennia of indigenous culture. The Inca temples were torn down and replaced with Spanish-style buildings on Inca foundations. The region's gold and silver were systematically seized, its languages disappeared, and the population declined by more than 90 percent, not through the use of force by the Spanish—although force was widely used—but as a result of diseases such as smallpox and measles that the Europeans brought with them.

Whether the outcome would have been different had Atahualpa used his enormous army to stop a handful of Spanish soldiers in their tracks we shall never know, but his decision to meet Pizarro in Cajamarca plaza handed the Inca Empire to the Spanish on a plate.

HENRY VIII WANTS A SON

1534

MOTIVATION

Anger

Charity

Envy

Faith

Gluttony

Greed

Hope

Lust

Pride

Sloth

Main Culprit: Henry VIII

Damage Done: The course of development of the Christian Church in England was changed for ever

Why: Henry could not gain the Pope's approval to nullify his first marriage and undertake a second, so he denied the authority of the Pope and became head of the Church in England

By the ordinance and sufferance of God we are king of England, and the kings of England in time past have never had any superior but God alone. Wherefore know you well that we shall maintain the right of our crown and of our temporal jurisdiction as well in this point as in all others.

Henry VIII, November 1515

While the Protestant Reformation was in full swing in Germany, England was being ruled by King Henry VIII, who had ascended to the throne in 1509. A few days before his coronation Henry was married to Catherine of Aragon, the widow of his elder brother Arthur, who had died after being married to her for only five months. According to the law of the Catholic Church, a man may not marry his brother's widow, consistent with Leviticus 20:21, which reads, "If a man takes his brother's wife, it is impurity. He has uncovered his brother's nakedness; they shall be childless." However, Pope Julius II gave Henry a special dispensation to marry Catherine on the grounds that her marriage to Arthur had never been consummated and that the marriage had not, therefore, been valid.

KING HENRY VIII
Although he was critical of Martin Luther and the Protestant Reformation, when it suited his personal ambition Henry was willing to reject the authority of Rome.

Catherine was, by all accounts, a remarkable woman. Five years Henry's senior, she was attractive, intelligent, and well educated, and she impressed all who met her. She had acted as the Spanish ambassador to England (Europe's first female ambassador) before her marriage to Henry, and as his queen consort she was appointed regent in 1513 while Henry was in France. During that time the Scots invaded England and Catherine rode north in full armor, despite being pregnant, and oversaw the English victory at the Battle of Flodden Field. She had only one fault in Henry's eyes—she didn't bear him a son that survived infancy. After six pregnancies, their only surviving child was a girl, christened Mary, and Henry was determined to have a male heir so that there could be no dispute over the succession to the throne or the continuance of the Tudor line.

In 1525, when Catherine was 40 years old and unlikely to bear further children, Henry VIII found himself strongly attracted to one of his wife's maids of honor, the young Anne Boleyn, whom he pursued enthusiastically. She, however, refused to follow in the footsteps of her elder sister, Mary, with whom the king had already had an affair lasting several years (Mary may even have borne him two children, including a son, whom the king did not acknowledge). For Anne it was marriage or nothing, and so the king put into operation a plan that he may have had for some time. He would apply to Pope Clement VII to have his marriage to Catherine of Aragon annulled (the Roman Catholic

Church prohibits divorce), declared null and void on the grounds that Catherine's marriage to Arthur (Henry's late brother) had in fact been consummated and that the dispensation from Pope Julius II had been obtained under false pretences. The passage in Leviticus therefore held true and their union had been "blighted in the eyes of God." This would mean, of course, that Catherine and Henry had been living in sin since 1509 and that their daughter Mary was illegitimate, but that was a small price to pay for being able to marry Anne and produce a male heir to the throne. As it turned out, however, obtaining an annulment was not to prove so easy.

In 1527, bypassing Cardinal Thomas Wolsey, the papal legate as well as an important figure in matters of state in England, Henry VIII sent an envoy to Rome to petition Pope Clement VII for an annulment as well as a dispensation to marry any woman, even one with whom there was an affinal relationship, albeit through an unlawful connection. This was clearly a reference to Anne being the sister of Henry's former mistress, just as he was the brother of Catherine's former husband: the last thing he needed was another cursed marriage.

"THE KING'S GREAT MATTER"

Unfortunately, when the king's envoy reached Rome the city had just been sacked by the forces of Emperor Charles V and the Pope was effectively a prisoner, so he was in no position to give a definitive answer. The envoy returned to England, and Henry then passed the matter over to Cardinal Wolsey, who in turn made a strong case to the Pope and even suggested that a papal representative attend an ecclesiastical court in England to resolve the question there. The Pope refused, and prohibited Henry from remarrying until a decision had been made in Rome. Angry at Thomas Wolsey's failure, the king dismissed the cardinal from public office. (Wolsey was later arrested for siding with the Pope and plotting against Anne, and he would probably have been executed had he not died of natural causes in 1530.)

The Pope, in the meantime, was in an invidious position. Emperor Charles V held considerable power over him and, as the nephew of Catherine of Aragon, Charles was opposed to the annulment. Furthermore, the Protestant reformers, critical of papal infallibility and claiming that popes actually made decisions that best suited them, would be given further ammunition if Pope Clement VII were to overturn the earlier dispensation and state that Pope Julius II had erred. Equally anxious not to anger Henry VIII, the Pope delayed making any decision.

Henry then began to take matters into his own hands, banishing Catherine from court and bringing in Anne Boleyn in her stead. He appointed Sir Thomas More, who supported Henry's contention that his marriage to Catherine had been invalid, as Lord Chancellor in place of Thomas Wolsey, and the Boleyn family's own chaplain, Thomas Cranmer was appointed as the new Archbishop of Canterbury, with the Pope's approval.

THE BREAK WITH ROME

Henry VIII had been a devout Catholic and had even written a book criticizing Martin Luther's attacks on the Church, but now he was no longer willing to submit to the authority of Rome. In 1532, several acts were brought before Parliament by the pro-Reformation (and pro-Anne Boleyn) lawyer Thomas Cromwell (Thomas was clearly a very popular name in the late 15th century) in which the king's supremacy over the Church was recognized, and at the end of that year Henry and Anne were married in secret. A few weeks later, in January 1533, they were married in public in London, and in May a special court, headed by Archbishop Cranmer, declared Henry's first marriage to be null and void. This annulment was itself declared null and void by Pope Clement VII, and he excommunicated both Henry and Cranmer. In June, Anne was made queen consort in Catherine's stead, and three months later she gave birth to a girl, the future Queen Elizabeth I.

Henry's formal rejection of the authority of Rome occurred in November 1534, when the English Parliament passed the Act of Supremacy that declared the monarch to be "the only supreme head on earth of the Church in England." Refusal to accept the Act became a crime under the Treason Act, and Sir Thomas More, who refused to deny the authority of the Pope, lost his head as a result.

His was not the only blood to be shed over the issue of religion in England in the years that followed. The Church of England became strongly Protestant under King Edward VI (Henry's son by Jane Seymour, his third wife), but Roman Catholicism was restored for a short time under Catherine's daughter, Queen Mary, who became known as "Bloody Mary" for her persecution of the Protestants (almost 300 of whom were burned at the stake). Under Queen Elizabeth I, the Act of Supremacy and the Act of Uniformity established the independence and the form of the Church of England. The authority of the Holy Church of Rome over England was permanently ended, as a direct result of Henry VIII's insistence on marrying Anne Boleyn and the Pope's refusal to grant him an annulment. The Anglican Communion, of which the Church of England is the mother church, now has some 80 million adherents worldwide, is the third largest church after the Roman Catholic and Eastern Orthodox Churches.

ANNE BOLEYN
Despite his original infatuation, when Anne failed to produce a male heir, Henry had her tried for high treason and convicted. Anne was beheaded on May 19, 1536.

MOTIVATION

Anger

Charity

Envy

Faith

Gluttony

Greed

Hope

Lust

Pride

Sloth

PHILIP II OF SPAIN LAUNCHES THE ARMADA

1588

Main Culprit: King Philip II of Spain

Damage Done: The sinking of half the Spanish fleet and the deaths of some 16,000 Spanish sailors and soldiers

Why: King Philip's planned invasion of England was ill considered and poorly planned

My loving people ... I am come amongst you, as you see, at this time, not for my recreation and disport, but being resolved, in the midst and heat of the battle, to live and die amongst you all; to lay down for my God, and for my kingdom, and my people, my honour and my blood even, in the dust.

I know I have the body but of a weak and feeble woman; but I have the heart and stomach of a king, and of a king of England too, and think foul scorn that Parma or Spain, or any prince of Europe, should dare to invade the borders of my realm.

Not doubting but by your obedience to my general, by your concord in the camp, and your valour in the field, we shall shortly have a famous victory over those enemies of my God, of my kingdom, and of my people.

From Queen Elizabeth I's speech to her forces gathered at Tilbury, in August 1588.

If there's one thing we can learn from our journey through history's disasters, it is that when a person in absolute authority gets a bee in his bonnet (and it usually is a he), there is little that anyone can do to prevent him pursuing it, no matter how predictable the unfortunate outcome may be. The defeat of the Spanish Armada by the English navy in 1588 has been hailed as a glorious event in British history and as Queen Elizabeth I's finest hour, but King Philip II of Spain's planned invasion of England was flawed from the outset. Bad management and even worse weather merely compounded the problem.

Since the death of his wife, Queen Mary (with whom he had been the joint ruler of England) in 1558 and the coronation of Mary's sister, the Protestant queen Elizabeth I, relations between England and Catholic Spain had deteriorated considerably. Catholics did not recognize Elizabeth's right to the throne, since she was the daughter of Henry VIII and Anne Boleyn, a union that the Catholic Church deemed illegitimate. Elizabeth had further antagonized the Catholics by declaring the Church of England to be the official church, and by supporting Protestantism in France and in the Netherlands. The signing of the Treaty of Nonsuch in 1585, which pledged England's financial and military support for the Protestant Dutch against the Spanish, was seen by King Philip as a declaration of war. The restoration of a Catholic monarchy was undoubtedly one of the principal motives behind King Philip II's plan to invade England, and in this he had the support of Pope Sixtus V, but it would also enable him to cut off aid to the Protestants in the Low Countries and put an end to the piracy of such privateers as Sir Francis Drake, who had repeatedly raided Spanish ships in the West Indies and in the Atlantic, seizing goods, gold, and treasure that were destined to fund the Spanish king's empire building.

PHILIP II OF SPAIN
Philip was a staunch defender of Catholicism in Europe, and throughout his reign Spain was at war with various countries. He also extended Spanish influence around the globe.

Queen Elizabeth was aware of Philip's planned invasion, and in the spring of 1587 Drake sailed south with four naval vessels and some twenty merchant vessels and small armed sailing boats to the Atlantic coast of Spain, where they inflicted such heavy damage on the Spanish fleet assembled in Cadiz harbor that the invasion had to be postponed for a year, during which time England was able to prepare. Drake referred to the attack as "singeing the king of Spain's beard."

It had been King Philip's intention that the campaign be commanded by the renowned admiral the Marquis of Santa Cruz, who had been an avid supporter of the plan, but he died in February of 1588. The king had already chosen his replacement—the Duke of Sidonia Medina, a strongly Christian aristocrat with little military experience who had never been to sea, but a man who could be expected to comply with the king's wishes. The Armada, composed of more than 130 ships and carrying 8,000 sailors and 18,000 soldiers, left the Portuguese port of Lisbon at the end of May 1588. The fleet was to sail to Flanders on the European coast opposite the southeast tip of England and escort an army of 30,000 soldiers across the Channel and up the Thames to land near London. The Duke of Parma would have the men ready and waiting to put to sea in barges and meet up with the fleet.

Held back by adverse winds, it took the Armada almost eight weeks to reach the southwest tip of England, where they were spotted by lookouts on July 19. Part of the English preparations had been the construction of a series of beacons along the south coast and then north to London. The first was lit and then each one in turn, alerting Sir Francis Drake, whose fleet was stationed in Plymouth, and, within a short space of time, the queen herself. Held in the harbor by a flooding tide, the British fleet could not put to sea for a few hours, giving Drake, it is said, time to finish the game of bowls that he was playing. The Spanish considered attacking the English ships in the harbor, but as the king had expressly forbidden tackling the British navy, Sidonia Medina vetoed the plan. A little initiative might have been a good thing at this point.

THE FIRST WAS LIT AND THEN EACH ONE IN TURN, ALERTING SIR FRANCIS DRAKE, WHOSE FLEET WAS STATIONED IN PLYMOUTH, AND, WITHIN A SHORT SPACE OF TIME, THE QUEEN HERSELF.

The two navies engaged in battle twice as the Spanish made their way eastward, first on the morning of the 21st and again on the 23rd. Little damage was inflicted on either side, but the weaknesses of the Spanish force were obvious. Firstly the Spanish fleet was not designed to do battle. The large galleons, whose purpose was to act as troop transporters, were slow and cumbersome. In order to protect them, the fleet had to travel in a crescent formation with the larger ships at the center protected by the smaller vessels forming the horns. The Spanish fighting tactics traditionally involved bringing their ships alongside the enemy vessels, boarding them, and then fighting at close quarters. The faster and more maneuverable English ships were able to avoid being boarded and instead sailed in to fire broadsides and then moved out of range.

On July 27 the Spanish fleet reached Calais and, as there was no harbor deep enough for the ships to enter, hove to off the coast in their defensive formation. As the problem of communicating with the forces on land had not been thought through, only now did Sidonia Medina learn that neither Parma's army nor their transport barges were ready, and it would be several days before they could meet the Armada and make the crossing. That would be a long time to remain vulnerable.

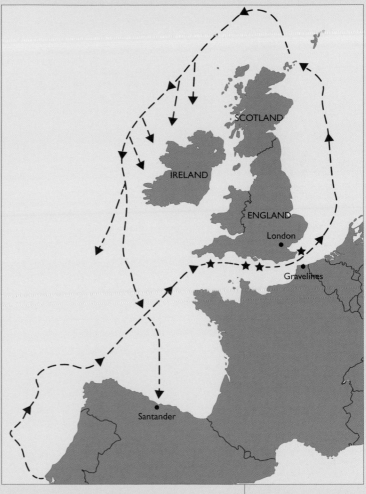

In the middle of the night the English, who were upwind of the Spanish, sent blazing fireships to drift into the moored ships of the Armada. The Spanish cut their anchor ropes and scattered, and although no ships were burned the fleet had lost its protective crescent shape and was unable to regain it as the wind blew them further along the coast. The English ships followed and, in an engagement known since as the Battle of Gravelines, they fired on the Spanish fleet throughout the day from upwind, sinking or grounding five ships and damaging many more.

It was clear to Sidonia Medina that all hope of meeting up with Parma's army was lost and that the only option was to head back to Spain,

★ Battles in the Channel

DOOMED VOYAGE
With their passage south blocked by the English navy, the Spanish ships made their way around the British Isles, and many were wrecked by storms on the rocky west coast of Ireland.

SIR FRANCIS DRAKE
Although he was regarded as a pirate by the Spanish, Drake was a hero in Britain. He was knighted in 1581 aboard his ship *The Golden Hind* after completing a circumnavigation of the globe.

but the English navy now stood in the way of a return journey southwestward along the Channel and into the wind. The Armada headed north on a route that would ultimately take them around the top of Scotland and then south past the west coasts of Scotland and Ireland. Unfortunately, a combination of the North Atlantic current and exceptionally severe westerly winds drove the ships toward land, and many were unable to prevent themselves being wrecked on the rocky and treacherous coast. Of the 130 ships and 26,000 men that had set sail from Lisbon, only 67 ships and 10,000 men returned.

CHARLES I'S CAVALIER ATTITUDE TOWARD PARLIAMENT
1625–1649

MOTIVATION

Anger

Charity

Envy

Faith

Gluttony

Greed

Hope

Lust

Pride

Sloth

Main Culprit: Charles I

Damage Done: He embroiled England in a bitter civil war, was found guilty of treason for overstepping the limits of his authority, and was beheaded by the English Parliament

Why: He believed that the divine right of kings gave him the power to overrule the wishes of the people

For the people—and truly I desire their liberty and freedom as much as anybody whomsoever— but I must tell you that their liberty and their freedom consists in having of government those laws by which their life and their goods may be most their own. It is not for having share in government, sirs, that is nothing pertaining to them.

King Charles I, on the scaffold, January 30, 1649

In England in the 1700s, religious struggles were still ongoing, and there were fears that King Charles's personal agenda—which he pursued despite Parliament's objections—might lead to a return of Catholic influence. His fervent ambition to rule as absolute monarch, his high-handed dismissal of the will of Parliament, and his collusion with the Scots in an attempt to overthrow the government backfired completely. Found guilty of treason, he was executed, and for a few years England became a republic for the only time in its history.

Charles was born in Scotland in 1600, the second son of James VI of Scotland. When James moved south to London to become James I of England in 1603, his eldest son and heir, Henry, traveled with the family but the sickly three-year-old Charles stayed behind in Scotland, too weak to travel. His life changed dramatically, however, when Henry

died and Charles, then aged 12, became heir to the throne. Charles was crowned on the death of his father in 1625, and shortly afterward he married Princess Henrietta Maria, the youngest daughter of King Henry IV of France, and a Catholic. The strongly Protestant English Parliament agreed to the marriage only on condition that restrictions placed on Catholics would not be eased, but in a secret marriage treaty Charles had promised that they would indeed be eased. He had also promised that England would help France suppress the Protestant Huguenots, whom England had supported since the reign of Queen Elizabeth I. These and other actions by the king led members of the House of Commons, among whom there were several Puritans, to fear that Charles was leading the English Church in the direction of Catholicism.

KING CHARLES I
Like his father, King James I of England, Charles believed implicitly in the divine right of kings, and had no intention of allowing Parliament to control him in any way.

When the king asked Parliament for money to fund a war against Spain (in order to help his brother-in-law, Frederick V, in Germany), the House of Commons voted to grant him far less than he wanted and also to impose restrictions on the king's right to customs duties (restrictions that he then ignored). The war against Spain was led by George Villiers, the Earl of Buckingham, a close (some say very close) friend of James I, who had become Charles's confidante and advisor with considerable influence over the king. When he returned to England after a disastrous campaign, Parliament sought to impeach him, but instead Charles appointed him Chancellor of Cambridge University. When Parliament protested that Buckingham was an unsuitable and unacceptable adviser to the king, he simply dissolved Parliament.

Ignoring his earlier promise to the king of France, Charles was now persuaded to go to war against the French in order to protect the Huguenots, Protestant rebels who were under siege from the Catholics in the French coastal town of La Rochelle. The king appointed Buckingham as Admiral of the Navy, but the expedition was a dismal failure, and Buckingham was more unpopular than ever when he returned to England. Shortly afterward, he was assassinated and, although it was probably the act of a single person, Charles blamed Parliament, and especially his chief opponent, Sir John Eliot.

During the next session of Parliament, in 1629, many of the members wished to pass a resolution concerning the king's unauthorized collection of customs duties, as well as discussing issues of religion, but the king tried to cut the debate short by calling for an adjournment. The members then physically prevented the Speaker of the House from rising, giving them time to voice a number of resolutions critical of the king, which met with broad approval. Outraged by this affront to his authority, the king not only dissolved Parliament but also had eight of the members arrested, including Sir John Eliot, who spent the rest of his life in the Tower of London, dying in 1632.

DURING THE NEXT SESSION OF PARLIAMENT, IN 1629, MANY OF THE MEMBERS WISHED TO PASS A RESOLUTION CONCERNING THE KING'S UNAUTHORIZED COLLECTION OF CUSTOMS DUTIES.

This time the king had no intention of recalling Parliament. He would rule alone, as was his right. Although he did a fairly good job over the next 11 years, and the country prospered under his benign, if autocratic, rule, his lavish spending on works of art and ostentatious architectural projects smacked of arrogance and a waste of public money, and there was a groundswell of animosity throughout the country. As usual, religion and money were the two principal causes of discontent. In the absence of Parliament, King Charles needed revenue of his own, and so in 1634 he demanded that English seaports pay ship money, a tax designed to be levied only during wartime. When he extended this tax to properties inland in 1635, it met with considerable resistance. On the religious front, William Laud, the Archbishop of Canterbury, wanted to unite the Scottish and English churches, and to this end he imposed upon the Scots the Church of England's Book of Common Prayer.

© Getty Images

THE KING'S ADVISER
Thomas Wentworth was
a strong supporter of the
king's absolute power, but
Charles was unable to
prevent Parliament from
sentencing him to death.

Perceiving this as a move toward Catholicism, the Scottish Presbyterians called for the Scottish bishops to be deposed and the prayer book to be abolished.

In 1640, Thomas Wentworth, Earl of Strafford, who had replaced Buckingham as the king's chief adviser and was strongly supportive of Charles's goal of absolute monarchy, encouraged Charles to put down the Scottish rebellion. However, Charles had to raise further funds to do this and he had no means of doing so without asking Parliament for the money, so he recalled Parliament. Led by John Pym, Parliament refused to cooperate until the king put an end to the ship tax and implemented a number of other reforms. Surprise, surprise, after just three weeks King Charles dissolved Parliament yet again (this was known as the Short Parliament!), but this time, having no other options, he had to back down, recalling Parliament six months later. It was the start of the "Long Parliament."

Now Parliament and the king were at loggerheads. John Pym had the Earl of Strafford arrested, charged with high treason, and imprisoned in the Tower of London. He was found guilty and sentenced to death, but the death warrant had to be signed by the king, which he refused to do. However, with threats being made against his wife and children, he had no choice and finally signed it. Strafford was duly dispatched.

Parliament now served the king with a list of grievances, which included a call for the king to dismiss his ministers, whom Parliament felt were providing the king with poor advice. Asserting his divine right, the king refused to be told that he could not choose his own counsel, and when Parliament threatened to impeach the queen, Charles ordered the arrest of five members of Parliament, including the man he considered to be the ringleader, John Pym. Parliament refused to hand them over and, when the king ordered their arrest, they fled.

The English Parliament was now determined to place limits on the king's power, and in 1642, fearing that the king might use the county militia against Parliament (there was no standing army), the House of Commons tabled the Militia Ordinance, legislation enabling them to implement their own choice of lieutenants over the military, and the law was passed without royal assent. It was the first step toward civil war. By the fall of 1642, both Parliament and the Royalists (or Cavaliers) had raised and armed their own armies, and the First Civil War was fought over the next three and a half years, with the Royalists faring worst. During this period, the parliamentarians, or Roundheads, formed the New Model Army, a full-time professional army. After escaping from the Siege of Oxford in April 1646, Charles surrendered to the Scottish Presbyterian army, which handed him over to Parliament. He was then confined in a series of locations, ending up in Carisbrooke Castle on the Isle of Wight. From here he arranged a deal, known as the "Engagement," with the Scots whereby he would establish Presbyterianism in return for the Scots invading England and restoring him to the throne. The Second Civil War began in July 1648, and the Scots duly played their part, but they were defeated at the Battle of Preston in August and the Royalist cause was lost.

TREASON TRIAL

Left to its own devices, the Long Parliament would have voted to accept the king's proposals for reform and for terms under which he would be allowed to return to the throne, but the commanders of the New Model Army—notably Oliver Cromwell—stepped in and took control of Parliament. In January 1649, the House of Commons agreed to set up a court to try the king for treason, having used his position to pursue personal goals and having entered into a treaty with the Scots against the English people. He was held personally responsible for the two civil wars and for all the death and suffering that they caused.

Still convinced of his position and authority under the divine right of kings, Charles refused to acknowledge the legitimacy of the High Court of Justice or its right to bring a king to trial, and he refused to plead his case. On January 27, 1649, he was found guilty and sentenced to death. He was beheaded three days later. The monarchy was at an end . . . at least for the next 11 years. The Commonwealth of England, and later the Protectorate under Oliver Cromwell and then his son Richard, gave way to the election of a predominantly Royalist Parliament in 1660, and the following year Charles II, eldest son of Charles I, took his place on the throne. The monarchy was back, albeit in a less powerful form.

MOTIVATION

Anger

Charity

Envy

Faith

Gluttony

Greed

Hope

Lust

Pride

Sloth

NAPOLEON AND THE LOUISIANA BARGAIN-BASEMENT PURCHASE

1803

Main Culprit: Napoleon Bonaparte

Damage Done: Deprived himself of money that would have helped to fund his ambitions in Europe

Why: Probably because he was so anxious to get one up on England

I know that the acquisition of Louisiana has been disapproved by some ... that the enlargement of our territory would endanger its union.... The larger our association the less will it be shaken by local passions; and in any view is it not better that the opposite bank of the Mississippi should be settled by our own brethren and children than by strangers of another family?

Thomas Jefferson

When Napoleon sold the Louisiana Territories to the United States of America in 1803, it was the first time that land had changed hands on this scale as the result of a negotiation rather than an act of war. Napoleon had good reasons—political and financial—for ceding the territory to the US, but he misjudged badly when he set the price.

The Louisiana Territories in what is now the central USA were first claimed by the French in the late 1600s, and the region was named "la Louisiane" in honor of King Louis XIV. The territory was handed over to the Spanish in 1762, shortly before the French lost the last of their possessions in the New World, but then, in 1800, in secret and under pressure from Napoleon Bonaparte, France's First Consul, Spain signed the Third Treaty of San Ildefonso, agreeing to return the old French colonial territory to France. La Louisiane was more than just what is now the US state of Louisiana—a great deal more. The territory stretched from southern Canada in the north to the Gulf of Mexico in the south, and from the Mississippi in the east to the Rockies in the west, occupying almost a quarter of the area of the USA today. It contained the whole of the present-day states of Arkansas, Iowa, Kansas, Missouri, Nebraska, and Oklahoma, as well as parts of what are now Colorado, Minnesota, Louisiana, Montana, New Mexico, North and South Dakota, Texas, and Wyoming, not to mention parts of the Canadian provinces of Alberta and Saskatchewan. This gigantic area, more than 800,000 square miles (1.3 million km²) had tremendous potential for settlement and agriculture, but the Mississippi and the port of New Orleans were of particular strategic importance for the Americans. In 1795 the US had negotiated an agreement with the Spanish—Pinckney's Treaty—allowing US vessels to use the port and to store goods there ready for shipment. The treaty also gave the Americans the right to navigate the Mississippi, which had become a vital conduit for US exports of agricultural produce, as well as for supplying the most westerly US territories, to the east of the river. When the news leaked out that France once again had possession of the territory, and especially when Napoleon sent soldiers to New Orleans in 1801, it sparked deep concern throughout the American people, who

NAPOLEON BONAPARTE
Aware that war with Britain was imminent, and unable to defend the Louisiana Territory militarily, Napoleon sold the land to the USA at a knockdown price.

feared a French invasion that might lead to the freeing of their slaves in the south.

President Thomas Jefferson immediately took steps to secure US access to the Mississippi, sending lawyer and diplomat Robert Livingston to Paris with authority to negotiate the purchase of New Orleans and the land around it for the sum of $10 million. Livingston was later joined in this mission by US founding father and later president James Monroe, and by Pierre du Pont, a French acquaintance of Jefferson living in the US, and it was du Pont who first raised the possibility of buying more than just New Orleans.

Napoleon had his own strategic reasons for wanting to control New Orleans, which is why he had negotiated its repossession from the Spanish. He had a vision of rebuilding France's empire in the New World, centered on the Caribbean island colony of Saint-Domingue, and he needed a mainland base. However, he first needed to reclaim Saint-Domingue, which had been free of French control since a widespread slave rebellion in 1791. Napoleon's forces succeeded in regaining the colony in 1802, but when it became clear that they intended to reintroduce slavery, rebellion broke out again. The French army, already ravaged by yellow fever, was finally defeated in 1803, and Napoleon abandoned his dream of a French empire in the west. The revolt of the slaves of Saint-Domingue—the only such rebellion ever to succeed—led to the establishment, in 1804, of the New World's first independent black state: Haiti.

THE FRENCH ARMY, ALREADY RAVAGED BY YELLOW FEVER, WAS FINALLY DEFEATED IN 1803, AND NAPOLEON ABANDONED HIS DREAM OF A FRENCH EMPIRE IN THE WEST.

Napoleon's reason for wanting to control New Orleans had evaporated, and he also feared that the US (and/or Great Britain) might be willing to fight for control of the territory, so Jefferson's overtures were both timely and welcome. Jefferson was, in fact, equally unwilling to go to war with France, but in Europe war between Britain and France was imminent. Napoleon was already planning an invasion of Britain and he needed cash to fund it, which was an additional reason to sell the Louisiana Territories.

In fact, the land was not technically France's to sell, as Spain had not finalized arrangements for the transfer, which gave Napoleon an added incentive to resolve the matter quickly. On April 11, 1803, against the advice of his foreign minister, Napoleon instructed his treasury minister to offer the Louisiana Territories to the Americans for the sum of $15 million. When he received the offer, Livingston was stunned. He only had the authority to spend $10 million on New Orleans and its surroundings, and he had no way of communicating with America quickly, but he had no doubt that Jefferson and the US government would be more than happy to spend 50 percent more to gain such a vast tract of land—530 million acres (an area greater than the United States at that time) at a cost of less than

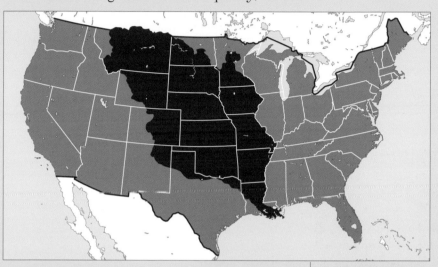

3 cents an acre! It was too good to be true, and Livingston accepted before Napoleon could reconsider. On April 30, Livingston, Monroe, and the French treasury minister Barbé-Marbois signed the Louisiana Purchase Treaty. As well as being the largest land deal in history it was also the greatest bargain (at least until Russia sold Alaska to the US in 1867 for about 2 cents per acre), and Livingston was justifiably proud of the achievement, saying, "We have lived long, but this is the noblest work of our whole lives. . . . From this day the United States take their place among the powers of the first rank." Napoleon demonstrated equal prescience when he said, "This accession of territory affirms forever the power of the United States, and I have given England a maritime rival who sooner or later will humble her pride."

Surprisingly, the treaty that Livingston and Monroe sent back to the US for ratification was not received enthusiastically by everyone (although it would seem that no one quibbled about the price!). Jefferson himself,

EXPANDING WEST
The Louisiana Territories, shown here in darker red, more than doubled the size of the US at the time, which occupied only the area to the east of this. The western portion was under Spanish control.

COMMEMORATION
The centenary of the
Louisiana Purchase was
celebrated in a series of
postage stamps featuring
Monroe, Livingston, Jefferson,
and, seen here, a map
showing the territory.

who took a very rigid approach to interpreting the US Constitution, had misgivings about his constitutional right to buy land for the United States and felt that an amendment might be needed. There were concerns that the purchase might antagonize the Spanish and start a war, and indeed the Spanish did raise objections, as the region had not been properly surveyed and its borders were therefore unclear. There was also the question of whether the 100,000 or so people who inhabited the territories, many of them French speaking, would or should be given all the rights of US citizens. Nonetheless, Jefferson pressed ahead, the US Senate ratified the treaty in October 1803, surveying expeditions (including that of Lewis and Clark) were sent out, and Spain and the US came to an agreement about the borders. The rest, as they say, is history.

One very fundamental question that was not broached at the time was whether, in the first place, France had any rights of ownership to land occupied for millennia by Native Americans, or whether the US had in fact only bought the right to claim the land. In the event, the United States gained land rights in the region from the native people piecemeal through military force, relocation, and treaty negotiation.

NAPOLEON'S SECOND BITE AT THE APPLE

1815

MOTIVATION

Anger

Charity

Envy

Faith

Gluttony

Greed

Hope

Lust

Pride

Sloth

Main Culprit: Napoleon Bonaparte

Damage Done: Landed himself in permanent exile in a very inhospitable place

Why: Couldn't resist attempting to regain power in France, and misjudged the political climate

Men who have changed the world never achieved their success by winning the chief citizens to their side, but always by stirring the masses. The first method is that of a schemer and leads only to mediocre results; the other method is the path of genius and changes the face of the world.

Napoleon Bonaparte

In 1804, the year after the Louisiana Purchase, Napoleon succeeded in reinstating the hereditary monarchy in France, with himself as Emperor Napoleon I and his wife Josephine as empress. In the following years, through a combination of astute political alliances and superb military strategy he extended French influence throughout Europe and beyond, but the Peninsular War against Spain and Portugal, the disastrous retreat from Russia, and the capture of Paris by the Sixth Coalition of allied forces in 1814 led to his defeat. King Louis XVIII ascended to the throne as the constitutional monarch, and Napoleon was exiled to the island of Elba, off the northwest coast of Italy. He was given sovereignty over the small Mediterranean island and its 12,000 inhabitants and he retained his title of emperor and his personal guard, but for most people this would have spelled the end of any aspirations to be the ruler of the French Empire, let alone the world. Napoleon, however, wasn't most people. Neither his ambition nor his ego would allow this to be the end.

Within a few months of his arrival on Elba Napoleon had reorganized the government administration on the island, improved agriculture and mining, and mustered a small army. The news that was reaching him from France, of general dissatisfaction with the rule of the new Bourbon king, convinced him that if he could return home then the people and the army would rally to him, but the waters around the island were being patrolled by the British and the French, preventing his escape. The opportunity arose on February 26, 1815, when the guard ships were absent, and Napoleon and 600 of his soldiers sailed from Elba on ships that had been made ready in the preceding weeks. On March 1 they disembarked on the south coast of France, close to Cannes.

SWELLING THE RANKS

Avoiding the most obvious route by marching through the Alps, his army moved northward, its numbers swelling as they went, and when they encountered the supposedly royalist 5th and 7th Infantry Regiments the soldiers all joined Napoleon's forces. When confronted by troops at Lyon, it is said that Napoleon walked to within firing range, ripped open his coat, and challenged the soldiers to shoot their emperor. To cheers of "Long live the emperor," the men joined him.

On March 20, 1815, Napoleon and his army entered Paris, from which King Louis XVIII had fled the previous day, and he resumed his position as the country's leader without a shot having been fired. So far, so good, but his enemies were on the warpath. A week earlier, on hearing that Napoleon was on his way to Paris, the countries represented at the Congress of Vienna (Russia, Prussia, Austria, Britain, Portugal, Spain, Sweden, and Bourbon France) had declared him to be an outlaw, effectively declaring the War of the Seventh Coalition, and five days after his enthusiastic welcome in Paris the main protagonists pledged 150,000 troops each. The invasion of France was planned for July 1, giving the coalition time to assemble their troops, although an Anglo-Allied force, under the command of the Duke of Wellington, and the Prussians, under Field Marshall von Blücher, would be ready sooner. The downside of the delay was that it would give Napoleon, who could only muster a much smaller army, three months to prepare and swell his ranks.

In the event, Napoleon chose to take the initiative and attack before the Austrian and Russian forces were ready. His strategy was to drive his forces between the armies of Wellington and Blücher—which were quartered south of Brussels, in what was then the United Kingdom of the Netherlands—and prevent them combining and outnumbering his own troops, and then to inflict such heavy losses on each of them that the coalition would come to the negotiating table. Well, that was the plan.

With his army divided into three parts—left and right wings, commanded by Marshals Ney and Grouchy respectively, and a reserve force under his own command—Napoleon crossed the border into the Netherlands on the morning of June 15, and the following day Grouchy's right wing and part of the reserve attacked the Prussians at Ligny. Although the French troops won the battle (with great losses on both sides), they were unable to prevent a substantial part of the Prussian army from making an orderly retreat toward the north.

PRUSSIAN ATTACK
In the fighting between the French and Prussian forces, the village of Plancenoit changed hands five times. Only one-twentieth of the French Young Guard were alive and uninjured at the end of the fighting.

Ney's left wing, meanwhile, was ordered to take the crossroads at Quatre Bras, to the west of Ligny, which was being held by Dutch forces under the command of William, Prince of Orange. The Dutch were greatly outnumbered and were gradually being pushed back until reinforcements arrived and Wellington took command, regaining Quatre Bras. It was clear to Wellington, however, that without the help of the Prussians they could not hold Quatre Bras and he therefore ordered his troops to fall back—also to the north. When Napoleon's troops advanced on Quatre Bras the following afternoon, the 17th, there was no one there. Wellington and his Anglo-Dutch army were close to the town of Waterloo—a name that Napoleon would come to remember—and his men were drawn up along a 2.5-mile (4-km) battle front, largely hidden by a long, low ridge. Blücher's army was a few miles to the east, at Wavre, and early on the morning of the 18th Blücher was able to promise Wellington that he would send reinforcements.

The Battle of Waterloo did not begin until midday, because Napoleon needed the ground to dry before he could move his heavy guns on it. Wellington's men withstood the onslaught of the French throughout the afternoon, with both sides launching infantry and cavalry attacks, and in the meantime Grouchy's troops had engaged the Prussian army at Wavre. Although the French overcame them, the Prussians had tied up a significant proportion of the French forces and given Blücher time to move the promised reinforcements to the west. In the evening they reached Waterloo and broke through the French right flank. Wellington then responded with an attack from the front and the French army fled southward in confusion, pursued by the coalition forces.

WATERLOO
British troops in square formation are charged by French cuirassiers, armored cavalrymen, during the Battle of Waterloo.

The Battle of Waterloo, in which more than 100,000 soldiers died, was Napoleon's last battle and the end of his career. He reached Paris on June 21 and attempted to rally support against the approaching coalition forces, but the country was in no mood to listen. The following day he abdicated in favor of his four-year-old son (who was in Austria), and on the 25th the provisional government asked him to leave the city, which he did. He made his way to Rochefort on the Atlantic coast, intending to escape to the US, but there he found a British naval blockade in place. Caught between the devil and the deep blue sea, he finally surrendered to Captain Frederick Lewis Maitland of the Royal Navy aboard HMS *Bellerophon* on July 17, 1815.

He was taken to the UK, where he was imprisoned and then transported to exile on the island of St. Helena. If Elba had been rather small and a little unexciting, St. Helena was a hundred times worse. Located 1,200 miles (2,000 km) off the west coast of Africa in the middle of the South Atlantic, this craggy volcanic rock, with an area of just 50 square miles (130 km^2), was Napoleon's open prison for the rest of his life, which proved to be less than six years. He died on May 5, 1821.

ST. HELENA WAS NAPOLEON'S OPEN PRISON FOR THE REST OF HIS LIFE, WHICH PROVED TO BE LESS THAN SIX YEARS.

MOTIVATION

Anger

Charity

Envy

Faith

Gluttony

Greed

Hope

Lust

Pride

Sloth

BRITISH TROOPS MASSACRE WORKERS AT "PETERLOO"

August 16, 1819

Main Culprits: The magistrates of Manchester, England

Damage Done: 15 killed, hundreds injured

Why: The ruling class protecting its interests and privileges

Everything is almost at a standstill, nothing but ruin and starvation stare one in the face. The state of the district is truly dreadful.

Joseph Johnson, *Manchester Observer*, 1819

In the early 19th century, the conditions under which the working-class people of Manchester lived and labored—assuming they had a job—were undeniably grim. Southern Lancashire had long been the center of a flourishing textiles industry, and in the early 18th century this was a cottage-based industry in which the women and children in a family would spin the wool and cotton into yarn that was then woven into cloth on hand-operated looms, usually by the men. During the second half of the century all that changed, thanks to the development of a range of technological innovations that constituted the first wave of the Industrial Revolution, most notably John Kay's flying shuttle, which speeded up the weaving process, Richard Arkwright's water-powered spinning frame, and James Hargreaves's multi-spindled "spinning jenny." Together with the introduction of water and steam power and improvements in iron smelting, these inventions spelled the end of the domestic textiles industry in northwest England, and the cottage workers of the area—unable to compete with mass-produced goods—flooded into the growing industrial towns of northwest England to work the machines in the cotton mills under poor conditions and for low pay. In towns such as Rochdale, Blackburn, and especially Manchester—the first truly industrial city, second in size only to London in the early 1800s—workers were crowded into low-quality housing built by the factory owners. As capitalism took hold, traditional social relations were being rapidly swept aside and an industrial working class was coming into being.

SMOKING CITY
William Wylde's *View of Manchester from Kersal Moor* captures the contrast between the English countryside and the smoking chimneys of the world's first industrialized city.

After Waterloo and the end of the Napoleonic Wars, many thought that conditions would improve, but if anything they worsened. During the war, with the doors effectively closed on imports of grain, the large landowners had experienced a period of unprecedented profits as wheat prices reached an all-time high, making bread, a staple of the working-class diet, an expensive commodity. Fearing, quite rightly, that the return of imported grain would bring down the price, they successfully persuaded the British government (which was little more than a coterie of the rich and powerful, many of them landowners) to

CORN LAWS

pass the Corn Laws, imposing high taxes on imported grain and keeping prices artificially high once the war was over.

With no further need to clothe and supply a large army or navy, the end of the war also meant a dramatic decline in demand for cotton goods, and many workers found themselves without jobs as the cotton mills reduced their output. The Combination Acts of 1799 and 1800 that prohibited trade unions and collective bargaining were another cause for anger among the British workers, and calls for parliamentary reform to give working people real representation in government were also high on the agenda. Between 1815 and 1818 these many grievances found expression in a number of large-scale political rallies, marches, and pickets that took place throughout Yorkshire and Lancashire. Many of these were broken up by police and local yeomanry, volunteer regiments used to support the civil authority, and there was a growing presentiment among the ruling classes—already shaken by events in France—that revolution was in the air.

STOKING THE FIRE

This, then, was the backdrop against which a notorious radical orator by the name of Henry Hunt was invited to speak at what was expected to be a very large outdoor gathering in St. Peter's Field in the center of Manchester on August 16, 1819. The primary purpose of the rally was to call for parliamentary reform, and the organizers—the Manchester Patriotic Union Society—were adamant that it should be peaceful, making it known that no one should bring a weapon or commit any breach of the peace that might give the authorities an excuse to use force. "Cleanliness, Sobriety, Order and Peace" was the order of the day. Even the Home Office had issued instructions that the meeting should not be broken up by violence, and that legal means should be used to arrest the speakers and ringleaders. This was not, however, how the city's magistracy—charged with the administration of civil law and composed of members of the landowning families—saw the situation.

Fearing possibly for their personal safety and certainly afraid of the long-term threat that such gatherings posed to their wealth and privilege, "the great and the good" of Manchester made sure they had as many police and soldiers on hand as possible. The magistrates' plan was to arrest Henry Hunt and the rest of the "rabble rousers" and to use whatever force might be needed to do so. To this end, in addition to 400 special constables, they brought in four squadrons of cavalry of the 15th Hussars (600 men), several hundred infantrymen, a detachment of the Royal Horse Artillery with two small cannons, 400 men of the Cheshire Yeomanry cavalry, and 120 cavalrymen of the Manchester and Salford Yeomanry. This latter regiment had been formed following political riots a couple of years earlier and it comprised local shopkeepers and small business owners (including several publicans) who were generally young, inexperienced, right wing, and vehemently opposed to the political views being espoused by the Radicals and the working people.

The sky on August 16 was cloudless, and throughout the morning thousands of people from within Manchester and from the surrounding towns, dressed in their best clothes, made their way to St. Peter's Field in organized groups. It has been estimated that by 11 o'clock the throng, by now pressed shoulder to shoulder, numbered at least 60,000— probably the largest gathering that England had ever seen. Fearing that it would be impossible to move through the crowd to arrest the speakers, the magistrates sent in the 400 special constables to form two lines and create a corridor between the podium and the house in which they were staying.

Henry Hunt and several other speakers, as well as a number of newspaper reporters, made their way to the podium at about 1:20pm to rapturous applause and the speeches began. Within ten minutes, however, the chairman of the magistrates, William Hulton, decided that "the town was in great danger" and instructed the chief constable to move in and arrest the speakers, but the chief replied that he would need help from the military. Hulton then penned two messages calling for military assistance, sending one to Manchester's military commander, Lieutenant-Colonel George L'Estrange, and the other to Major Thomas Trafford, commander of the Manchester and Salford Yeomanry. Trafford received the message first and set off with his troops at a gallop, knocking down a woman in the street and causing the death of her two-year-old son when he was flung from her arms. After speaking with Hulton, Trafford ordered his second in command, a Manchester factory owner called Hugh Birley, to lead 60 of the mounted yeomanry along the police corridor and clear the way to the speakers' platform but

A PUBLIC MASSACRE

when the horses became hemmed in and began to rear, the inexperienced cavalrymen—some of whom may well have been drinking in the nearby hostelry—began to strike out at the protesters with their sabers.

BLOODSHED
Published shortly after the massacre, this depiction of the Hussars attacking the protesters was dedicated to Henry Hunt and to the many casualties.

Finally reaching the platform, Captain Birley and the deputy constable, Joseph Nadin, proceeded to arrest everyone there—speakers, organizers, and members of the press. As they attempted to make their way back to the edge of the field, the angry crowd tried to bar their way, at which point Hulton told L'Estrange, who had arrived with the 15th Hussars, that the yeomanry were under attack and ordered him to disperse the crowd. The mounted Hussars formed a line and charged into the crowd, sabers drawn, from the east side of the field while the Cheshire Yeomanry Cavalry did the same from the south side. The crowd attempted to flee, but the main route out of the area was blocked by soldiers standing with fixed bayonets and panic ensued. The men of the Manchester and Salford Yeomanry were by now out of control and were hacking at the crowd with their swords.

By the time the people had managed to leave, at least 11 men, women, and children lay dead on St. Peter's Field, and more than 400 were injured, many of them seriously. There followed a night of riots and clashes as the once-peaceful protesters vented their rage.

The following day the people of London learned what had happened, thanks to a journalist, Richard Carlile, who had avoided being arrested and had made his way to London overnight. The authorities responded by confiscating all remaining copies of his report and eventually imprisoning him. In Manchester, James Wroe published an account of the attack and, alluding to the fact that the 15th Hussars had been at the Battle of Waterloo, referred to the event as the Peterloo Massacre. His pamphlet on the subject remained in circulation for many weeks and he, too, ended up in prison.

For those who had attended the rally, there was a price to pay. Many lost their jobs as a result of having been present. Some of the wounded were even turned away from hospitals by doctors who disagreed with their politics. Several of the organizers and speakers, including Henry Hunt, were imprisoned. Through the Home Secretary, Lord Sidmouth, the Prince Regent expressed his gratitude to the Manchester magistrates for the way in which they had handled the matter, and the government soon introduced the Six Acts—measures intended to prevent further mass meetings and to suppress left-wing newspapers.

Nonetheless, if the heavy-handed response of the ruling class and the military was intended to put an end to working class demands, it did not actually achieve its goal. Indeed, news of the Peterloo Massacre provoked widespread anger across the country and served to draw members of the middle class toward the cause of the working people. The events in St. Peter's Field can be seen as an important milestone on the road that ultimately led to a more representative and democratic form of Parliament.

MOTIVATION

Anger

Charity

Envy

Faith

Gluttony

Greed

Hope

Lust

Pride

Sloth

SANTA ANNA ATTACKS THE ALAMO

February 23–March 6, 1836

Main Culprit: Antonio López de Santa Anna, commander of the Mexican army

Damage Done: His army slaughtered hundreds of US settlers at the Alamo, raising support for the settlers' cause and leading to independence for Texas

Why: To enforce Mexican government authority over the "Texian" settlers

To the People of Texas & all Americans in the world—Fellow citizens & compatriots—I am besieged, by a thousand or more of the Mexicans under Santa Anna—I have sustained a continual Bombardment & cannonade for 24 hours & have not lost a man—The enemy has demanded a surrender at discretion, otherwise, the garrison are to be put to the sword, if the fort is taken—I have answered the demand with a cannon shot, & our flag still waves proudly from the walls—I shall never surrender or retreat then, I call on you in the name of Liberty, of patriotism & everything dear to the American character, to come to our aid with all dispatch.

From a letter by William B. Travis, February 24, 1836

The "Mexican Empire" gained its independence from Spain in 1821, and the new government was soon encouraging settlers to move into the northeastern part of the Mexican state of Tejas, or Texas, offering land and tax concessions. Many Americans seized the opportunity, and by the mid-1830s US settlers, who went by the name of "Texians," outnumbered Mexicans by a factor of 4:1. The Mexican government soon introduced a range of measures to halt this disequilibrium, banning further immigration and ending tax concessions. These added to the settlers' growing list of grievances against the Mexican government, which included having to swear allegiance to, and pay a tithe to, the Catholic Church and being prohibited from using slave labor, which the settlers regarded as essential for the profitable growing of cotton. Mexico's government was also becoming increasingly centralized, in contravention of Mexico's constitution of 1824, and soon the settlers began to call for an end to these laws and for greater federal control over their own affairs (though not for independence from Mexico). Hostility between the settlers and the government escalated as the Texians formed committees to organize their activities and began to raise their own militia, and at the beginning of October 1835 the first skirmish of the Texas Revolution took place between the Texian and Mexican armies at Gonzales. Over the ensuing weeks, the Texians had several military successes, culminating in the siege of San Antonio de Bexar. Forced to withdraw from the town to the nearby Alamo mission, the Mexican troops subsequently surrendered on terms that included leaving Texas. The Texians then stationed a garrison there and increased the fortification of the sprawling mission by mounting cannons left by the Mexican army and building walkways inside the high surrounding walls from which rifles could be fired.

To the Texians, it appeared as though they had succeeded, but the Mexican president, Antonio López de Santa Anna, had in the meantime quit his post and taken command of an "Army of Operations" to put down the rebellion once and for all. He had also pushed through a resolution (later conveyed in no uncertain terms to US President Andrew Jackson) stating that foreigners found taking up arms against the Mexican authorities would henceforth be treated as "pirates." This

SANTA ANNA
Antonio López de Santa Anna stood down from his position as President of Mexico in order to lead a force against the rebellious Americans.

meant that the Mexican army would be taking no prisoners and would execute any Texian soldiers it captured.

By the end of 1835 this army was more than 6,000 strong, and through January and February the Mexican troops made their way northward in exceptionally wintry conditions, some of the soldiers succumbing to disease and hypothermia. While part of the army traveled up the coast, engaging detachments of the Texian army and inflicting a series of defeats on them, some 1,500 troops headed directly for San Antonio de Béxar, the scene of the Mexican army's earlier embarrassing surrender, reaching the river south of the town in the last week of February.

At the start of the year, the Texian garrison at the Alamo, under the command of Colonel James C. Neill, had numbered fewer than 100 men, and in mid-January Neill had sent out a request to Sam Houston, one of the Texian army commanders, asking for reinforcements, ammunition, and supplies. Unable to provide what was needed, and acknowledging that the Alamo would be unable to hold out for long against the Mexicans, Houston decided that the post should be abandoned and sent 30 men, headed by the pioneer Jim Bowie, to remove the cannons and destroy the "fort." Unfortunately, when they reached the Alamo there were no animals there to haul the guns and so, recognizing the importance of preventing San Antonio from falling to the Mexicans, Bowie decided to remain at the fort with his men. He, too, requested troops and supplies, but little was forthcoming. In early February a further 30 men under Lieutenant Colonel William B. Travis arrived, and Davy Crockett arrived with a few more volunteers a few days later, but the garrison still numbered less than 200 men. When Neill left the Alamo on February 11 to get further supplies, he put Travis in command, but the garrison overruled the decision and put Bowie in charge instead. In the end the two shared command.

THE BATTLE OF THE ALAMO On February 23, 1836, the 1,500-strong Mexican contingent took the town of San Antonio de Bexar. They also took the Texian garrison at the Alamo by surprise, and no real preparations had been made for a siege. What cattle they could find were quickly brought into the compound, as were the families of volunteers living in Bexar itself. Bowie and Travis sent out envoys to Santa Anna to discuss terms for a surrender, but when they learned that any surrender must be unconditional (i.e. they could expect to be "put to the sword"), they fired the largest cannon in reply.

During the first week of the siege, the Alamo was subject to a steady bombardment from the Mexican cannons, and many of their own balls were fired back at Santa Anna's troops, but the Texians had too little powder to keep up constant cannon fire. Two groups of reinforcements reached Santa Anna, more than doubling his troop numbers to over 3,000, while only a handful of Texians managed to reach the Alamo.

On the night of March 5, the Mexican bombardment ceased and the exhausted Texians rested, but at 5:30am, under cover of darkness, the Mexicans launched their attack. Initially the Texians held them off valiantly, but they were overcome by sheer force of numbers, and once the walls were breached they retreated to the fortified barracks while the women and children sought refuge in the chapel. The Mexicans turned the Texian cannon on the barracks and blew the doors in before loosing volleys of musket fire and then rushing the trapped soldiers. True to Santa Anna's word, within an hour of the initial attack the Mexican soldiers had killed every one of the men, including seven who were captured but whom Santa Anna ordered to be executed. The bodies that littered the mission compound were repeatedly bayoneted and shot. The women and children were spared, apart from one boy who was mistaken for an adult. Casualty figures for the Mexican troops are hard to estimate, but it is thought that some 500 of Santa Anna's soldiers were killed in the storming of the Alamo Mission.

It was now Santa Anna's intention to demolish the rest of the Texian army, under the command of Sam Houston. He assumed that the size of his own army, together with his reputation after the massacre at the Alamo, would persuade the Texian army and the settlers to abandon their rebellion, but in fact the opposite occurred. Incensed by the slaughter of their countrymen, volunteers flocked to join Houston, and the army's numbers swelled as Santa Anna pursued it northeastward along the coast toward Louisiana. The two armies met on April 21 at the San Jacinto River, in what is now Harris County, Texas. Confident that Houston would not attack the much larger Mexican force, Santa

JIM BOWIE
The pioneer, who took joint command of the small force at the Alamo, had been taken ill and was killed in his bed after shooting several of his assailants.

REPERCUSSIONS

Anna stood his men down before noon prior to launching his own attack, but he was mistaken. The Texian army charged the Mexican camp in the afternoon with a battle cry of "Remember the Alamo!" and in less than half an hour they had killed or captured the entire Mexican army. Santa Anna was taken prisoner and forced to sign what were later to become known as the Treaties of Velasco. It was the beginning of the road to independence for Texas.

BRITAIN INVADES AFGHANISTAN

March 1839

MOTIVATION

Anger

Charity

Envy

Faith

Gluttony

Greed

Hope

Lust

Pride

Sloth

Main Culprit: Lord Auckland, Sir William Hay Macnaghten

Damage Done: More than 16,000 soldiers and civilians were massacred by Afghan tribesmen as they tried to flee the country

Why: Britain wished to prevent Russia from gaining influence in Afghanistan that might enable it to threaten British supremacy in India

... a war begun for no wise purpose, carried on with a strange mixture of rashness and timidity, brought to a close after suffering and disaster, without much glory attached either to the government which directed, or the great body of troops which waged it. Not one benefit, political or military, has Britain acquired with this war. Our eventual evacuation of the country resembled the retreat of an army defeated.

British Army chaplain Reverend G. R. Gleig, writing in 1843 on his return from Afghanistan

The first half of the 19th century saw the gradual development of what was to become known as the "Great Game," as Britain and Tsarist Russia played political chess on the map of Central Asia. With Russia extending its sphere of influence southward, Britain feared that India, its greatest colonial possession, could be the ultimate target. Control of Afghanistan, reasoned British intelligence, was vital to retaining the jewel in Queen Victoria's crown, and in 1809, when a joint invasion of India by the forces of Napoleon and Tsar Alexander I seemed possible, the British signed a treaty with the Afghan leader Shuja Shah Durrani by which other foreign powers would be prevented from passing through Afghanistan. He was deposed shortly afterward and fled into exile in India. Subsequent leaders were less willing to observe the terms of the treaty, and in 1838 the British received news that the Russians were making overtures to the Afghan ruler, Dost Mohammad. Perceiving this as a significant threat, the governor-general of India, Lord Auckland, sent an envoy to Dost Mohammad with a request to distance himself from the Russians, but the request was refused. Lord Auckland, on the advice of Sir William Hay Macnaghten, decided to take military action and to put Shuja Shah Durrani back on the throne. This was against the advice of another political officer, Sir Alexander Burnes, who believed the best policy would be to support Dost Mohammad and keep him on the British side.

ALEXANDER BURNES
The Scottish political aide, seen here dressed in the costume of Bukhara, advised against reinstating Shuja Shah. He was killed in the Afghan insurrection.

© Getty Images

In late 1838, some 20,000 East India Company British and Indian soldiers, together with almost twice as many support staff and families of the soldiers, made the arduous march from India through the Bolan Pass into Afghanistan. Taking Kandahar in April and Ghazni in June, and leaving garrisons in both cities, the army reached Kabul in August 1839. Dost Mohammad fled and Shuja Shah Durrani returned to the throne, a puppet leader who would protect British interests with guidance from William Macnaghten and Alexander Burnes. Dost Mohammad later gave himself up to the British and went into exile in India.

The operation appeared to have gone smoothly, and there had been very few casualties. Macnaghten sent the majority of the troops back to India and the rest settled down to a comfortable British colonial lifestyle, but within a year things started to go wrong. It became clear that Shuja Shah was far less popular than Dost Mohammad, that he had a tenuous grip over this large and mountainous country, and that the British presence was seen as an occupation. Akbar Khan, the son of Dost Mohammad, was encouraging rebellion against the British among the rural tribespeople and a guerilla war was breaking out. When the British government stopped paying money to various tribal leaders to keep the peace (money that was being paid at Macnaghten's request), matters deteriorated further, and during the spring and summer of 1841 the situation became increasingly tense. Surprisingly, command of the army was handed over at this point to the aged General William Elphinstone, who was both incompetent and unwell.

On November 2, 1841, on the instructions of Akbar Khan, who now had considerable support, a nationwide uprising began. In Kabul, the home of Sir Alexander Burnes was stormed and he and his aides were murdered, but Elphinstone took no action in retaliation. The following week the fort in which the army's supplies were held was taken by rebels. In an attempt to rescue the situation, Macnaghten offered Akbar Khan the throne of Afghanistan in return for allowing the British to remain in the country. At the same time he paid out money to have him assassinated, a double-cross that, unfortunately, Akbar Khan discovered. When Macnaghten and three officers met with Akbar Khan close to the British army compound outside Kabul on December 23 they were killed by Akbar Khan himself, who reputedly placed the barrel of a gun in Macnaghten's mouth and blew his brains out. The body was then dragged through Kabul market, as that of Burnes had been.

Again Elphinstone took no action but instead agreed to hand over the British army's gunpowder, muskets, and cannons to the tribal chiefs in return for the troops' safe conduct out of Afghanistan. On January 6, 1842, about 4,500 British and Indian soldiers, together with 12,000 camp followers, departed from Kabul in the direction of Jalalabad, 90 miles (145 km) to the east over several high passes. It was the middle of winter. The Afghans reached the first snowy pass before them, and on January 9, one-quarter of the British and Indian soldiers and civilians

FLIGHT OF THE BRITISH

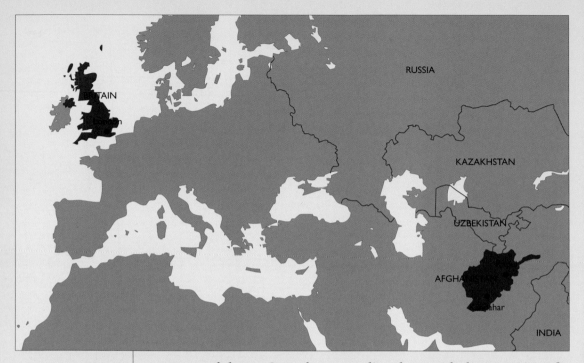

RUSSIA

KAZAKHSTAN

UZBEKISTAN

BRITAIN

London

AFGHANISTAN

Kandahar

INDIA

GATEWAY
From a political perspective, Afghanistan offered access to India from the north through Kazakhstan and Uzbekistan. To Russia and Britain it was a pawn in the "Great Game."

were gunned down. Over the succeeding days, with the exception of a few ransom-worthy officers' wives who were taken hostage, almost the entire group of 16,500 people was steadily massacred as they struggled through the rocky, freezing terrain. On January 13, the last 40 men, mainly members of the 44th Regiment of Foot, were surrounded on a hill close to the village of Gandamak. It is said that they were offered a chance to surrender, to which one of the soldiers replied, "Not bloody likely." Nine were taken prisoner, and the rest were slaughtered. Only one British soldier, Assistant Surgeon William Brydon, reached Jalalabad, having been hidden by an Afghan shepherd who had then given the severely injured man his horse.

The destruction of the retreating regiments by Afghan tribesmen was the most humiliating and tragic episode in British colonial military history, and it could not go unavenged. Akbar Khan was now in power, and in April Shuja Shah was assassinated. British relief forces were sent to the garrisons still holding Jalalabad and Khandahar, and Akbar Khan's rebels were defeated in a battle near Jalalabad. In August a British force retook Ghazni from the rebels and another inflicted a final defeat on Akbar Khan. In September Kabul was captured, the British and Indian prisoners being held there were released, and the city's market area was razed to the ground as a punishment. Freed by the British, Dost Mohammad returned to power in Afghanistan, and in 1845 Akbar Khan died, probably poisoned by his father.

For the time being, Britain backed away from playing an active role in the politics of Afghanistan, but this was not the last time that a foreign invader would come to grief in this wildly inhospitable and fiercely independent country.

GHAZNI CITY
The British garrison in Ghazni was defeated by Afghan forces, but the city was retaken when the British returned and its fortifications were demolished.

MOTIVATION

Anger

Charity

Envy

Faith

Gluttony

Greed

Hope

Lust

Pride

Sloth

TRAGEDY IN THE VALLEY OF DEATH

October 25, 1854

Main Culprits: Lord Raglan and Captain Nolan, and a feud between Lords Lucan and Cardigan

Damage Done: 118 men of the Light Brigade were killed and 127 were wounded

Why: The initial order was vague, and personal animosities prevented clarification

Half a league, half a league,
Half a league onward,
All in the valley of Death
Rode the six hundred.
"Forward the Light Brigade!
Charge for the guns!" he said.
Into the valley of Death
Rode the six hundred.

"Forward, the Light Brigade!"
Was there a man dismay'd?
Not tho' the soldier knew
Some one had blunder'd.
Theirs not to make reply,
Theirs not to reason why,
Theirs but to do and die.
Into the valley of Death
Rode the six hundred.

From "The Charge of the Light Brigade" by Alfred Tennyson

The Charge of the Light Brigade, which took place on October 25, 1854, has been hailed as an example of supreme military bravery in the face of overwhelming odds, which it was, even if the blind following of orders was tantamount to suicide. It was also a monstrous blunder precipitated by an ambiguous command and festering personal animosity between key officers. It costs the lives of hundreds of men.

In September 1854, French, British, and Turkish troops landed on the west coast of the Crimean Peninsula, which juts into the Black Sea from the coast of the Ukraine, with the aim of taking the important naval base of Sevastopol from the Russian Imperial Army. Bypassing the city and defeating the Russians at the River Alma, the British set up their supply base in the coastal town of Balaclava, a few miles to the south of Sevastopol, before laying siege to it. On October 25 the Russian commander Prince Menshikov, with an army of 20,000 infantry and 3,000 cavalry, together with 76 guns, advanced on Balaclava from the northeast, intending to take the British base and threatening to cut off the only supply route between Balaclava and Sevastopol. This route, the Woronzoff Road, ran along the top of a ridge known as the Causeway Heights. The North Valley, to its north, separated it from the Fedioukine Hills, and another valley lay to its south with hills beyond. Work was in progress to fortify the Causeway Heights by the building of six redoubts, entrenched defensive positions, equipped with naval guns to protect the base at Balaclava, but it was far from complete. Five hundred Turkish soldiers were manning the first redoubt but, after an artillery bombardment that caused heavy losses to the Turks, the advancing Russians took it, and the garrisons in the other redoubts soon fell back to the south, toward Balaclava.

MENSHIKOV
Prince Alexander Sergeyevich Menshikov was commander-in-chief of the Russian forces in the Crimea but was removed from his command after defeats in the Battles of Alma and Inkerman, which followed the Battle of Balaclava.

The Russians also took up positions along the Fedioukine Hills to the north, and 3,000 of their cavalry came along the North Valley and then over the Causeway Heights heading for Balaclava just as the 900-strong British Heavy Brigade of cavalry moved east along the South Valley. Neither knew of the other's presence until the Russians crested the ridge and began their descent, when they found the columns of the British cavalry crossing their path. Under the command of Major General

James Scarlett, the Heavy Brigade wheeled to their left, formed a line facing the Russian cavalry, and attacked. After a short struggle, the Russian cavalry fled back over the Causeway Heights into the North Valley, where 670 cavalrymen of the Light Brigade were ideally positioned to attack the Russians on their flank. The Earl of Cardigan, however, instructed them not to attack, claiming to have been told by his superior, Lord Lucan, that they were not to take offensive action. The Russian cavalry continued to the east end of the valley and formed up behind a battery of heavy artillery.

This was not the first time that the cavalry had been prevented from using their strengths and skills to best advantage. In the battles that had taken place the previous month on the army's march south, Lieutenant General the Earl of Raglan, the commander of the British army, had held them back, and the blame for their inaction then had fallen on the cavalry commander, Lord Lucan, who had received the nickname "Lord Look-On" as a result. This irritant was to prove an important element in the debacle that followed.

Meanwhile, as the majority of the Russian cavalry had been descending from the Causeway Heights only to be routed by the Heavy Brigade, a smaller force of their cavalry had advanced directly south toward Balaclava, and the 93rd Highlanders had successfully halted their progress by forming a line and firing one or two volleys at them from a distance. It had been enough to turn them back, and a war correspondent with *The Times*, William Russell, later referred to this gallant defense by a row of red-coated soldiers, rifles raised with bayonets fixed, as a "thin red line tipped with steel." It was a phrase that was to go down in history.

THE CHARGE OF THE LIGHT BRIGADE

From his position on high ground at the west end of the North Valley, on the Sapouné Ridge, Lord Raglan could see that the Russians were taking the guns on the Causeway Heights, an action that would be seen as a victory for the Russians. Since no other troops were available, he decided to send the Light Brigade, still positioned at the west end of the North Valley, to attack them, and he dictated an order to that effect. The order read, "Lord Raglan wishes the cavalry to advance rapidly to the front, and try to prevent the enemy carrying away the guns. Troop of horse artillery may accompany. French cavalry is on your left. Immediate." The order was carried to the Light Brigade by Captain Lewis Nolan, a vehement advocate of making full use of the cavalry and a vocal critic of Lord Lucan for that reason. Nolan galloped down from the ridge and handed the order to Lord Lucan—and here the confusion began. The Russians at the gun emplacements on Causeway Heights could not be seen from the valley floor, and the order therefore made no sense to Lord Lucan. On being asked to explain which guns and what enemy were being referred to, it is reported that Nolan (who knew precisely what had been meant) gave a vague wave of his arm in the direction of the far end of the valley, where the Russian cavalry and artillery were positioned a mile away, and said curtly, "There is your enemy. There are your guns, My Lord." He gave no further clarification and rode away to talk to other officers.

Lucan, who was aware of the criticism that had been leveled at him and presumably did not wish to appear hesitant, then ordered Lord Cardigan to charge the Russian position. Had relations between these two men been better, there could have been some discussion at this point. They were brothers-in-law but Cardigan had separated from Lucan's sister and there had been no love lost between them for decades. Cardigan gave the order, and the cavalry mounted and set off down the valley, with Lord Lucan and the Heavy Brigade behind them. Lord Raglan and his party on the Sapouné Ridge, watching the Light Brigade riding eastward and then entering the mouth of the valley rather than swinging to their right to ascend the Causeway Heights, could only look on in horror as the tragedy unfolded. To the cavalry's left, Russian infantry, cavalry, and artillery occupying the Fedioukine Hills opened fire; to the right, the Russians troops that had taken the redoubts on the Woronzoff Road opened fire; and ahead of them the Russian guns blazed. In a hail of rifle bullets and shells, the horsemen quickened their pace as their colleagues fell all around them. Captain Lewis Nolan, apparently realizing the mistake that was being made, galloped to the head of the cavalry waving his sword and rode across in front of Lord Cardigan,

© Getty Images

CHARGE FOR THE GUNS!
Fired upon from three sides, the valiant cavalrymen of the Light Brigade rode right through the Russian guns and into the soldiers beyond.

presumably to remedy the error, but he was struck down by shrapnel from an artillery shell.

Lord Lucan and the Heavy Brigade had pulled up when the scale of the rifle- and gunfire had become apparent, but the Light Brigade charged on at a full gallop, right through the heavy guns and into the Russian cavalry. They succeeded in pushing them back, but were finally forced to retire back down the valley, still under heavy fire (although the French cavalry had, in the meantime, successfully taken on the Russian troops on the Fedioukine Hills) and under attack from Russian cavalry units that had descended from the ridges on either side.

OF THE 670 MEN THAT CHARGED DOWN THE "VALLEY OF DEATH," LESS THAN 200 MADE IT BACK.

Of the 670 men that charged down the "Valley of Death," less than 200 made it back. Almost 250 had been killed or wounded, the rest had been taken prisoner, and 475 horses had died. An unclear and uninformative order, compounded by a string of petty personal vendettas, had led to the most avoidable disaster in British military history. Incidentally, the Earl of Cardigan, who had ridden at the head of the charge and entered the fray against the Russian cavalry, survived unscathed and is said to have had a champagne dinner aboard his yacht in Balaclava harbor that evening.

THE ASSASSINATION OF TSAR ALEXANDER II

March 13, 1881

MOTIVATION

Anger

Charity

Envy

Faith

Gluttony

Greed

Hope

Lust

Pride

Sloth

Main Culprit: The revolutionary group The People's Will

Damage Done: Led to even greater repression by the Tsarist regime and slowed the pace of political reform

Why: The People's Will were dissatisfied with the pace of change under Tsar Alexander II

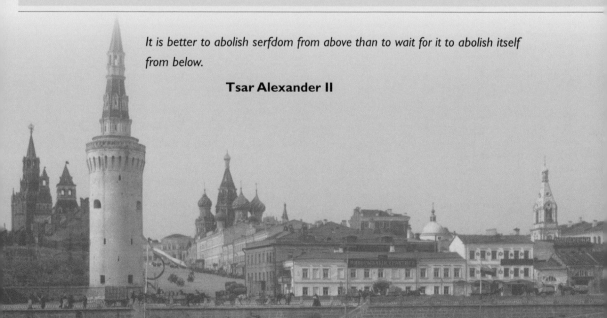

It is better to abolish serfdom from above than to wait for it to abolish itself from below.

Tsar Alexander II

Alexander, born in Moscow in 1818, became Tsar of Russia in March 1855 on the death of his father, Tsar Nicholas I. The Crimean War was in its second year. Six months after his accession, Sevastopol was captured, and the following year the Treaty of Paris put an end to Russian dominance in the Balkans. The country that had considered itself the major power in Europe had been revealed as seriously backward, not just militarily (the army was composed entirely of long-service soldiers and had been unable to raise new recruits as reinforcements), but economically and politically. While western European states reaped the economic benefits of rapidly expanding industrialization and burgeoning capitalism, industrial output in Russia was falling and agricultural production, which relied on traditional peasant technologies, was stagnant. More than a third of the country's population of 62.5 million were serfs—slaves who were literally owned by the nobility who owned the land on which they worked.

YOUNG ALEXANDER
As a boy, Alexander was tutored by the Romantic poet Vasily Zhukovsky, which may have tempered the influence of his autocratic father and made him a more liberal Tsar.

Discussions concerning the possible emancipation of the serfs had been underway in government circles since the 1830s, but no progress had been made under Tsar Nicholas I. Now three leading reformers brought their ideas to the new Tsar, suggesting that changing the status of the serfs to that of a land-owning peasantry could lay the foundations of a market economy. Although he himself was no liberal-minded reformer, Tsar Alexander II was an astute statesman. He understood that the feudal system was a brake on the development of Russia, and a committee was formed to look into improving the conditions of the peasants. The nobility were willing to accept that the serfs be freed, but were not willing to see their land given away. However, they had little choice as a large proportion of their estates and the majority of their serfs (who were a form of property) had been mortgaged either to the banks or to the state. The Emancipation Manifesto, providing the legal framework for the reforms, was adopted in February 1861, freeing the serfs, giving them the right to marry or start a business without permission of the landowner, and granting them the rights to buy half of the land that they worked. Since they could not afford to pay for it, the government advanced money in the form of government bonds to the landowners (holding back any debts they may have) and the serfs were to pay back the money, with interest, over a period of 49 years. The transition was far from problem-free, but it was a major step forward for the country.

In the following years Tsar Alexander oversaw the introduction of a wide range of reforms, including the creation of local councils with the power to manage transport, education, and health in their areas (although only the wealthy could be elected to the councils), a restructuring of the military, and the expansion of industry and the railroads. However, while conservatives lamented the rapid pace of the reforms, radical groups saw them as too little and too slow. A group calling itself Land and Liberty demanded the wholesale handover of lands to the peasants, and some advocated terrorism as a means to achieve change.

In April 1879, a former student, acting alone, fired a revolver repeatedly at the Tsar but missed. He was arrested and later hanged. Later that year, the terrorists in Land and Liberty formed a splinter group called The People's Will, questioning the very basis of political power in Russia and calling for revolutionary change and an end to the Tsarist autocracy. The People's Will made the assassination of the Tsar a priority. In October they attempted to blow up the train in which the Tsar was traveling, but failed. The following year a carpenter in the group took a job in the Tsar's Winter Palace in St. Petersburg and managed to secrete a large quantity of explosives beneath the dining room. At 6:30 on the evening of February 17, when the Tsar was expected to be dining, this was detonated, but he had been delayed and escaped the blast. Sixty-seven members of the household were not so fortunate.

THE PEOPLE'S DEMANDS

The People's Will now informed the Russian government that they would call off their campaign of terror if the government instituted free elections and put an end to censorship. If limited social reform was on the Tsar's agenda, dramatic political reform was not, although he did order the release of several political prisoners and instructed his Minister of the Interior to suggest some revisions to the constitution. He also gave him the task of eliminating The People's Will organization. When the proposed revisions, giving the local councils more power and the ability to send delegates to a newly created national assembly, threatened to reduce his own authority he suggested that the minister look again.

Impatient at the delays, The People's Will planned another assassination attempt, and on March 13, 1881, they succeeded. As the Tsar's bullet-proof carriage, accompanied by armed Cossacks on horseback and followed by police officers in sleighs, reached a corner close to the Catherine Canal in St. Petersburg, a member of the group, Nikolai Rysakov, threw a bomb that detonated and seriously injured one of the Cossacks. Ignoring advice to remain in the carriage and stepping out to comfort the dying man, the Tsar received the full blast of a second bomb hurled by another terrorist, Ignaty Grinevitsky, who died in the blast. The Tsar, his legs blown off and his torso ripped apart, was taken by sleigh to the Winter Palace, where he died shortly afterward.

REFORMER
As Tsar Alexander II's Minister of the Interior, Count Loris-Melikov was the architect of a range of reforms. When these reforms were shelved by Alexander III, Loris-Melikov resigned.

As it turned out, Alexander II had, the previous day, approved draft plans for the creation of an elected assembly, or Duma. On his ascent to the Russian throne, his eldest son, Tsar Alexander III, rejected these plans and substantially reversed many of the reforms introduced by his father, including reducing the power of the local councils.

The "what-ifs" of history are, of course, unanswerable, but the assassination of Tsar Alexander II in 1881 certainly cut short a process of change in Russia that had the potential to improve the lives of millions. His death plunged the country back into a period of autocratic repression that was finally replaced by Communism, with all its imperfections. The Duma was finally introduced after the Russian Revolution in 1905.

AUSTRIA'S MAYERLING INCIDENT

January 29–30, 1889

MOTIVATION

Anger

Charity

Envy

Faith

Gluttony

Greed

Hope

Lust

Pride

Sloth

Main Culprit: Crown Prince Rudolf of Austria, or did someone else shoot him?

Damage Done: Hopes of a more liberal Austro-Hungarian leadership died with Rudolf. His father's empire-building heightened tensions in Europe

Why: The assassination of the new heir, Archduke Franz Ferdinand, by Serb nationalists triggered World War I

Dear Stephanie, you are now rid of my presence and annoyance; be happy in your own way. Take care of the poor wee one, she is all that remains of me. To all acquaintances . . . say my last greetings. I go quietly to my death, which alone can save my good name. I embrace you affectionately. Your loving Rudolph.

Text of Crown Prince Rudolf's final letter to Princess Stephanie

ILL MATCHED
Crown Prince Rudolf and Princess Stephanie, seen here at their engagement, were married in 1881. Less than eight years later he was dead, probably at his own hand.

The facts of the Mayerling Incident are largely clouded in mystery and will probably never be known, but certainly Crown Prince Rudolf of Austria and his teenage lover, Baroness Mary Vetsera, died that night. If the version of events that was made public at the time—that it was a murder-suicide—was true, then Rudolf's final gunshot was to echo down the years, leading to the end of the Hapsburg dynasty and ultimately to World War I, or at least the manner in which it started.

Prince Rudolf was the only son of Emperor Franz-Josef of Austro-Hungary and Empress Elisabeth of Bavaria. In 1881, when he was 22 years old, he made a "good" marriage to Princess Stephanie of Belgium, who was not yet 17, and although they were initially happy together, the couple proved to be ill suited. Stephanie was extremely conventional, even boring, and, as her mother-in-law put it, "a moral heavyweight," whereas Rudolf was far more impulsive and liberal in his thinking. By the time their first and only child, a girl named Elisabeth Marie, was born in 1883, the two were drifting apart, a process that accelerated when the promiscuous Rudolf gave his wife a venereal disease that precluded the possibility of producing an heir to the Hapsburg throne. She openly began an affair with a Polish count and Rudolf continued to entertain a series of mistresses, including the 17-year-old Baroness "Mary" Marie Alexandrine von Vetsera. It is thought that they met in the fall of 1888, but according to an account written by his sister-in-law some 30 years later, Rudolf told her the affair had actually begun at least two years earlier, when Mary was just 15. This might explain his decision to buy the manor house at Mayerling, in the Vienna Woods, in 1888 and to transform it into a hunting lodge. It would have provided the couple with a secluded, and rather grand, love nest.

Telling his family that he was planning to spend the following day hunting, Rudolf spent the night of January 29, 1899, at Mayerling, but when his valet came to wake him in the morning he found the prince's bedroom door locked. Unable to raise a response, the valet and Rudolf's hunting buddy, Count Josef Hoyos, who had also spent the night there, used an axe to break the door. In the dim light of the shuttered room they found Mary lying on the bed and Rudolf sitting (or lying) beside it on the floor. Both were dead and, seeing a glass on the bedside table, Count Josef concluded that poison was the cause.

The count made his way to Vienna as quickly as possible to inform the emperor and empress of the tragedy. They were, of course, shattered by the news, but the emperor had the presence of mind to call the Minister of Police and have Mayerling and the surrounding area cordoned off. A statement was made to the press to the effect that Prince Rudolf had died of an aneurism (Catholics don't commit suicide) and a doctor was sent to ascertain the exact cause of death, which apparently turned out to be gunshot wounds. It appeared that Rudolf had shot Mary in the head and then, having sat beside the body for some hours, shot himself. The body of the young baroness was quickly removed from the house by her uncles and was buried with unseemly haste in the cemetery of a nearby monastery.

Journalists, however, soon discovered that the body of Rudolf's mistress had also been found in the room and that this was probably a murder-suicide. Although the imperial household did all it could to suppress the story, the emperor had difficulty persuading the Church to allow Rudolf's body to be buried in the Imperial Crypt in Vienna, since a suicide may not receive a Christian burial. Finally a dispensation was given on the basis that Rudolf had died while in an unbalanced mental state.

A range of doubts has been raised concerning precisely what did happen that night and why. According to one report only one bullet had been fired from the gun found beside the prince, and according to another, six bullets had been fired, neither of which would account for two bullet wounds. The strange adventures that later befell the body of Mary also threw up conflicting evidence. Her coffin was opened by occupying Russian troops in 1946, and when her remains were being reinterred in 1955 it was observed that there was no bullet-hole in the skull. Rather, there were signs that she may have been struck by a blunt instrument, an unlikely way for her lover to have killed her. Her skeleton was again dug up in 1991, this time by a fanatical furniture dealer, and a medical

DEAR STEPHANIE
The note that Rudolf left suggests he did intend to commit suicide, but it gives no reason why he felt he should take his own life.

WHAT REALLY HAPPENED?

examination at that time was inclusive because part of the skull was now missing. Then there is the question "why?" It is said that there had been an argument a few days earlier between Rudolf and the emperor, who insisted that Rudolf end the affair—would that be a good enough reason for a suicide pact, given that their affair was widely known? Then again, it is known that a few months earlier Rudolf had proposed a suicide pact to his other mistress at the time, an actress by the name of Mitzi Kaspar. She had refused the honor, but perhaps Mary was more romantically minded. It was also suggested that Mary may have been pregnant and had died having an abortion, or that she took poison, the bereft prince then killing himself.

UNDER WRAPS
For the lying-in-state of Crown Prince Rudolf at the Hofburg in Vienna, his head was wrapped in a bandage to hide the damage caused by the bullet.

A wholly different scenario is recounted in great detail by a German spy writing at the time. According to him, the couple were gunned down by three men who arrived at the lodge on the evening of the 29th. The tragedy, in this case, was a political assassination carried out either by the French, who (it is posited) had tried unsuccessfully to involve the prince in a plot to overthrow his pro-German father, or by Austrian agents who were concerned that the liberal-minded Rudolf intended to allow Hungary too great a degree of autonomy.

As the only son of the emperor and empress, Rudolf was heir to the Hapsburg throne, and he himself had no male offspring. The next in line was therefore Emperor Franz Josef's younger brother, Archduke Karl Ludwig, but he quickly renounced his right to the succession in favor of his eldest son, Archduke Franz Ferdinand. The assassination of the Archduke in Sarajevo in 1914, which triggered World War I, spelled the end of the Hapsburg monarchy. Had Rudolf lived to become emperor, he would undoubtedly have been more liberal than his father and may have taken a more enlightened approach to the competing nationalist aspirations in the region, and the course of European history may have been significantly different.

THE GERMAN NAVY SINKS THE *LUSITANIA*

May 7, 1915

MOTIVATION

Anger

Charity

Envy

Faith

Gluttony

Greed

Hope

Lust

Pride

Sloth

Main Culprit: The German navy

Damage Done: Hundreds of civilians lost their lives, and the US was ultimately drawn into the war

Why: Germany was anxious to prevent war materials reaching Britain, and wanted to get even for the British naval blockade that was starving Germany

Whatever be the other facts regarding the Lusitania, the principal fact is that a great steamer, primarily and chiefly a conveyance for passengers, and carrying more than a thousand souls who had no part or lot in the conduct of the war, was torpedoed and sunk without so much as a challenge or a warning, and that men, women, and children were sent to their death in circumstances unparalleled in modern warfare.

**President Wilson's "Reply to Berlin" (No. 1803),
Department of State, Washington, June 9, 1915**

The sinking of the British passenger liner RMS *Lusitania*, torpedoed by a German submarine on May 7, 1915, with the loss of more than 1,000 lives, including more than 100 American citizens, sent a wave of horror and anger through the Allied countries, but especially the neutral US. Despite claims by Germany that the vessel was in truth a military ship, this act of aggression against civilians undoubtedly boosted anti-German sentiment in the US and played an important role in ultimately drawing the US into the war.

RMS *LUSITANIA*
One of only a small group of four-funneled liners, the *Lusitania* was highly distinctive. The U-boat captain knew what he was aiming at when he fired the torpedo.

The Royal Mail Ship *Lusitania*, built in Scotland for the Cunard Line, was launched in 1906 and was at that time the world's largest ship, with a length of 787 feet (240 m) and a gross tonnage of more than 30,000 tons. She was also the fastest and most powerful; her 68,000-horsepower engines were capable of propelling her at 25 knots, and on her second east–west crossing she broke the transatlantic record, taking less than five days. Her construction was partly funded by the British government on the understanding that she be fitted with gun mounts and that in the event of a war or other emergency she would be turned over to the government and converted into an armed merchant cruiser. In fact she remained with Cunard after the start of World War I, carrying passengers across the Atlantic between Liverpool and New York City.

As the war progressed and Britain enforced a naval blockade against ships potentially supplying Germany, so German naval—and particularly submarine—interventions against shipping in the Atlantic and around the shores of Britain increased. Although the Hague Convention asserted that unarmed merchant ships should not be fired upon, Germany, in response to the British declaration that the North Sea was now a war zone, announced in February 1915 that all the waters around Britain were henceforth a war zone, that British merchant shipping would be targeted, and that it might not always be possible to warn or evacuate vessels before firing on them. The British then advised all its merchant ships to ram or fire upon any submarine sighted, which was a considerable disincentive for submarine commanders to take the risk of surfacing and warning would-be targets.

Transatlantic passenger services continued even though the possibility of German submarine, or "U-boat," attack was increasing. As if to announce Germany's intentions, in the days before the *Lusitania's* 202nd Atlantic crossing, a warning advertisement appeared in several New York newspapers. It read:

> NOTICE !
>
> Travelers intending to embark on the Atlantic voyage are reminded that a state of war exists between Germany and her allies and Great Britain and her allies; that the zone of war includes the waters adjacent to the British Isles; that, in accordance with formal notice given by the Imperial German Government, vessels flying the flag of Great Britain or of any of her allies, are liable to destruction in those waters and that travelers sailing in the war zone on ships of Great Britain or her allies do so at their own risk.
>
> Imperial German Embassy,
>
> Washington, D.C., April 22, 1915

The Cunard Line was at pains to reassure passengers that the speed of the *Lusitania* —almost twice that of a U-boat— and her watertight bulkheads made her safe from being sunk by the German navy and, although there was concern, very few passengers took the threat seriously or canceled their bookings.

On May 1 she sailed out of New York bound for Liverpool with a crew of 694 and 1,265 passengers, of whom 159 were Americans. Her passenger list boasted a host of the wealthy and the famous, from bankers and industrialists to artists, writers, designers, musicians, and socialites.

Her captain, William Thomas Turner, was under instructions to keep her speed up, to avoid sailing close to headlands, where submarines might lie in wait, and to sail a zigzag path if confronted with the immediate danger of a submarine. Her crossing of the Atlantic was uneventful, but throughout the week the British Admiralty had been aware of a German submarine, U-20, operating in the Irish Sea. On May 5 the

SMS U-20
The German submarine U-20, seen here (second from left) moored in Kiel harbor in 1914, was later scuttled after grounding off Jutland, Denmark.

U-boat sank the merchant schooner *Earl of Lathom* after ordering her crew to abandon ship, and on the 6th the U-20 sank two 6,000-ton ships and missed two others. Warnings were broadcast by the Royal Navy to all shipping, and Captain Turner took the precaution of closing the *Lusitania*'s watertight doors, doubling the lookout, and preparing the lifeboats for launching. As the *Lusitania* reached the southern coast of Ireland on the morning of May 7 she was forced by misty conditions to slow down to 15 knots, and when a further radio warning was received, the captain altered course to pass closer to the Irish coast. He did not, however, adopt a zigzag course. As the weather cleared, the ship's speed was increased to 18 knots.

THE SHIP GOES DOWN

In the early afternoon, the submarine U-20, captained by Walther Schwieger, surfaced some 10 miles (16 km) south of the Old Head of Kinsale, a headland on the south coast of Ireland, and at 1:20pm the highly recognizable outline of the *Lusitania* was sighted approaching from the west. Submerging to periscope depth, the submarine came within 800 yards (730 m) of the oncoming liner and at 2:10pm a single torpedo was fired.

Spotting the approaching tell-tale stream of bubbles, a lookout aboard the *Lusitania* shouted a warning, but it was too late to do anything. Seconds later the torpedo struck the starboard side of the ship beneath the waterline behind the bridge with a loud explosion, blowing a large hole in the hull. A second, even greater, explosion followed immediately, blasting steel and debris into the air, and within minutes the ship began to list to starboard and the bow began to go down. The captain issued instructions to turn toward the land, but the ship would not respond. Nor could the engines be put into reverse to slow the ship down, which made it impossible to launch the lifeboats immediately. As the ship slowed, the severe list to starboard prevented lifeboats on the port side from being lowered properly, as they scraped down the sloping hull and caught on the protruding rivets. Those on the starboard side, swung out on their davits, were too far from the deck for the fleeing passengers to reach them or, because the bow of the ship was tilted down, hit the sea at such an angle that they filled with water. (The recurring difficulty of launching lifeboats from a listing ship was seen again when the *Costa Concordia* luxury cruise ship grounded off the coast of Italy in 2012.) In less than 20 minutes from the time of the impact, the *Lusitania* had sunk, the huge downdraft of the hull dragging people under the water. Only six of the ship's 48 lifeboats reached the water successfully, and the vast majority of the passengers were drowned or found themselves struggling in the cold sea. Responding to the ship's SOS, vessels from the nearest Irish ports made their way to the scene to rescue survivors, but at the final count only 764 passengers and crewmembers, out of a total of 1,959 people, survived, and almost 900 bodies were never recovered. Only 11 of the 139 Americans on board survived.

LOSS OF LIFE
Almost two-thirds of the *Lusitania*'s passengers and crew drowned, largely because the lifeboats could not be launched properly from the listing ship.

Germany and Austria applauded the actions of Kapitänleutnant Schwieger and immediately justified the sinking of *Lusitania* by claiming that she was armed, that she was carrying troops, and that her cargo included large quantities of munitions which had caused the second explosion. The international community, on the other hand, reacted with outrage. Although the *Lusitania* had been fitted with gun mounts, she certainly had no guns on board, and nor was she carrying troops. As far as munitions were concerned, her manifest revealed that she had been carrying more than four million rounds of rifle cartridges and over a thousand empty shell cases, as well as fuses, but neither Cunard nor US customs classified these as munitions. (The second explosion was put down to the igniting of coal dust in the boiler rooms, although it now seems more likely that it was caused by a steam explosion when high pressure steam lines ruptured.) No one in the US or among the Allied countries accepted that such a cargo justified the killing of more than 1,000 civilians.

In the words of former President Roosevelt, "This represents not merely piracy, but piracy on a vaster scale of murder than old-time pirates ever practiced. . . . It is a warfare against innocent men, women, and children traveling on the ocean, and our own fellow countrymen and countrywomen, who were among the sufferers. It seems inconceivable that we can refrain from taking action in this matter, for we owe it not only to humanity, but to our own national self-respect." This was fighting talk, and even though neither the American public nor its leaders were willing to go to war at that time, the sinking of the *Lusitania* had certainly raised the possibility. US President Woodrow Wilson—recognizing that unrestricted submarine warfare against the world's shipping represented a new and ugly turn in the war— sent several strongly worded notes to the German government making it clear that the sinking of merchant and neutral shipping was unacceptable. In September 1915, fearing that the US might join the war against them, Germany backed down and the German Chancellor and Kaiser Wilhelm II issued instructions, against the wishes of the German Admiralty, forbidding U-boats to fire on neutral ships without warning. The fear of U-boat attacks on transatlantic shipping subsided, and it was enough to placate the US for the time being, but in January 1917, with the war going badly for Germany on the Western Front, unrestricted submarine warfare was seen as vital to that country's war effort, and the policy was reversed. The German military were sure that this would not cause America to declare war. They were wrong. Woodrow Wilson broke off diplomatic relations with Germany, but this had no effect on their decision, and within two months seven US merchant ships had been sunk. On April 6, 1917, America entered the war. It was the culmination of a process that had started with the sinking of the *Lusitania*—a decision that Germany was to regret.

THE GERMAN MILITARY WERE SURE THAT THIS WOULD NOT CAUSE AMERICA TO DECLARE WAR. THEY WERE WRONG.

THE TREATY OF VERSAILLES

January 18, 1919

MOTIVATION

Anger

Charity

Envy

Faith

Gluttony

Greed

Hope

Lust

Pride

Sloth

Main Culprits: The Allied Powers

Damage Done: The terms of the Treaty of Versailles inadvertently created the conditions that were to lead to the outbreak of World War II

Why: The treaty neither made Germany an equal partner in a peaceful Europe nor crushed it so definitely that it could never again use military aggression to fulfill territorial ambitions

The lofty aims which our adversaries first set before themselves in their conduct of the war, the new era of an assured peace of justice, demand a treaty instinct with a different spirit. Only the cooperation of all nations, a cooperation of hands and spirits, can build up a durable peace. We are under no delusions regarding the strength of the hatred and bitterness which this war has engendered, and yet the forces which are at work for a union of mankind are stronger now than ever they were before. The historic task of the Peace Conference of Versailles is to bring about this union.

From a letter by Count von Brockdorff-Rantzau (leader of the German Peace Delegation) to Georges Clemenceau (president of the Paris Peace Conference) on the subject of peace terms, May 1919.

© Getty Images

In the early hours of the morning of November 11, 1918, the Allied Powers and the Central Powers agreed to a cessation of hostilities on general terms dictated by the Allies, and the Germans were in no position to refuse to sign. It took a further six months for the Allies—principally Britain, the US, and France—to determine between themselves the fine detail of a final peace treaty. Britain wanted Germany to be a buffer against Communism, the US was looking for a long-lasting peace in Europe without American involvement, and France sought to regain its former power at the expense of Germany. There were inherent conflicts between their aims, but at last the Treaty of Versailles and the demands that it made upon Germany appeared to present a workable compromise. Two decades later, that compromise failed: an ideology far more frightening than Communism reared its ugly head; war returned, involving the US once again; and France paid a high price for its revenge.

PEACE WITHOUT VICTORY?

The Paris Peace Conference, charged with working out the details of the peace treaty, was convened in January 1919 and involved representatives of 25 nations, but the prime movers—the "Big Four"—were France, Italy, the US, and Britain. Several months prior to the signing of the armistice, US President Woodrow Wilson had put forward his list of "Fourteen Points," which he felt were necessary in order to secure a lasting peace, referred to as a "peace without victory." These principally called for the restoration of territories to their pre-war (and, in the case of Alsace-Lorraine, pre-Franco–Prussian War) borders, arms reductions, self-determination for specific ethnic groups, and freedom of navigation in the seas and through the Dardanelles. When the armistice was signed, Germany had been led to believe that these would form the basis of any peace treaty, but the European members of the "Big Four" had other ideas. The Allies negotiated separate treaties with the Ottoman Empire, Austria, and Hungary, but in the Treaty of Versailles, Germany was singled out for especially harsh treatment.

Germany was required to cede portions of its claimed territory to Poland, France, Denmark, Belgium, and Czechoslovakia. The industrially important coal- and steel-producing German Rhineland, which borders France, was to be demilitarized and occupied by Allied forces for the next 15 years. Germany's colonies in Africa and the Pacific were taken from it and were shared out between several of the Allied countries.

Key elements of the treaty were designed to prevent Germany from rebuilding its military might, and this included restricting the size of the German army to 100,000 troops, severely limiting the size of its navy, in terms of both the number of troops and the number and size of its ships, and forbidding Germany to have an armed air force. A prohibition was placed on the import and export of armaments, the manufacture of weapons was restricted, and poison gas, submarines, and tanks were forbidden. The terms might have been more severe had it not been for Britain's desire for Germany to remain strong enough to resist the spread of Communism from Russia.

Western Europe lay in tatters. Ten million soldiers and almost as many civilians had been killed. Towns and villages had been pulverized. Millions of people were displaced or homeless. Roads, railroads, bridges, farms, and industries had been destroyed. The cost of the mayhem was huge, and the question of reparations was high on the list of priorities for many of the war-torn countries, but especially for France.

MAKING GOOD THE DAMAGE

With the aim of making Germany responsible for paying for the damage, Article 231 of the Treaty of Versailles, which became known as the "Guilt Clause," read, " . . . Germany accepts the responsibility of Germany and her allies for causing all the loss and damage to which the Allied and Associated Governments and their nationals have been subjected as a consequence of the war imposed upon them by the aggression of Germany and her allies." It was a condition of the peace terms that was to rankle above all others.

When it came to determining the actual amount of reparations to be paid, neither Britain nor the US wished Germany to be brought to its knees, preferring it to remain an important trading partner and recognizing that destroying its economy could lead to political and social unrest. Nonetheless, the price demanded—$53.7 billion—was high, although it was reduced to $31.4 billion two years later (the equivalent of $385 billion today). Even at the time, it was realized that Germany would be unable to repay the level of reparations demanded.

ARMISTICE
The *New York Times* announces the signing of the armistice and highlights the political disorder already breaking out in Germany.

Prior to the signing of the armistice, Kaiser Wilhelm II abdicated (the treaty would require that he be tried for war crimes) and power was handed over to a government headed by the new Chancellor, Friedrich Ebert, a member of the left-wing Social Democratic Party. It was he who signed the armistice agreement, and in February 1919 he was made first president of the Weimar Republic. When the terms of the Treaty of Versailles were revealed later that year, his first question was directed to the military. If Germany were to refuse to sign, and hostilities were resumed, would its army be strong enough to respond? The answer was a resounding "no." Germany accepted the Treaty of Versailles—which became known as the Diktat, since Germany had had no say in its composition and no choice but to accept it—and the recriminations began.

CHANCELLOR
Friedrich Ebert signed the armistice on behalf of Germany and was made the country's first president the following year, with the difficult task of trying to achieve political harmony.

Humiliated by the ignominy of the defeat and by the punitive nature of the peace terms, the military, the right wing, and very soon the German people, began to blame the German left. As memories of the terrible situation that had existed in 1918 receded, the Social Democrats became accused of having stabbed Germany in the back. Germany's loss of its raw materials and industry, and the swingeing cost of the reparations, had serious economic repercussions and led to hyperinflation, mass unemployment, and social unrest. The political climate was ripe for extreme nationalistic right wing ideologies such as *Nationalsozialismus* (National Socialism), or Nazism as it is better known, which called for the terms of the Treaty of Versailles to be revised, for Germany to rearm, for the payment of reparations to cease, and for the repossession of the Rhineland. Promising the restoration of Germany's honor and hegemony, and the downfall of its internal enemies—Communists, Jews, Social Democrats—Hitler rose to power during the late 1920s and early '30s. Germany's fledgling democracy, politically isolated from the rest of Europe, could do little to resist the tide, and in 1933 Hitler became German Chancellor, ushering in the Third Reich and a totalitarian state. The process of rearmament that had already begun under the Weimar Republic (in contravention of the Treaty of Versailles) was accelerated, and on September 1, 1939, Germany invaded Poland. Two days later Britain and France responded by declaring war on Germany, and Europe was soon being torn apart again, followed shortly by much of the rest of the globe.

STALIN'S FIRST FIVE-YEAR PLAN

1929–1933

MOTIVATION

Anger

Charity

Envy

Faith

Gluttony

Greed

Hope

Lust

Pride

Sloth

Main Culprit: Josef Stalin

Damage Done: He used a policy of collectivization to starve millions of Ukrainians to death

Why: To break the national spirit of the Ukrainian people

On one side, millions of starving peasants, their bodies often swollen from lack of food; on the other, soldiers, members of the GPU [Soviet secret police] carrying out the instructions of the dictatorship of the proletariat. They had gone over the country like a swarm of locusts and taken away everything edible; they had shot or exiled thousands of peasants, sometimes whole villages; they had reduced some of the most fertile land in the world to a melancholy desert.

Malcolm Muggeridge, "War on the Peasants," in *Fortnightly Review*, May 1, 1933

© Getty Images

JOSEF STALIN
The Soviet leader saw collectivization as an opportunity not only to get rid of "class enemies" but also a means to crush the fiercely independent Ukrainian people.

Large scale social engineering almost invariably has unintended and detrimental, even horrific, consequences for the people affected, as we shall see in the policies and programs of the Chinese leader Mao Zedong (see pp. 180–183), but in the case of Josef Stalin's first Five-Year Plan the dreadful consequences may not have been accidental. There was certainly no attempt to change the course of events when, in the first years of the 1930s, it became obvious that his planned collectivization of the farms of Ukraine was causing famine on an unprecedented scale. Indeed, the policy was implemented with even greater vigor, turning a very bad decision into deliberate "death by starvation," or *holodomor* in Ukrainian. Stalin's attempted genocide is an unpleasant truth that the world community has been strangely unwilling to discuss or even accept as fact.

When Stalin came to power, industrialization was central to his drive to make the Soviet Union a global power, and his first Five-Year Plan (1929–1933) set out targets for massive increases in the production of iron, steel, coal, oil, and electricity. It was his intention to expand heavy industry and make the Soviet Union self-sufficient in raw materials, industrial goods, and, importantly, armaments. The year after its introduction, Stalin expanded the plan to include the collectivization of farms throughout the USSR. Lenin had distributed privately owned land among the peasants, who now grew crops and raised animals in traditional ways on a small scale, but now Stalin saw this as an obstacle to true socialism, as well as an impediment to efficient food production. Collectivization—amalgamating the small peasant-run farms into large collectively run operations—would facilitate mechanization, reduce the number of people working on the land (and make them available as a labor force for the new heavy industries), and increase production to feed the growing urban population.

CLASS WAR

Hand in hand with the policy of collectivization, Stalin announced that the kulaks—wealthier peasants who hired the labor of others, owned machinery, or sold their surplus on the market—were class enemies and must be removed. In his own words, "Now we have the opportunity to carry out a resolute offensive against the kulaks, break their resistance, eliminate them as a class and replace their production with the production of [communal and state-owned collective farms]." As a policy, this went far beyond taking their land and livestock. That was just the start. Hundreds of thousands, if not millions, of kulaks were sent to work in labor colonies, deported to areas outside the agricultural regions, shot, or imprisoned. Stalin was willing to push through the policy of collectivization at any price, and in many parts of the Soviet Union the price was very high. Ironically, the Ukraine, a huge area of fertile agricultural land, witnessed more suffering than anywhere else as a result of falling production. It was no accident.

The Ukraine had been fiercely independent in spirit since the end of Tsarist rule, when it had declared itself a people's republic and fought a four-year battle against both Lenin's Red Army and the pro-Tsar White Army that ended in a Soviet victory. The Ukraine become the bread-basket of the USSR, but it retained a strong nationalism and pride in its culture, language, and religion. To Stalin this was unacceptable, and in 1929 several thousand academics, intellectuals, and cultural leaders were deported or executed. Now collectivization offered a further opportunity to break the spirit of the Ukraine.

As peasants were deprived of land and livestock, taken for the collective, many fought to retain what they had worked so hard to achieve. Those who resisted were labeled as kulaks and were deported or shot. Some refused to hand over the grain they had cultivated. Others slaughtered their animals sooner than have them taken. Reprisals followed quickly, but the net affect was a fall in agricultural production and a drop in the number of animals, cattle falling by 30 percent and sheep by almost 60 percent.

HOLODOMOR
Ignored by habituated passersby, the corpses of people starved to death by Stalin's imposed famine lie on a sidewalk in Kharkiv in 1933.

In order to put an end to the resistance, Stalin took one simple step. He ramped up the grain quotas demanded by the state, increasing them by more than 40 percent in 1932. That year there was a good harvest but until the state's requirements were fulfilled, the peasants were allowed no grain, and as a result there was simply nothing for them to eat. The grain was transported away and much of it was sold on the world market, the money fueling the industrialization program.

Communist Party officials, the military, and the secret police carried out a virtual war on the peasantry, executing or deporting anyone found in possession of even a handful of grain. People who were not visibly malnourished were suspected of theft or hoarding food. Military blockades were set up to prevent anyone from leaving the affected areas or food from entering, and the Ukraine was turned into a virtual concentration camp.

GENOCIDE | Between 1932 and 1933 as many as 15 million people are thought to have starved to death throughout the USSR, more than a third of these being Ukrainians. When officials within the party organization pointed out the terrible famine that was occurring, they were accused of anti-Soviet propaganda, and there was a purge of the Communist bureaucracy. The Soviet Union declared outright that there was no problem, closing the door on any possible international aid. It is even thought that some Western journalists, aware of what was happening but threatened with being denied access to Soviet news sources, chose not to cover the story. The international community was, nonetheless, generally aware of what was happening — if not the full scale of it — but took no action against the USSR, unwilling to jeopardize the lucrative trade agreements that flowed from the Soviet industrialization program.

By the end of 1933, figuring that the Ukraine was finished as a cultural entity and would offer no further obstacle to complete collectivization, Stalin eased up on food restrictions. It is estimated that between 10 and 20 percent of the population of the Ukraine had died as a result of his ruthless policy. Only since the break-up of the Soviet Union in 1991 and the advent of Ukrainian independence have the full facts begun to emerge, and even now only a handful of countries has been willing to recognize Stalin's forced famine as an act of genocide.

HITLER INVADES THE SOVIET UNION

June 22—December 5, 1941

MOTIVATION

Anger

Charity

Envy

Faith

Gluttony

Greed

Hope

Lust

Pride

Sloth

Main Culprit: Adolf Hitler, against the advice of his military command

Damage Done: Operation Barbarossa resulted in literally millions of casualties on both sides, and Germany gained nothing by it

Why: Hitler underestimated the Red Army and was confident that the campaign would be over before winter. It wasn't

We only have to kick in the door and the whole rotten structure will come crashing down.

Adolf Hitler, June 22, 1941

© Getty Images

Greed and pride are woefully inadequate terms to describe Hitler's motivation for invading the Soviet Union in 1941. In his book *Mein Kampf*, written in 1925, he had already made it clear that he believed Germany needed, and should take, the territories to its east in order to provide its citizens with the living space (Lebensraum), natural resources, and agricultural land that they deserved. When he finally put this plan into action—in Operation Barbarossa, as it was codenamed— it led to the greatest loss of human life ever seen on the planet, as well as the untold suffering of millions of survivors. It also planted the seeds of the Holocaust. In return, Germany gained absolutely nothing and ultimately lost the war as a direct result of the failed invasion.

LOOKING EAST

In the two years after the start of World War II, the Axis powers had taken control of almost three-quarters of Europe, and Nazi Germany's next logical targets were Britain and the Soviet Union. In the second half of 1940 Britain had repulsed the German Luftwaffe and the country's morale had not been broken despite extensive bombing. Hitler's next option was a seaborne invasion, but the English Channel and the strength of the British navy presented a major obstacle. Besides, Britain had little to offer in the way of materials or space.

Invading the Soviet Union was the obvious choice, given its resources (Germany was in desperate need of oil and other raw materials) and the fact that Hitler despised Communists, Jews, and Slavs, not to mention Stalin, whose ideology was diametrically opposed to that of the Nazis. Moreover, despite the fact that Germany and the Soviet Union had signed the Molotov–Ribbentrop non-aggression pact in 1939, Hitler had good reason to suppose that Stalin would eventually choose to profit from the weakened condition of war-torn Europe and make its own territorial claims. The longer he delayed, the stronger and more organized the Soviet army would be.

Even the Allies could see the logic behind Hitler's decision to invade, but when it came to the details of the plan Hitler confronted a level of opposition from within his own ranks. Whereas the military were in favor of a concerted attack on Moscow to destroy Russia's nerve center and the heart of Communism, Hitler proposed to attack along the entire length of the Eastern Front, from the Baltic in the north to the Black Sea in the south with a three-pronged assault. Army

Group North was to move through the Baltic states (recently ceded to Russia under the Molotov–Ribbentrop Pact) to take Leningrad, Army Group Center was to advance through Belorussia and capture Moscow, and Army Group South was to cross the agricultural and mineral-rich Ukraine, taking Kiev, Stalingrad, and the oil fields of the Caucasus. Hitler's view prevailed.

The success of Operation Barbarossa depended upon it being accomplished quickly through the famed *blitzkreig* ("lightning war") strategy—using an overwhelming military force, in the air and on the ground, to smash through the enemy's lines at high speed and then keep going. The strategy relied upon the enemy being taken by surprise and being unable to respond quickly and effectively. Remarkably, despite the decoding of secret messages concerning the invasion, repeated warnings from Soviet spies, the massing of German troops on the Polish border, and repeated reconnaissance flights over Soviet territory, Stalin refused to believe that an attack was imminent, and to this extent the Germans did maintain the element of surprise. However, he did believe that war against Germany was inevitable once Britain had been overrun, and vast numbers of troops were already assembled behind the Russian border.

WEHRMACHT
Hitler sent a huge number of troops into Russia, but they were spread over several fronts and they met far more resistance than he expected.

As for its ability to respond, Hitler had a good many reasons to suppose that the Soviet army was weak and disorganized, not least being the fact that Stalin had carried out a purge of the Red Army in the late 1930s in which the majority of its generals, admirals, and commanders had been removed and tens of thousands of soldiers had been executed. (The result was a command structure largely composed of young and inexperienced men unwilling to act without explicit orders.) Above all, Hitler's contempt for Communism led him to suppose that the Soviet structure would collapse once initial defeats had been inflicted.

Operation Barbarossa, the largest military operation in history, began at 3am on Sunday, June 22, 1941. The troop numbers on both sides are almost unimaginable, with more than 3 million German and Axis troops confronting more than 2 million Soviet troops. The rapid advance of

TAKEN PRISONER
A Russian soldier shepherds a German prisoner of war. Russians taken prisoner by the Germans were not afforded the protection of the Geneva Convention.

the Axis forces and their resounding victories in the first few days appeared to fully justify Hitler's optimism. Within three days the Luftwaffe had destroyed more than 3,000 Soviet planes, with minimal losses of their own. In the first week of the offensive more than half a million Soviet soldiers were killed, wounded, or captured, and the three Army Groups achieved all their immediate campaign objectives. Indeed, their advance was so rapid that in the north, although they were almost within striking distance of Leningrad, the panzer (tank) groups had to wait a week for the infantry divisions to catch up, which gave the Soviets an opportunity to strengthen the defense of the city.

During the course of July, German progress slowed dramatically. In the north a period of heavy rain turned the roads into mud, and the German tanks, with their narrower tracks, were less able to deal with the conditions than the Soviets'. The German troops had also outpaced their supply lines and had to wait for munitions and other supplies to reach them. Furthermore, Soviet resistance was far greater than predicted, and the Soviet armies, although they had suffered terrible losses, were being replenished by new reserves.

A FATAL DELAY

On July 15 the Germans captured the city of Smolensk, and by the end of the first week in August the road to Moscow was open for them. What happened next can be seen, with hindsight, as a turning point in the campaign, if not in the war as a whole. Hitler, reasoning that depriving the Soviet army of its supplies would give Germany the advantage, made the decision to send panzer divisions from Army Group Center southward to support the advance in the Ukraine. This meant delaying the advance on Moscow, and his commanders were adamant that this was a mistake, that taking Moscow—the center of communication and munitions production—was the highest priority, but they were overruled. Once Kiev had been taken, on September 19, the panzers returned northward to Army Group Center and the advance on Moscow recommenced on October 2, but it was a delay that the Russian winter would not forgive.

As the German forces approached Moscow, the weather steadily deteriorated. Neither the men nor their equipment were prepared for temperatures that fell to -40°F (-40°C). The supply lines were now so long, and so subject to attack by Russian partisan forces, that it was difficult to get fuel and munitions through. Food was in short supply, and winter clothing wasn't even on the list of priorities. By early December, although German troops were within sight of the spires of the Kremlin, some divisions had been reduced to half their strength by the terrible conditions. Machinery began to malfunction as oil thickened and grease froze, and the Luftwaffe planes were unable to fly. The Soviet troops, on the other hand, had quilted clothing, thick boots, and fur hats, and their equipment was designed for this climate. On December 5, the half a million Soviet troops massed around Moscow launched a successful counter-attack that drove the Germans back some 200 miles (320 km). Moscow would not fall to the Nazis, and although the war on the Eastern Front would last for another three years, it would end with the Soviet flag being raised in Berlin.

MOTIVATION

Anger

Charity

Envy

Faith

Gluttony

Greed

Hope

Lust

Pride

Sloth

JAPAN ATTACKS PEARL HARBOR

December 7, 1941

Main Culprits: Emperor Hirohito and Japanese Imperial General Headquarters

Damage Done: Killed more than 2,000 US servicemen and women, but ultimately led to the defeat of Japan

Why: Intended to prevent the US standing in the way of Japan, the attack actually drew the US into World War II

To have the United States at our side was to me the greatest joy. Now at this very moment I knew the United States was in the war, up to the neck and in to the death. So we had won after all!... Hitler's fate was sealed. Mussolini's fate was sealed. As for the Japanese, they would be ground to powder.

Winston Churchill, recalling his feelings on receiving a phone call from Roosevelt informing him of the attack

Japanese planes—fighters, dive-bombers, and aerial torpedo planes—attacked the US Pacific Fleet in Pearl Harbor, on the Hawaiian island of O'ahu, shortly before 8am on the morning of December 7, 1941. In less than an hour and a half, 2,400 people were killed, nine ships were sunk, and 21 were seriously damaged. The following day Franklin D. Roosevelt referred to the event as "a date which will live in infamy." In the words of a Japanese admiral, "We won a great tactical victory at Pearl Harbor and thereby lost the war."

Although the time and the place of the attack took the Americans completely by surprise, the US had been expecting an act of war by the Japanese for months, if not decades. Relations between the two countries had been especially tense since the Japanese invasion, in 1931, of Manchuria in northwest China. Throughout the 1930s the nationalist-dominated Japanese government had been increasing the country's military strength and implementing a policy of imperial expansion that threatened the colonial interests of the US, Britain, France, and the Netherlands. When Japan attacked China in 1937, pitching those two countries into full-scale war, the US and other Western powers supplied financial and military aid to China, but in 1940 and 1941 Japan moved into north and south Indochina (now

JAPANESESQUADRON
More than 400 Japanese planes were involved in the aerial attack on Pearl Harbor, bombing, strafing, and dropping torpedoes to destroy the US fleet.

Cambodia, Laos, Vietnam, Burma, and Thailand), cutting off the supply route into China. In the meantime, Japan had signed the Tripartite Pact with Germany and Italy, whereby the three countries promised to come to each other's aid if they found themselves at war with countries considered neutral. This was clearly intended to keep America out of the war, but with Nazi aggression to its east and Japanese expansion to its west, the US was being forced to move from its neutral position. Already it was directly aiding Britain with financial and material support and by protecting merchant ships supplying Britain across the Atlantic. Now the US imposed trade sanctions on Japan, froze Japanese assets in the US, and on August 1 placed an embargo on all its fuel exports to Japan (which constituted 80 percent of that country's total supply).

Diplomatic discussions took place over the next few months but no progress was made.

Plans to launch an attack on Pearl Harbor had been under discussion since the start of 1941, and on November 5 the Japanese emperor Hirohito gave his approval for the planned attack to go ahead, but in a last diplomatic effort Japan submitted two proposals to the US. The first, made the following day, offered a partial withdrawal of Japanese from China. The second, presented on November 20, offered a withdrawal from southern Indochina on condition that the US discontinue its aid to the Chinese Nationalist Government of Chiang Kai-shek and restore oil supplies to Japan. Both of these were rejected by the US, and plans for a counter-proposal were dropped when it was learned that Japan was planning for war and had already dispatched warships to Indochina. On November 26 Japan was presented with a proposal known as the Hull Note, named after Secretary of State Cordell Hull. It contained a US demand for the complete withdrawal of Japanese troops from both China and French Indochina, and Japan interpreted this as an ultimatum. In fact, a fleet of six aircraft carriers carrying more than 400 planes for the attack on Pearl Harbor was already en route across the Pacific. It was not recalled.

There is no doubt that President Roosevelt and Secretary of War Henry L. Stimson were aware that a surprise attack by the Japanese was likely, not that the US was ready and willing to go to war with Japan. The hope was that Japan would make the first act of aggression, enabling the US to respond, but that the US would not have to pay too high a price. It was not thought, however, that the target would be Pearl Harbor (Thailand and the Philippines were considered more likely), and no preparations for an attack were made. In fact, the US base was very ill prepared in several ways:

- No troops were on operational alert.
- Because of concerns about possible sabotage, the planes of the Air Corps had been parked wingtip to wingtip in the center of the airfield, away from the perimeter, and could not be scrambled in a hurry.
- The harbor itself was thought to be safe from attack by

air-launched torpedoes given the shallowness of the water, and therefore no torpedo netting had been deployed. (In fact, the British had demonstrated the previous year that torpedoes could be used in water of a comparable depth when they sank half the Italian fleet in the port of Taranto using modified aerial torpedoes, but the warning wasn't heeded. The Japanese, on the other hand, had learned the lesson.)

• For fear of causing undue alarm among the civilian population, the mobile anti-aircraft guns had not been deployed around the island, and the shells were being stored in armories.

• There were very few long-range reconnaissance aircraft at the base and therefore few reconnaissance missions—which could have detected the approaching Japanese fleet—were being flown.

The first wave of the air attack comprised 183 planes—bombers (some armed with modified torpedoes), dive bombers, and fighter planes—that proceeded to bomb and torpedo the battleships—especially the destroyers—in the harbor, and to dive-bomb and strafe the onshore bases. A second wave of some 170 planes followed, and there was little that the US forces could do to respond. The scene was one of devastation, and the loss of life was terrible, but the real cost to the US was far less than the Japanese had hoped for. In many respects, the lack of preparedness on the part of the Americans proved to be a blessing. Had the fleet put to sea to meet the oncoming attack vessels, the loss of life would have been far greater, and so would the loss of vessels. As it was, many members of the ships' crews were ashore at the time and several of the ships, having sunk in shallow water rather than the open ocean, were recovered and repaired within a few weeks.It was also fortunate for the US that the three aircraft carriers of the Pacific Fleet were away at the time. As the war in the Pacific developed, aircraft carriers, rather than destroyers, proved to be the key to success, and those of the US had suffered no damage.

DESTROYED
The Japanese attack sank four US naval battleships and three destroyers. On the land, 188 planes were destroyed and 155 were damaged.

Japan had assumed that the Pacific Fleet would be so crushed that the US would have to negotiate a settlement and leave Japan to achieve its goals in the Pacific, but the gamble hadn't paid off.

AMERICAN INTERVENTION

On the international front, events moved quickly. The day after the attack, the US received notice of Japan's declaration of war (it had been meant to arrive shortly before the attack began, but due to the Japanese Embassy's delays in decoding and delivering the message, it arrived late). In the US, outrage at the attack rapidly overcame popular opposition to entering the war, and America immediately declared war on Japan (as did Britain, Australia, and other Allied powers). In accordance with the Tripartite Pact, Germany and Italy then declared war on America, and the US responded in kind. America was to play an important role in the Allies' victory over Nazi Germany, but an even greater one in the Pacific War, ultimately leading to the ignominious surrender of Japan, more than two million of its citizens dead, its navy incapacitated, the Allies on the brink of invading the country, and the cities of Hiroshima and Nagasaki flattened by atomic explosions.

BRITAIN PARTITIONS INDIA

August 15, 1947

MOTIVATION

Anger

Charity

Envy

Faith

Gluttony

Greed

Hope

Lust

Pride

Sloth

Main Culprits: Hindus, Muslims, and the British government

Damage Done: Conflict between Muslims and Hindus led to widespread violence and thousands of deaths. The tensions and violence continue to this day.

Why: The British believed that separating the Muslims and Hindus geographically was the only way to avoid civil war in India

I would like to see Punjab, North-West Frontier Province, Sindh and Balochistan amalgamated into a single state. Self-government within the British Empire or without the British Empire, the formation of a consolidated North-West Indian Muslim state appears to me to be the final destiny of the Muslims, at least of North-West India.

Sir Muhammad Iqbal, president of the All India Muslim League, 1930

My whole soul rebels against the idea that Hinduism and Islam represent two antagonistic cultures and doctrines. To assent to such a doctrine is for me a denial of God.

Mohandas Gandhi

Whether Britain had any choice in 1947 but to end British rule and to split India into two separate states—predominantly Muslim Pakistan and predominantly Hindu India—remains a matter of contention. Communal violence was breaking out, civil war was looming, and there appeared to be no alternative. However, the speed with which this major political decision was implemented, and the consequent lack of preparation for what would follow, can certainly be criticized. The effect of partition led to the greatest migration of people ever seen and to terrible loss of life. The aftershocks are still being felt in the daily lives of the people of both countries.

Although some 1,300,000 Indians chose to serve in the British Indian army during World War I, there was already a growing Indian independence movement that sought to put an end to the domination of the country by the British Raj. This was especially evident in Bengal and Punjab.

GANDHI
An advocate of peaceful protest to attain independence, Mahatma Gandhi was strongly opposed to the partition of India. In January 1948 he was assassinated by a Hindu extremist.

In 1918, as incidents of terrorism increased, the British Imperial Legislative Council passed the Rowlatt Acts, allowing trial without jury and internment without trial for people suspected of sedition. Lawyer and human rights activist Mahatma Gandhi called for non-violent protest against these laws, but in the first week of April 1919 protests in several towns in Punjab flared into violent anti-British riots. In Amritsar, several Europeans were murdered and banks were looted and burned. On April 13, following the arrest of two Indian nationalists, at least 5,000 (and possibly as many as 20,000) peaceful protesters gathered on an enclosed area of wasteland in the city to voice their opposition, despite a ban on public meetings. Brigadier-General Rex Dyer, in the belief that India was on the brink of a full-blown rebellion that would threaten Britain's continued presence in India, led a force of more than 50 Ghurka and Sikh infantrymen to the protest and then ordered them to open fire on the packed crowd with rifles. By the time they had run out of ammunition, almost 400 men, women, and children were dead and some 1,500 had been injured. The Lieutenant Governor of the Punjab, Sir Michael Francis O'Dwyer, approved Dyer's orders as "correct action," and the British establishment initially accepted that the massacre had been necessary to quell a rebellion. The authorities later distanced themselves from Dyer's actions after the full details of what had happened became known, but the damage was done. It was a turning point in the relationship between India and the British Raj.

As a direct consequence of the Amritsar Massacre, Indian people flocked to join the Indian National Congress (INC), which had been founded in 1855 as a mouthpiece through which educated India might have a dialog with the British Raj about issues of government. Now it became a mass movement, transformed into a voice for Indian demands for independence. Although initial opposition to the Raj united Muslims and Hindus alike, their fears and ambitions soon diverged, and while the INC, with Gandhi as its president, remained the voice of the Hindus, the Muslim League, under the leadership of Muhammad Ali Jinnah, spoke for the Muslims. From the Hindu perspective, it was the Muslims, in the form of the Moghul Empire, who had been the occupying invaders before the British. The Muslims felt that in an independent India they would be ruled by a Hindu majority that already dominated the government bureaucracy, having availed themselves of educational opportunities to a greater degree than the Muslims.

During the 1920s and '30s, various measures were introduced to include Indians in the electoral process and in governmental decision making (except in the fields of defense and foreign affairs) but these fell far short of satisfying the nationalists, whose call now was for nothing less than dominion status for India and a complete end to British rule. When, in the 1937 provincial elections, Hindus won control in eight of the 11 provinces, Muslim fears of Hindu domination appeared justified, and the Muslim League began to demand a separate state of their own. Gandhi and the Congress Party were equally intent upon preserving Indian unity. Rivalry between the Hindus and Muslims continued to escalate.

At the end of World War II, the new Labour government in Britain was anxious to solve the "Indian problem" as soon as possible, and the religious issue posed the greatest stumbling block. A plan was put forward in which political power would be devolved as much as possible to the provinces, the idea being that in the few provinces that had a Muslim majority (in the northwest and the northeast of

THE CALL FOR PARTITION

© Allan Warren | Creative Commons

VICEROY OF INDIA
Lord Louis Mountbatten's
short schedule for British
withdrawal and the partition
of India was a contributing
factor in the chaos and
bloodshed that ensued.

India) this would be reflected in the decision making of the provincial government, and that there would be no need for a separate Muslim state. The idea was accepted in principle, and although the details could not be agreed, the head of the INC, Nehru, was invited to form an interim government. Although Nehru included two Muslims in his cabinet, the Muslim League under Muhammad Ali Jinnah were distrustful. When the INC rejected the Muslim League's call for a separate and independent Muslim state of Pakistan, the League called for a day of "direct action" to protest.

On the morning of the Day of Direct Action (August 16, 1946) sporadic acts of violence broke out in the city of Calcutta, where Hindus largely dominated the economy in a state—Bengal—that had a Muslim majority. In the course of the day the violence escalated dramatically, with groups of Hindus and Sikhs on the one hand and Muslims on the other attacking and literally hacking each other to pieces. The British were slow to bring in the military, and in the course of more than a week of rioting and looting an estimated 5,000 people were killed and as many as 100,000 were wounded. The violence also spread to other parts of India, and it became clear that a civil war was erupting. Despite having been developed and administered as a single entity for a century, a unified India after independence no longer looked like a viable possibility.

On June 4, 1947, the Viceroy of India, Lord Louis Mountbatten, announced the plan by which two independent dominions—India and Pakistan—would come into existence in just ten weeks' time, on August 15. The result was the beginning of a mass migration as Muslims and Hindus crossed the imminent borders, the mayhem heightened by the fact that the exact borders had not yet been determined. For months it had seemed probable that Punjab would be bisected, and it had been a focus of communal violence—killings, rape, and arson—since March. Now inter-religious atrocities here and in Bengal, where many people would also find themselves on the wrong side of a border, increased to a horrifying degree.

With due pomp and ceremony, the Dominion of Pakistan and the Union of India came into being on the 14th and 15th of August respectively, and full responsibility for managing the largest migration in history fell upon the shoulders of the newly formed governments. It is estimated that approximately 15 million people crossed the Pakistan/India borders in the months that followed, with roughly equal numbers moving in each direction. The army and the security services, in the process of being divided by religion and allocated to the new states, were unable to police the situation adequately, and at least half a million Muslims, Hindus, and Sikhs were hunted down and killed by marauding groups that attacked cross-border trains and buses, as well as refugees traveling by foot, all trying to make their way out of what had become, virtually overnight, enemy territory. The end of the Raj and the Partition of India may have been inevitable, but the speed with which they were accomplished had exacted a terrible human price.

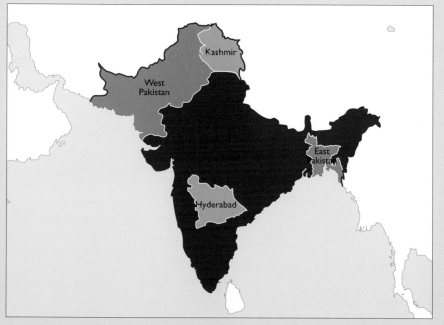

— Boundary of British India (1939)

■ Union of India

■ East/West Pakistan (1947)

■ States not included in the partition plan

DIVIDED

The greatest migration and the worst violence took place in the northwest, where Punjab was divided by the India/Pakistan border, and in the east, where the creation of East Pakistan split Bengal. Hyderabad became part of India in 1948, and Kashmir remains torn to this day, with control of the region being divided between Pakistan, China, and India.

MOTIVATION

Anger

Charity

Envy

Faith

Gluttony

Greed

Hope

Lust

Pride

Sloth

THE VIETNAM WAR

1955–1975

Main Culprits: American foreign policy hawks

Damage Done: Caused untold economic, ecological, and humanitarian damage to Vietnam, and embroiled the US in its longest and most unpopular war

Why: To try—unsuccessfully—to prevent the spread of Communist ideology

US objectives and concept of operations [are] to prevent Communist domination of South Vietnam; to create in that country a viable and increasingly democratic society, and to initiate, on an accelerated basis, a series of mutually supporting actions of a military, political, economic, psychological, and covert character designed to achieve this objective.

President J. F. Kennedy, May 1961

In the course of the Vietnam War, which started in 1955, the United States was drawn into an ever greater commitment of manpower and weaponry in its support for the Republic of Vietnam (South Vietnam) against the Communist-led Democratic Republic of Vietnam (North Vietnam). At one point, more than half a million US troops were on the ground, but they were unable to inflict defeat on the guerilla forces of North Vietnam. As public anti-war sentiment in the US grew, the government was eventually forced to acknowledge that a war that had lasted almost 20 years and cost the lives of almost 60,000 American servicemen could not be won. The last American troops were withdrawn in 1973, and the north and south were reunited as the Socialist Republic of Vietnam.

By the end of the 19th century, France exerted colonial control over much of what are now Vietnam, Laos, and Cambodia, an area known at the time as French Indochina. In 1941, during World War II, Ho Chi Minh returned from some 30 years overseas and led the Viet Minh independence fighters against the French and then, with support from China and the US, against the occupying Japanese. When Japan surrendered to the Allied Powers, many of the Japanese weapons ended up in the hands of the Viet Minh, who then opposed French attempts to reestablish control of the region.

FRENCH INDOCHINA
A soldier of the French Foreign Legion walks ahead of an advancing tank. The French were ultimately defeated by the Viet Minh.

The United States, led by Harry Truman, allowed the French to reassert their authority, and the French Indochina War began, but initially without active US support, as the US was generally opposed to European colonialism. However, as the spread of international Communism became a major issue in American foreign policy, the French war in Vietnam began to be seen in this light, and the US began to fund the French war effort. Nonetheless, the French were unable to defeat the Viet Minh, and in 1954 they suffered a crushing defeat in the Battle of Dien Bien Phu.

In peace negotiations carried out in Geneva, Switzerland, the French and the Vietnamese agreed to temporarily divide the north and south of the country along the 17th parallel, on the understanding that elections take place in 1956 prior to reunification.

The Viet Minh under Ho Chi Minh controlled North Vietnam, with their capital in Hanoi, while the southern State of Vietnam, with its capital in Saigon, was under the Emperor Bao Dai. His prime minister, Ngo Dinh Diem, soon deposed the emperor and took control himself. With US backing, he then reneged on the Geneva Accords and refused to participate in elections, as the US feared that Ho Chi Minh would win and the whole of Vietnam would then be under Communist control. According to the prevalent "domino theory," adjacent territories would then "fall" and America's greatest fears would be realized.

At this point the Viet Minh launched a march southward, but the movement was so weakened, after carrying out a self-harming purge of its less Communist members and instituting disastrous land reforms, that it proved ineffective as either a political party or an army.

DIRECT INVOLVEMENT

In 1955, in order to support the independence of South Vietnam, the US, under President Dwight D. Eisenhower, sent in its first group of military advisers—the first of many. The US-backed presidency of Ngo Dinh Diem was not only strongly anti-Communist but also tyrannical and corrupt, and any opposition was ruthlessly crushed. A South Vietnamese rebel group calling itself the Viet Cong and using guerilla tactics against the forces of Ngo Dinh Diem was quickly suppressed and driven into remote and inhospitable areas of the country, but after 1957 the North gave increasing support to the insurgency (against Ho Chi Minh's wishes). In 1959 the North Vietnam Communist Party authorized a "People's War" against the South, with support from the People's Army of Vietnam (PAVN), and set about improving a secret supply route between North and South, which became known as the Ho Chi Minh Trail.

In 1961, the year in which J. F. Kennedy's presidency began, violent attacks against the South increased dramatically, and although he was opposed to deploying ground troops, Kennedy sent in 18,000 advisors and began supplying South Vietnam with napalm incendiary jelly, defoliants such as Agent Orange, helicopters, and jet aircraft. These did little to lessen the successes of the Viet Cong, however, and the US began to lose faith in Diem's ability to defeat the Communist insurgency, which by now had Chinese backing. In 1963 Ngo Dinh Diem was murdered and his government was overthrown, to be replaced by a military coalition.

In the hope of a quick victory, the North Vietnamese PAVN increased its troop numbers to more than 300,000, and by the end of 1964 it looked as though the Saigon government might collapse. However, the administration of President Lyndon B. Johnson had found an excuse to use military force without having to ask for congressional approval to declare war. On August 2, 1964, the USS *Maddox* was maneuvering off the coast of North Vietnam when it was apparently attacked by three North Vietnamese torpedo boats. In the ensuing sea battle, involving US fighter-bombers and the firing of some 280 shells by the US destroyer, the Vietnamese ships were damaged, four of their crew were killed, and six were wounded. One of the US planes was damaged, and the USS *Maddox* was hit by a single bullet. Two days later the Maddox and another ship reported being attacked again.

Before the day was over, LBJ had broadcast the details to the American people, approved US Defense Secretary Robert McNamara's call for retaliatory air strikes against North Vietnam, and presented a resolution to Congress requesting the authority to conduct military operations in Southeast Asia, which Congress approved three days later. This was a turning point in the Vietnam War—and it was founded on a fiction. In the case of the first attack, it was later revealed not only that the USS *Maddox* had been inside Vietnamese territorial waters but that the US ship had fired the first shot. As for the second attack, it hadn't taken place at all. The USS *Maddox*'s captain blamed "freak weather effects on radar and overeager sonarmen" for the mistaken report. Robert McNamara had known this before Johnson gave permission for air strikes but hadn't told him.

ENGAGEMENT
Lyndon B. Johnson (center) and Robert McNamara (right) were selective in their use of the intelligence coming from the Gulf of Tonkin, and brought the US into the Vietnam War.

Be that as it may, Johnson now had the authority he needed, and the US began a campaign of bombing North Vietnamese cities and industrial targets. In the spring of 1965, 3,500 marines were sent in, by the end of the year there were 200,000 US troops in Vietnam, and this number eventually rose to more than 550,000.

This was not the kind of warfare that US troops had experienced before. Although there were some conventional battles, much of the

MUCH OF THE CONFLICT
TOOK PLACE IN DENSE
JUNGLE, GIVING THE
VIET CONG GUERILLA
FIGHTERS A DECISIVE
ADVANTAGE.

conflict took place in dense jungle, giving the Viet Cong guerilla fighters a decisive advantage. In an attempt to redress the balance, the US used napalm and defoliants in vast quantities to destroy vegetation, villages, and crops, theoretically leaving the Viet Cong with no cover, no food, and no rural support. In 1968 the Viet Cong adopted a new tactic.

The Lunar New Year celebrations fell on January 30 in 1968, and there was an agreed ceasefire in place. The Viet Cong, however, smuggled some 80,000 fighters, together with weapons and explosives, into 100 towns and cities across South Vietnam and launched a major offensive, shooting and bombing civilians, attacking air bases and the US Embassy in Saigon. The fighting continued for more than a week, and several thousand South Vietnamese were killed. Militarily, it was a disaster for the Viet Cong, who lost an estimated 45,000 soldiers, but it was a political triumph. Scenes of the carnage had been broadcast in the US, and support there for the war flagged while the anti-war movement gained momentum.

In January 1969, Richard Nixon became president, and after initially increasing American involvement (including a massive bombing campaign in Cambodia over what were thought to be Viet Cong headquarters), he implemented a policy of "Vietnamization," replacing US troops with Vietnamese counterparts and bringing the US soldiers home. In 1973 the signing of the Paris Peace Accords brought US involvement in the war to an end, although it was tacitly understood that without US support the Republic of Vietnam would soon be defeated. On April 30, 1975, Saigon fell to the North, and the two halves of the country were reunited as the Socialist Republic of Vietnam in 1976.

The war had cost more than 100 billion dollars, killed an estimated two million Vietnamese and 58,000 American soldiers, injured almost six times as many, deeply divided US public opinion—and achieved absolutely nothing.

FRANCE TRIES TO HOLD ON TO ALGERIA

1954–1962

MOTIVATION

Anger

Charity

Envy

Faith

Gluttony

Greed

Hope

Lust

Pride

Sloth

Main Culprit: The French government

Damage Done: Led to the first conflict in which torture and brutal urban terrorism played a major role

Why: France was loathe to abandon more than 1,000,000 French settlers in a country that would accept nothing less than independence

A free, open-minded, and absolutely impartial adjustment of all colonial claims, based upon a strict observance of the principle that in determining all such questions of sovereignty the interests of the populations concerned must have equal weight with the equitable claims of the government whose title is to be determined.

Point five of Woodrow Wilson's Fourteen Points

Putting aside the question of whether or not the French government was fundamentally mistaken in annexing a portion of North Africa and running it as a province of France, its response to Algerian demands for greater autonomy and ultimately for independence led to eight years of war and the deaths of thousands of native Algerians, European-Algerian settlers, and French military. Successive presidents failed to read the writing on the wall.

France first began its invasion of Algeria in 1830, and by 1847 some 50,000 French *colons* were settled in the country, farming formerly communal land that had been confiscated. In 1848 Algeria was declared to be a part of France, and it was the only French colonial possession to be treated as a province in this way. After World War I, in which many Algerians fought for France, an indigenous movement calling for more rights and a greater say in the running of their country began, and over the following decades several political parties were formed in Algeria with greater autonomy on their agenda.

SÉTIF MASSACRE

The call for independence gained considerable momentum after an event that took place on May 8, 1945. In the town of Sétif, a parade by some 5,000 native Algerians celebrating Victory in Europe Day turned into an anti-colonial demonstration, and in clashes with the French gendarmerie several protesters were shot and killed. In the riots that followed, more than 100 French settlers, or *pieds noirs*, were killed by Muslim Algerians. The French police and army then carried out reprisals, including the bombing of villages and the shelling of a coastal town by a naval gunship, in which several thousand Algerians were killed. The "Sétif Massacre" had a profound effect on relations between the two countries, and on the political climate to which Algerian soldiers fighting in the war returned.

Faced with demands for radical reform to give greater equality to the indigenous Algerian people, the French government offered a range of concessions, including giving French citizenship to all Algerians, but in 1946 the Democratic Union of the Algerian Manifesto called for Algeria to become an autonomous state with its own government within the French federal system, rather than being a province of France. The French government remained opposed, and as attitudes on both sides hardened, the movement for Algerian independence gained strength.

In the spring of 1954, the French lost the battle of Dien Bien Phu in Vietnam, and in the aftermath the newly appointed Prime Minister Pierre Mendès France (a consistent opponent of French colonialism) negotiated French withdrawal from Indochina. In Algeria, this prompted the Front de Libération Nationale (FLN) to launch armed attacks throughout the country on November 1, demanding a sovereign Algerian state. France responded by deploying troops, and French Foreign Minister François Mitterrand stated, "I will not agree to negotiate with the enemies of the homeland. The only negotiation is war!" Bloody All-Saints' Day, as it became known, marked the start of the Algerian War of Independence.

The war escalated in August 1955 when the FLN launched an attack on the town of Philippeville in which more than 100 people were killed, including Muslim politicians, in acts of extreme savagery. At least 1,000 (possibly several thousand) Muslim Algerians died in the acts of retaliation by both French troops and unofficial gangs of French *pied noir* settlers that followed swiftly. A year later, at the end of September 1956, the FLN began planting bombs in public spaces in Algiers, the capital city—the first time that this tactic had ever been used—with the intention of spreading insecurity among the public. It has been suggested that they were also deliberately inviting reprisals in order to win moderates over to their cause. The French, in turn, resorted to torture and summary execution in order to stamp out the terrorists. This had the unintended effect of fueling a growing anti-war movement in France, and the French government now found itself caught between the conflicting wishes of its citizens at home and the more than one million French *pieds noirs* in Algeria.

A BRUTAL WAR
The soldiers of the FLN used inhuman means, such as decapitation and mutilation, in their pursuit of independence. The French responded with torture and summary execution.

On May 13, 1958, French military leaders in Algeria and French settlers, fearing that the socialist government in France was about to embark on the road to Algerian independence (Morocco and Tunisia had already gained their independence in 1955 and 1956 respectively), carried out a coup and an army junta seized power in Algeria. They demanded that Charles de Gaulle be installed as the French leader, in the belief that he would ensure the continued occupation of Algeria and

FRENCH PARATROOPERS
FROM ALGERIA TOOK
THE FRENCH ISLAND
OF CORSICA, AND ARMY
LEADERS DECLARED
THAT UNLESS POWER
WAS HANDED OVER TO
DE GAULLE THE ARMY
WOULD REVOLT AND
SEIZE PARIS.

its further integration with France. On May 24, French paratroopers from Algeria took the French island of Corsica, and army leaders declared that unless power was handed over to de Gaulle the army would revolt and seize Paris. They weren't kidding, and 15 hours before the deadline for implementing "Operation Resurrection" the government voted to hand power over to de Gaulle, which he accepted. This marked the end of the French Fourth Republic, and the move was seen as a breakthrough by Algerians and French on both sides of the Mediterranean. In June, de Gaulle visited Algeria, espousing "French Algeria" and proposing a range of reforms to improve the situation for native Algerians, as well as giving all the right to vote in a referendum on a new French constitution the following year. At the same time, the French military continued the war against the FLN and its military wing, the Armée de Libération Nationale (ALN). The FLN continued the terrorism in Algeria in an attempt to force the population to boycott the referendum, and the ALN brought the terrorist war to France.

The political climate in France, meanwhile, was moving toward support for a much greater degree of autonomy for Algeria, especially among the left-wing parties, and the mood internationally—including within the UN and NATO—was increasingly critical of France's continued colonial domination, especially given the brutal methods being used to enforce it. In 1959 de Gaulle raised for the first time the possibility of "self-determination" for Algeria. Horrified that a negotiated settlement and Algerian independence were now on the agenda, French reservists and *pieds noirs* staged an insurrection in Algiers early in 1960, but the army and police, under orders not to fire on the rioters, remained loyal to the government. The ringleaders were arrested but were later involved in forming the French terrorist Organisation de l'Armée Secrète (OAS).

The situation in Algeria was chaotic, with the OAS and FLN fighting each other and both using terrorist tactics against French government supporters in Algeria. There were also internecine feuds between radical groups within the independent Algeria movement and among the French-Algeria supporters. In France the battles were political, as new parties formed in support of French Algeria on one side and in opposition to the war and the manner in which it was being conducted on the other.

In January 1961, a referendum on independence for Algeria was held in which three quarters of the electorate in France and Algeria voted in favor. This gave de Gaulle the mandate he needed, and he entered into supposedly secret talks with the FLN, but senior figures in the French army were determined to prevent France from abandoning its Algerian *départements*. In April they organized a coup that became known as the Generals' Putsch, intending to take control of Algeria first and then Paris. On the night of April 21, with the support of 1,000 soldiers, they arrested key civil and military personnel in Algiers and took control of the country, but the French Premier had received intelligence reports on the mutiny and was able to arrest its leaders in Paris, as well as closing all airfields around Paris and ordering the army in France to resist the coup. President de Gaulle made a speech on radio calling upon all French people to come to the aid of their country, and commanding army conscripts not to accept orders from the rebel officers. By April 26 the putsch had been crushed.

© AFP | Getty Images

CEASEFIRE
As the French Minister for Algerian Affairs, Louis Joxe was a senior negotiator of the Évian Accords between France and the FLN, signed at Évian-les-Bains in 1962.

Talks between the French government and the FLN continued, and in the course of 1961 the details of French withdrawal from Algeria were worked out in the Évian Accords, with an agreed ceasefire to take effect on March 18, 1962, but the fighting was by no means over. The FLN embarked on a bombing campaign in France, and when some 20,000 pro-FLN Algerians held a march in Paris in October 1961 the French police, apparently under orders from Prefect of Police Maurice Papon, carried out a massacre of some 200 Algerians, throwing the bodies into the River Seine.

In the first half of 1962, the right-wing OAS and *pieds noirs* made a last attempt to prevent the implementation of the ceasefire and the creation of an independent Algeria in which the French Algerians would be an unsupported 10 percent minority. In March 1962, the month in which the ceasefire came into effect, the OAS exploded more than 3,000 bombs in a campaign of urban terrorism designed to provoke the FLN group into breaking their part of the bargain, but they were largely unsuccessful. The French army and police were also targeted, as was de Gaulle himself. On their way from central Paris to Orly airport on

August 22, he and his wife survived one of many assassination attempts when OAS gunmen opened fire on the presidential car, riddling it with 140 bullets and killing two motorcycle bodyguards.

EXODUS AND INDEPENDENCE

Following further referenda on Algerian independence in France and Algeria, where the vote in favor was almost unanimous, de Gaulle declared Algerian independence on July 3, and although the Évian Accords guaranteed protection for the *pieds noir*, they were already leaving the country in droves, taking heed of the Algerian nationalists' maxim *La valise ou le cercueil*—"the suitcase or the coffin." Their fears proved to be well founded, as the FLN began a concerted campaign of violence against the settlers, beginning with a massacre of Europeans in the town of Oran in which hundreds were killed. Within the year almost the entire French-Algerian population of over one million people had fled Algeria for France, the antagonism against them exacerbated by the continued terrorism of the OAS.

In the context of changes taking place around the world, the end of French colonial domination of Algeria had always been inevitable, but the presence of such huge numbers of settlers made the dynamics of the country, and of French withdrawal, different from those of almost any other territory. The intensity of the antagonism on both sides led to violence and terrorism on an unprecedented scale, and it has been estimated that casualties during the war and in its aftermath may have been as high as a million Muslims and 27,000 French. The aftershocks are still being felt in French society today.

THE USA AND THE BAY OF PIGS

April 1961

MOTIVATION

Anger

Charity

Envy

Faith

Gluttony

Greed

Hope

Lust

Pride

Sloth

Main Culprit: The US government

Damage Done: The failed invasion brought Cuba and the USSR closer and revealed US involvement

Why: The US was responding to the perceived threat of Communism

The evidence is clear and the hour is late. We and our Latin friends will have to face the fact that we cannot postpone any longer the real issue of survival of freedom in this hemisphere itself. On that issue, unlike perhaps some others, there can be no middle ground.

President John F. Kennedy, Statler Hilton Hotel, Washington, D.C., 1961

When John F. Kennedy became president of the USA in January of 1961 he inherited a plan, developed by the CIA and approved in its basic form by President Dwight Eisenhower, to bring about the overthrow of the recently installed Communist regime in Cuba and establish a government friendly to the US. Kennedy's decision to go ahead with the plan, despite contrary advice from senior government officials and mounting evidence that the plan was flawed, led to the "Bay of Pigs" invasion of Cuba on April 17, a disastrous fiasco that left the US with egg on its face and pitched Cuba into an even closer embrace with the Soviet Union.

In January 1959, the Cuban dictator Fulgencio Batista had been overthrown in an armed revolt led by Fidel Castro, who was now prime minister of the Communist-dominated Cuban government. In the US, the sweeping reforms taking place in Cuba, the curtailing of civil rights, the imprisonment and execution of many thousands of dissenters, and the closening relationship between Castro and Nikita Khrushchev, head of the Soviet Union, raised fears—disproportionate fears, some might say—about the growing influence of Communism in the region. The US was also experiencing a massive influx of exiles from Cuba. It was against this background, and fresh from a decade of the Red Scare and McCarthyism, that Eisenhower had approved the CIA's plan, as well as a budget for its implementation, and from March 1960 the CIA had been recruiting and training Cuban exiles who were to execute an invasion of their homeland.

JOHN F.KENNEDY
The new president went along with the plan to support an invasion of Cuba. It failed to achieve its objective and attracted international disapproval.

The plan relied upon the invasion force successfully establishing itself on the island and the Cuban people and some of the military supporting the invasion, creating a popular uprising that would overthrow Castro and his government. Crucially, "deniability" had to be maintained—there could be no evidence that the US was directly involved—and with a plan on such a large scale this was a tall order. Within the White House fears were expressed that there was insufficient anti-Castro sentiment within Cuba and that the role of the US could not be kept secret. The US would then be seen to be violating a host of international agreements as well as elements of its own constitution.

The training of some 1,400 Cuban exiles took place, nonetheless, throughout 1960 at several US military bases in Florida, Panama, and Guatemala, where the CIA had previously assisted in the overthrow of a democratically elected socialist government. When Kennedy moved into the Oval Office he gave his approval for the training of what had become known as Brigade 2506 to continue. Elaborate preparations were made to give the appearance that the affair involved only Cuban nationals, including the painting of six WWII B-26 attack bombers in the colors of the Cuban Air Force. A further 20 of these aircraft were prepared for the mission and the air fleet was assembled at a dedicated airfield constructed on the Pacific coast of Guatemala. Four freighters, chartered for use in transporting the brigade, were fitted with anti-aircraft guns, and landing craft were prepared.

The plan as it had originally been conceived was for the invasion force to go ashore at the port of Trinidad on the south coast of central Cuba. This would mean that they could, if necessary, find refuge in the nearby Escambray Mountains, where counter-revolutionary forces were already active. When this location was vetoed by the State Department, the CIA opted instead to stage the night landings in a swampy area some 60 miles (97 km) to the west, around the Bay of Pigs (Bahía de Cochinos). There was an airfield there and, being more remote, there was less likelihood that Cuban forces would be able to respond quickly to the invasion. However, the force would be a long way from any kind of refuge.

SELECTING A SITE

The date for the invasion was set for April 17, 1961. Although the exact date was kept under wraps, the planned operation was an open secret, with articles even appearing in the US press, including the *New York Times*. There is evidence that Castro knew of the planned invasion as early as October 1960, that Cuba and the Soviet Union had more detailed information in the days prior to the invasion, and that the CIA knew they knew but did not inform President Kennedy.

At dawn on April 15, eight CIA B-26 bombers in Cuban Air Force colors took off from Nicaragua and bombed three Cuban airfields to put as many planes out of action as possible. The Cuban exile pilots reported a major success, but reconnaissance the following day revealed that they had largely missed their targets. However, Kennedy ruled against a further bombing run for fear that US involvement would be too obvious. In a propaganda ruse, another of the disguised planes, bearing the same number as one of the planes used in the bombing, and with one of its engine cowlings deliberately riddled with bullet holes, was flown to Miami where its Cuban pilot was granted political asylum, giving the impression that he had defected and that the raids on the Cuban airfields had been carried out by disaffected Cuban Air Force personnel.

Havana

Bay of Pigs

Guantánamo Bay

BAHÍA DE COCHINOS
The CIA's choice of the Bay of Pigs for the landings proved to be unfortunate. The coast was reef-strewn and the bay was surrounded by swamps.

When, at the United Nations, Cuba accused the US of orchestrating the bombing, the US Ambassador to the UN, Adlai Stevenson, was able to show photographs of the "Cuban" bomber on the runway in Miami and deny that the US had had any involvement. It was soon pointed out, however, that the nose of the plane differed from the planes used by Cuba, suggesting that the US was behind the event. Stevenson had made his statement in good faith, but within a few hours it was obvious to all that he had been duped by the CIA and the White House, where Kennedy had referred to him as "my official liar."

The troops of Brigade 2506 had embarked onto the transport vessels in Nicaragua on April 14 and were now headed for Cuba, accompanied by seven US Naval destroyers. Leaving their escort some 65 miles (105 km) south of Cuba, the Cuban Expeditionary Force vessels reached the landing zone shortly before midnight on the night of April 16 and the landings began. A small military post was captured, but not before the militia there had radioed the armed forces and told them of the invasion. The landings took longer than expected, being hampered by the darkness and by the presence of coral reefs that damaged the boats as they went ashore, and the Cuban forces responded much more quickly than expected. At dawn, six Cuban planes attacked the landing vessels and one, the *Houston*, carrying men, supplies, and ammunition, was hit by rocket fire and forced to beach. The remaining troops on board went ashore without adequate equipment. An hour later, an airdrop of Brigade 2506 paratroopers and heavy equipment failed when the equipment fell irretrievably in the surrounding swamp and the troops were unable to secure the road. Castro mobilized an estimated 20,000 troops, and hundreds of Cuban militia reached the nearby town of Palpite by midday, forcing the invading troops to flee to the west. Over the next few days the fighting continued, with US planes carrying out raids on Cuban supply convoys, including one that included civilians. However, the Cuban Air Force dominated the skies, despite their losses in the airfield bombings. By the 19th it was clear that the invasion force was in serious trouble and the White House authorized an air cover operation, sending in six unmarked US fighter planes, crewed by pilots contracted by the CIA, to defend the brigade's B-26s, but the bombers arrived an hour after the fighter planes (probably due to a mistake about time zones) and two were shot down. The invasion force was overwhelmed the following day, with 100 killed, almost 1,200 taken prisoner, and a few dozen escaping to the coast to be picked up by waiting US ships. On the Cuban side, 176 soldiers were killed and several hundred were wounded.

The prisoners were held for more than 20 months, returning to the US in late December 1962 in exchange for more than $50 million dollars' worth of medicine and baby food supplied by US manufacturers at the request of the US government.

The failed coup not only caused the US government severe embarrassment—the US was seen to have lied repeatedly to the UN and to have broken several international treaties, as well as elements of its own constitution—but it also increased support for the new government in Cuba. Che Guevara is said to have sent a note to President Kennedy thanking him for the Bay of Pigs operation and saying, "Before the invasion, the revolution was weak. Now it's stronger than ever." Furthermore, the Bay of Pigs strengthened ties between Cuba and the Soviet Union and may have helped to bring about the Cuban Missile Crisis, bringing the world to the brink of nuclear war.

THE INVASION FORCE WAS OVERWHELMED THE FOLLOWING DAY, WITH 100 KILLED, ALMOST 1,200 TAKEN PRISONER.

MOTIVATION

Anger

Charity

Envy

Faith

Gluttony

Greed

Hope

Lust

Pride

Sloth

MAO ZEDONG'S GREAT PROLETARIAN CULTURAL REVOLUTION

1966–1976

Main Culprit: Mao Zedong, Chairman of the Communist Party of China

Damage Done: Subjected millions of people to torture and forced labor; many thousands were killed; the vast wealth of Chinese art and culture was destroyed

Why: To purge the country of people whose ideology differed from that of their great leader

It is up to us to organize the people. As for the reactionaries in China, it is up to us to organize the people to overthrow them. Everything reactionary is the same; if you do not hit it, it will not fall. This is also like sweeping the floor; as a rule, where the broom does not reach, the dust will not vanish of itself.

Mao Zedong, 1945

After organizing the Long March, the retreat of the Communist Red Army (later the People's Revolutionary Army) from the forces of the Kuomintang (Chinese Nationalist Party), Mao Zedong rose to become Chairman of the Chinese Communist Party in 1943. Under his leadership, the People's Republic of China was established in 1949 and dramatic land reforms were carried out in which land was taken from the landowners and distributed among the peasants. In order to involve the peasantry in the revolution, Mao encouraged them to kill the landowners and wealthy peasants who had been oppressing them, and it is estimated that at least a million people died as a result.

FORWARD MARCH

A second round of reforms, known (ironically, as it turned out) as the Great Leap Forward, took place in the late 1950s with the aim of establishing a modern Communist society and increasing the production of grain and steel. This involved promoting small-scale industrialization in the rural areas, banning private farming, and "collectivizing" the small farms into large, ultimately mechanized and hopefully efficient, communes. Large-scale state-funded industrial projects were also undertaken, and largely untested innovations in crop growing were encouraged. The results were disastrous.

Millions of peasants were moved into industrial work and into the urban areas, and state employment almost doubled between 1957 and 1960, to more than 50 million. This placed a huge burden on food resources but, combined with exceptionally poor weather conditions, the new agricultural system actually caused a decrease in the amount of grain being grown. This fact was largely disguised, as each level in the management hierarchy systematically exaggerated production figures, too frightened to admit the truth. This led to unsustainable demands for grain by the state and left too little to feed the rural population in many areas. Referred to officially as the Three Years of Natural Disasters, the Great Chinese Famine that resulted from the policy decisions of the Great Leap Forward caused the death by starvation of an estimated 30 million people between 1959 and 1961.

Undaunted by the failure of this experiment in social engineering, in 1966 Mao Zedong launched the Great Proletarian Cultural Revolution.

© Getty Images

MAO ZEDONG
Ostensibly intended to achieve high ideological goals, the Cultural Revolution provided Mao with the means to regain personal authority that had been shaken by the Great Leap Forward.

Fearing that China was being diverted from the path of true socialism by the re-emergence of a bourgeois elite and the insidious spread of capitalism (and possibly wishing to regain his personal prestige and authority), he mobilized the country's youth to root out counter-revolutionary elements within society and purify the party through violent class struggle. Students everywhere—some 20 million of them—left school and formed units of the Red Guard in towns and cities across China. They threw themselves into the task of challenging and exposing anyone whose background was anything other than wholly Communist or who appeared to be tainted with the old values of Chinese culture—artists, writers, intellectuals, and anyone with an academic qualification were among those targeted. Millions were forced into manual labor and many tens of thousands were killed. The Red Guard, who had acquired weapons from the military, had become judge and, quite literally, executioner, and Mao issued explicit instructions to the police not to interfere with their good work. Religion, too, was targeted, with temples and churches being taken over and even torn down. Works of art, books, and historical cultural artifacts were systematically looted and their owners incarcerated or sent for re-education. The political hierarchy from top to bottom was purged of anyone whose views, now or in the past, failed to accord with those of Mao, and any opposition to the Cultural Revolution itself was quickly crushed. Most of Mao's political rivals were deposed, but the Communist Party bureaucracy was so disrupted that it virtually ceased to function.

WARRING FACTIONS   In 1967, the Red Guard began to factionalize as groups vied with each other for ideological purity and tried to outdo each other in their zeal to rid the country of "class enemies." There were pitched battles between rival Red Guard units involving thousands of armed students, and in 1968 Mao sent in the People's Liberation Army to bring an end to the disorder. The army took control of schools, factories, and government buildings, introducing revolutionary committees to take over the task of local administration.

In an attempt to bring an end to the chaos and put the excesses of the Red Guard in the past, Mao instituted a program called Down to the Country, which involved the forced displacement of millions of students from the towns and cities to some of the most remote rural areas of

China, ostensibly to learn from the workers and farmers. The same year saw a concerted campaign to strengthen further the fervent personality cult of Chairman Mao, and every Chinese citizen was expected to carry a copy of the Little Red Book of his quotations.

In 1969 Mao declared an end to the Great Proletarian Cultural Revolution, but by now millions had been displaced, imprisoned, or executed, and the country had been riven by widespread betrayal, torture, rape, and mental and physical harassment. China's great cultural history had been largely destroyed, industrial output had fallen by more than 10 percent since 1966, and political instability was to plague the country until after the death of Mao in 1976, when more moderate leaders began to turn China toward a more market-oriented economy. The Cultural Revolution, which had been intended to revitalize China, is now referred to as the "decade of chaos."

PROPAGANDA
A Beijing poster in 1967 declares, "We have to be good soldiers of Mao Zedong, we have to listen to his words, we have to follow his instructions and read his books."

MOTIVATION

Anger

Charity

Envy

Faith

Gluttony

Greed

Hope

Lust

Pride

Sloth

CHARLES DE GAULLE FACES DOWN THE STUDENTS

May 1968

Main Culprit: Charles de Gaulle and his brand of authoritarian government

Damage Done: Caused a small student protest to escalate into violent mass demonstrations and a national strike that brought the French economy to a standstill

Why: A stubborn unwillingness to listen to those calling for a re-examination of the government's policies

In the afternoon, M. Mendès-France, the former President of the Council and, in his own right, probably the most universally respected political personality in the country, said that the Government must resign. By its comportment over the past 10 years, he said, the Government had created a revolutionary situation. It could no longer resort to force without releasing tragic consequences; nor could it begin a useful dialogue with the masses who were rising against its policy.... And he ended by paying tribute to the students and the young workers who had joined them to reawaken the nation.

Nesta Roberts, Paris, May 19, 1968, writing in *The Guardian*

Charles de Gaulle came to power in France in 1958, being inaugurated as the first president of the Fifth French Republic the following year, and brought welcome stability to a country that was tired of political infighting and indecision. He was re-elected in 1965, but his highly conservative and ultra-nationalistic style of politics was increasingly at odds with the changing times. This was an era of social change in Europe and the US, of anti-Vietnam demonstrations, flower power, freedom of expression, pop music, and the mini-skirt—which, incidentally, his equally conservative wife Yvonne tried to persuade him to ban in France.

Against this backdrop there was growing discontent, particularly among students, with repressive aspects of the state, which controlled radio and television, with Western capitalism, and with de Gaulle's authoritarian style of government, especially in the fields of employment and education.

The events that were to shake French society to its core began on March 22, 1968, when some 150 students occupied a building in the University of Paris Nanterre to protest against the French class system and government control of educational funding, and the university administration responded by calling in the police. The protest ended peacefully, but the conflict continued for several weeks until, on May 2, the administration closed the university and threatened to expel the ringleaders.

UNSWERVING
The political demands of the Paris students and the authoritarian leadership style of General Charles de Gaulle met head on in the spring of 1968.

The following day, students at the Sorbonne declared their solidarity with the Nanterre students and occupied a number of buildings. Police then invaded the university and it, too, was shut down. This heavy-handed response exemplified state control of the education system, and on May 6 some 20,000 students from the national students' union, supported by teachers, marched on the Sorbonne and confronted the police, who reacted with a baton charge. The situation turned violent as protesters—with some support from the local people—built barricades and hurled chunks of broken paving slabs at the police, who fired tear gas into the crowd and arrested hundreds of students.

The following day the university students and teachers were joined by high-school students and workers in a rally at the Arc de Triomphe that called for the release without charge of all the arrested students, for an end to the police occupation of the Sorbonne, and for the reopening of Nanterre and the Sorbonne, none of which was granted.

FROM BAD TO WORSE

In the course of the following week, the numbers of protesters and the level of violence escalated dramatically, and the Latin Quarter of Paris became a battlefield, with protesters hurling Molotov cocktails and hundreds of police and demonstrators being injured. On the night of May 10, when negotiations once again failed, confrontations that lasted all night were covered live on radio, and television the following day carried footage of the events. The protesters had now occupied the Latin Quarter and forced the police to leave.

The Communist Party of France and the main trade unions, unwillingly drawn into the fray, called a one-day strike general strike for Monday May 13, and more than a million people thronged the streets of Paris while demonstrations sprang up in towns across the country. At this point Prime Minister Georges Pompidou agreed to the release of those who had been arrested and to the reopening of the Sorbonne, but the protesters were now in no mood for compromise, calling for a greater say in the workplace, in government, and in education. By the end of the week the Communist Party and the unions, which were seen as too willing to negotiate with the government, had lost control of the workers and more than two million were staging wildcat strikes. In the course of the next week, that number increased to a staggering 10 million—two-thirds of the entire French workforce. When the trades unions negotiated a highly beneficial pay deal with the employers, the workers rejected it, as they did a subsequent offer from the Ministry of Social Affairs. They were seeking much more fundamental reforms of workers' rights.

By now the government was considering the use of force to put down what amounted to a rebellion and what might soon become a revolution, and the army was placed on standby. General de Gaulle's prime minister, Georges Pompidou, suggested that he dissolve the National Assembly and call for a general election, but he thought his party would lose and therefore refused. On May 29, acknowledging that the nationwide strikes and demonstrations were a challenge to his legitimacy as president, General de Gaulle packed his bags and took his family to the French military headquarters in Germany. Here he was reassured that the armed services would support him and he was persuaded to return to France the following day. By this time almost half a million people were marching through the streets of Paris celebrating his departure, but the rest of the country was more subdued. De Gaulle's sudden disappearance had unnerved the people of France and given them pause for thought.

De Gaulle now accepted Pompidou's suggestion of dissolving the National Assembly and announced that there would be a general election the following month. He also stated that he would declare a national state of emergency unless there was a return to work.

The crisis was over. As the election campaign got underway, the strikes and demonstrations subsided. To the surprise of many, de Gaulle's Union for the Defense of the Republic party won a landslide victory in the elections as the nation recoiled from the vision of chaos conjured up by the events of the previous month. The new government soon announced significant reforms to the education system, including the opening of more than 60 new universities and the introduction of a more democratic system of governing councils.

The election result was not, however, a vote for Charles de Gaulle. France post-May 1968 was a different country, more willing to countenance its own social changes and embrace those taking place beyond its borders, and the traditionalist, authoritarian de Gaulle was of the old school. In 1969 he lost a national referendum on political reform on which he had staked his reputation, and he resigned as president.

GENERAL STRIKE
Protests that began in the universities of Paris soon spread to workers throughout the country and to a general strike and march in Paris that attracted more than a million people.

© Time & Life Pictures | Getty Images

MOTIVATION

Anger

Charity

Envy

Faith

Gluttony

Greed

Hope

Lust

Pride

Sloth

IDI AMIN EXPELS THE ASIAN POPULATION FROM UGANDA

1972

Main Culprit: Idi Amin, 3rd president of the Republic of Uganda

Damage Done: Amin supervised the killing and torture of tens of thousands of his compatriots, the deportation of the entire Asian community, and the destruction of the Ugandan economy

Why: Ignorance, paranoia, megalomania, and merciless bloodthirsty malice

His Excellency, President for Life, Field Marshal Al Hadji Doctor Idi Amin Dada, VC, DSO, MC, Lord of All the Beasts of the Earth and Fishes of the Seas and Conqueror of the British Empire in Africa in General and Uganda in Particular.

Title bestowed upon himself by Idi Amin. He had never received the DSO or MC, but gave himself a "Victorious Cross" and a Doctorate in Law. He also claimed to be King of Scotland.

The name of Idi Amin, the dictator of the East African country of Uganda from 1971 to 1979, is synonymous with corruption and inhuman brutality. During his years of rule at least 100,000, and quite possibly more than a quarter of a million, Ugandans were executed for their personal or political opposition, for being members of the wrong tribe, or simply as a result of their leader's paranoia. Thousands more were tortured or incarcerated. Uganda's economy went into a dramatic decline and suffered rampant inflation, fueled by Amin's capricious decision to expel Uganda's highly successful Asian population—all 50,000 of them—who were the mainstay of the country's trade and industry and also occupied key positions in the civil service. His action not only crippled the country but also caused untold hardship for the refugees.

Born in northern Uganda in about 1925, Idi Amin began his military career with the British Army, as a cook in the King's African Rifles. He rose through the ranks, fought for the British in Kenya during the Mau Mau revolt, held the title of Ugandan heavyweight boxing champion throughout the 1950s, and in 1961 he became a commissioned officer (only the second black Ugandan to do so) despite being almost completely uneducated and illiterate. In 1962 he led a force to northern Uganda to stop the theft of cattle by tribesmen from the Turkana region of Kenya. It later came to light that his troops had tortured, murdered, and even buried alive the cattle rustlers, but with Uganda about to be given its independence, and Amin being one of the country's few black officers, no action was taken against the overzealous leader of the "Turkana Massacre."

POWER MAD
With an overweening sense of self importance and a vicious sadistic streak, Idi Amin plunged his country into a decade of bloodshed, oppression, and economic chaos.

The new prime minister of Uganda, Milton Obote, clearly thought that Idi Amin displayed admirable qualities, for he made him Commander of the Ugandan Army and Air Force two years later, promoting him to Major General in 1968. However, relations between the two deteriorated and Amin was demoted in 1970. On hearing that Obote planned to arrest him on charges of embezzling of military funds, he made a preemptive strike and launched a successful military coup.

TAKING POWER

Promising elections and equality for all Ugandans, regardless of ethnic or tribal background, his self-proclaimed presidency was welcomed by the majority, but he soon showed his true colors. Obote supporters within the security services were rounded up, tortured, and executed. The army was purged of members of the Acholi and Lango ethnic groups, possibly as many as 6,000 of them, and their horribly mutilated bodies were dumped in forests and waterways. Anyone who spoke out against the atrocities became an immediate target, and that included the Anglican archbishop, Janani Luwum (whose body was found in a poorly simulated car crash), and Ben Kiwanuka, chief justice and leader of the Democratic Party.

ETHNIC CLEANSING Asians, almost all of them from India and Pakistan, had long constituted the largest non-indigenous ethnic group in Uganda, having been brought to Africa by the British Empire, and had faced considerable hostility under Obote's rule because of their economic success. Asians were involved in banking, clothing, farming, ranching, import/export, and some thriving industries, which gave rise to a great deal of envy, and Obote had capitalized on this to demonize the Asian community. To Amin they were a convenient scapegoat and a potential source of wealth, and in 1972 he announced that God had spoken to him and instructed him to expel all Asians from the country. Amin accused them of sabotaging the country's economy—which was far from the truth—and of sending all their money out of the country, which was partly true. The Asian population had been made to feel so insecure in Uganda that many had indeed chosen to send some of their hard-earned wealth overseas. On August 4 they were told they had to leave the country within 90 days, taking with them only what they could carry, or face the consequences. No compensation was offered for the businesses and homes they were being forced to abandon, and even as they were leaving on buses to get to the airport, valuables were taken from them. Many left with absolutely nothing and were forced to start from scratch in their new lives, about half of them in Britain (as they had UK passports), many in Canada and India, and the rest scattered around the globe.

© Getty Images

EXPELLED
Forced to leave their homes, businesses, and possessions in Uganda, many Asians, such as this family arriving in London, had to start again from nothing.

The majority of the businesses and land, houses, cars, and personal possessions that they left behind were divvied up between Amin and his supporters, especially members of the army whom he needed to keep on his side. It has been estimated that more than 5,000 business enterprises, including ranches and agricultural estates, were distributed in this way. At a stroke, Amin had virtually eliminated the Ugandan middle class, and their once-productive enterprises were now in the hands of individuals and organizations that had neither the expertise nor the experience to run them properly. Production, distribution, and imports were completely disrupted. Exacerbated by Amin's decision the following year to nationalize British-owned businesses (again, without any compensation, causing Britain to cut all ties with the country), the economic situation deteriorated rapidly. The civil service degenerated into chaos, annual inflation reached 1,000 percent, and even Uganda's principle export, coffee, went into decline because no money was reaching the growers.

THE CIVIL SERVICE DEGENERATED INTO CHAOS AND ANNUAL INFLATION REACHED 1,000 PERCENT.

In October 1978, diverting attention from the country's economic hardships, Amin invaded Tanzania, with help from Libyan forces, with the aim of annexing a portion of that country. Under the leadership of President Julius Nyerere, Tanzania responded with a force that included several thousand Ugandan exiles, and they successfully repelled Amin's troops, who were more focused on looting the towns and villages through which they passed than they were on fighting. The Tanzanian army advanced into Uganda, being joined by the Ugandan National Liberation Army, and in April 1979 the capital Kampala was taken. Amin fled to Libya, where he stayed for ten years, and then to Saudi Arabia, where he died in 2003.

As for the dispossessed Asian refugees, some have returned to their natal land since Amin's downfall, but most have remained in their new-found homes and flourished. In the UK, for example, Asian families from East Africa constitute the majority of small corner store owners, and a disproportionate number run their own multi-million-dollar businesses. For many countries, Uganda's loss has proved to be their gain.

MOTIVATION

Anger

Charity

Envy

Faith

Gluttony

Greed

Hope

Lust

Pride

Sloth

PRESIDENT NIXON AND THE WATERGATE AFFAIR

July 1972–August 1974

Main Culprit: Republican US President Richard Nixon

Damage Done: Was forced to resign to avoid impeachment; shook America's trust in its political system (but not before time)

Why: Condoned the use of illegal methods to try to scupper the Democrats in the forthcoming election, and participated in the cover-up

In any organization, the man at the top must bear the responsibility. That responsibility, therefore, belongs here, in this office. I accept it. And I pledge to you tonight, from this office, that I will do everything in my power to ensure that the guilty are brought to justice and that such abuses are purged from our political processes in the years to come, long after I have left this office.

Nixon's first Watergate Speech, April 30, 1973

It is amazing how often people in positions of power take risky decisions that they know could end in their downfall—and get caught. President Richard Nixon's use of wholly unethical undercover operations to spike the Democrats' election campaign and his collusion in a cover-up ultimately led to the greatest, and most public, fall from political grace in the history of America.

The "–gate" suffix that has been applied to the titles of so many scandals—from Irangate to Weinergate—has its origins in the Watergate Hotel and office building in Washington, D.C., where the Democratic Party had its headquarters in 1972. In the early hours of the morning of July 17, a security guard in the sixth-floor offices noticed that latches on several doors had been taped so that they would close without locking, and he called the police. Five men were caught photographing and stealing documents, and placing wiretaps on phone lines. They were arrested, indicted on a range of charges in September, and convicted the following January, but their discovery was the start of a trail that was ultimately to lead to the president.

The break-in was part of an election campaign plan to bug, spy on, and generally sabotage the Democratic Party, put together by the Republicans' "Committee for the Re-election of the President" (CRP), which included former Attorney General John Mitchell and Presidential Counsel John Dean. The break-in operation had been coordinated by G. Gordon Liddy, a former FBI agent, aided by E. Howard Hunt, a former CIA agent. They were both also involved in a secret security operation known as the White House Plumbers, the purpose of which was to prevent leaks of sensitive information from the president's administration to the media, and they had been using unorthodox methods to achieve their goals. The FBI quickly discovered Hunt's name in the address books of two of the burglars, so to prevent the truth coming out, President Nixon ordered his chief-of-staff to get the CIA to block the FBI's investigation on the grounds of national security.

FLEETING POPULARITY
According to the journalist Hunter S. Thompson, President Nixon was "a man with no soul, no inner convictions, with the integrity of a hyena and the style of a poison toad."

Two reporters with *The Washington Post*—Carl Bernstein and Bob Woodward—had already smelled a rat. With the help of an informant in the FBI (revealed more than 30 years later to be Mark Felt, the FBI's associate director), whom they referred to only as "Deep Throat," they soon began uncovering connections between the break-in and the Nixon administration. These included the fact that one of the burglars was a Republican Party security aide (strenuously denied by John Mitchell), that a check in the account of another burglar had originally been given to Nixon's campaign fund, and that when he was Attorney General, Mitchell had managed a fund that paid for secret information-gathering operations against the Democrats. By October, the FBI had established the connection between Watergate and a large-scale undercover operation in support of Nixon's re-election, but that didn't prevent him being re-elected the following month in a landslide victory.

By the spring of 1973, the word on everyone's lips was "cover-up," and at the highest levels. One of the burglars informed the judge who had tried him that he had committed perjury in the trial, and that he and the others had been under pressure to do so. Another of the burglars told US attorneys that John Dean and John Mitchell had been involved. Nixon's aides, meanwhile, were telling the Attorney General that no one in the White House had had any prior knowledge of the break-in.

In April, US attorneys informed the president that his two most important aides—John Ehrlichman and H. R. Haldeman—were involved in the cover-up, and Nixon then asked them for their resignations, going on TV to tell the nation what a difficult decision it had been. He also announced the departure of John Dean, whom he had fired.

THE SENATE WATERGATE COMMITTEE

In the meantime, the Senate had approved the convening of a special committee to investigate the Watergate affair, and it sat for the first time on May 17, 1973. The hearings were aired live on TV, shared between three networks. In June, a White House assistant revealed that President Nixon had had an automatic recording system installed in the Oval Office and other key areas, and that all conversations had been taped. The "Nixon tapes" were immediately subpoenaed, but the president refused to hand them over and ordered the special prosecutor to drop the subpoena—which he refused to do. Nixon then used strong-arm tactics to have the special prosecutor dismissed, a highly unpopular move that increased the public's negative perception of the president. Suspicions were heightened when Nixon's lawyers disclosed that there was an eighteen and a half minute gap in the tapes, and his secretary's explanation that she had accidentally erased this section was widely disbelieved.

By March of the following year, seven of Nixon's aides had been indicted for obstructing the Watergate investigation, and the noose was drawing tighter. Nixon narrowly missed being indicted with them, but he still maintained that he had known nothing about the break-in or the cover-up. In July 1974 the Supreme Court ordered Nixon to hand over the tapes to the special prosecutor, which he finally did at the end of the month, and even if the contents did not reveal an indictable offence, their tenor demonstrated the president's contempt for democratic government. It was clear, too, that he had approved of payments being made to defendants in the Watergate investigations, after the event if not before. In July the House Judiciary Committee began the procedure to impeach the president on the grounds of obstruction of justice, abuse of power, and contempt of Congress.

A tape made shortly after the break-in was released by the White House on August 5, and it was the clincher. It soon became known as the "smoking gun," because it contained conversations with the president in which Haldeman discussed the Watergate burglaries and outlined the cover-up plan, and Nixon gave his approval. There was now no doubt that he had been lying throughout the whole affair, and it was clear that the impeachment of the president would have more than enough support to succeed. On August 8, seated in the Oval Office, he announced his resignation to the American people.

Soon after taking over as president, former Vice-President Gerald R. Ford kindly pardoned Nixon of all charges in connection with the Watergate affair.

SUBPOENAED
In April 1974, during his address to the nation, President Nixon announced that he was finally handing over the transcripts of taped White House conversations.

MOTIVATION

Anger

Charity

Envy

Faith

Gluttony

Greed

Hope

Lust

Pride

Sloth

ARGENTINA INVADES THE FALKLAND ISLANDS

April 2, 1982

Main Culprits: General Leopoldo Galtieri and the military junta

Damage Done: Hundreds killed and injured

Why: To divert the attention of the Argentine people from social and economic problems at home and strengthen the position of the military government

They have retreated, our troops have reached the outskirts of Port Stanley. A large number of Argentinian soldiers have lain down their arms. White flags are flying over Port Stanley. Our troops have been issued the command to shoot only in self-defence. Discussions among the commanders on the capitulation of the Argentinian troops in the Falklands have begun.

British Prime Minister Margaret Thatcher, June 14, 1982

A satellite image reveals two large and ragged barren islands fringed by a few smaller barren islands, one of which is named Barren Island. From the ground the picture is only slightly different—these are soggy barren islands. So what could possibly have prompted the Argentine government to contest Britain's sovereignty of the remote and windswept Falkland Islands in the South Atlantic? There were actually several reasons, but one thing is certain: it was a bad decision.

After their discovery in the 16th century, these islands were claimed by the Spanish, the French, and the British, all of whom built settlements here in the course of the 18th century. In 1767, the French (who had named the islands Les Iles Malouines, in honor of the first French settlers, many of whom came from St. Malo in Brittany) conceded to the Spanish, who persuaded the British to leave in 1774. When Argentina gained its independence from Spain in 1816 it claimed the Islas Malvinas as their own but in 1833, after an altercation with America over fishing and hunting rights that resulted in US warships shelling the Argentine colony of Puerto Soledad, two British naval vessels successfully enforced a request that the Argentines leave. Maintaining that its claims to sovereignty had never been renounced, Britain claimed the Falkland Islands and in 1844 established a colony there, the immigrants coming largely from Scotland and Wales. Sheep farming became the staple of the economy, a harbor was built at Stanley, and the islands proved to have strategic importance during both the World Wars.

THE SEEDS OF WAR

© Chris Pearson | Creative Commons

PORT STANLEY
Despite their inhospitable appearance, the Falkland Islands became an important piece in the political games of both Britain and Argentina.

Throughout this time, the issue of the Malvinas continued to rankle in Argentina, and when the United Nations was formed in 1945, Argentina took its grievance to the UN, basing its claim to the islands on its geographical proximity and its inherited sovereignty from the Spanish, but with little success. Nonetheless, the issue became a popular and important one to the Argentine people. Britain, meanwhile, was able to point to more than 100 years of continuous and peaceful habitation by some 2,000 loyal and strongly pro-British Falkland Islanders in support of its own right to sovereignty.

In the early 1980s, when the Argentine ruling military junta was facing growing dissent from a populace suffering economic hardships and severely curtailed civil rights, General Leopoldo Galtieri saw the Malvinas as a means to divert attention from the shortcomings of the government and rally the people behind him. Assuming, perhaps not unreasonably, that Britain was unlikely to launch a military response to events on an insignificant group of rocks some 8,000 miles (13,000 km) from home, in the spring of 1982 Galtieri decided to invade the Falklands and impose Argentine sovereignty.

THE PRETEXT FOR INVASION

In March 1982, a group of some 40 workers employed by an Argentine scrap metal merchant arrived on South Georgia, a British territory 800 miles (1,300 km) from the Falklands. This was done with the knowledge of the British authorities, but when the Argentines planted their national flag the British responded by dispatching HMS *Endurance* from Stanley with half the garrison's forces—22 Royal Marines and one Lieutenant—with the intention of arresting and deporting the men. Argentina, however, sent a warship and landed 100 troops to "defend" its nationals, and the British forces had little choice but to move back and observe.

On April 2, using the incident as a pretext, Argentine amphibious craft landed 4,000 troops on East Falkland Island and the town of Stanley was occupied. On hearing this news, the marines on South Georgia surrendered to the Argentines. At this point Galtieri must have hoped that the matter was a *fait accompli*, but he had failed to take into account both the character of the British prime minister and her own need for popularity in the light of a forthcoming general election. There was also considerable baying from the right-wing press in the UK, expressing the fear that Britain was about to lose the last vestige of its imperial past.

Diplomatic efforts were launched immediately, and Britain moved deftly to gain support from NATO, the EEC, and the UN, which passed Security Council Resolution 502 on April 3, calling for an end to hostilities. At the same time, under the leadership of Margaret Thatcher, the decision was taken to launch "Operation Corporate," a potential military response, and a British naval taskforce, consisting of 20 warships (some of which were already at Gibraltar), eight

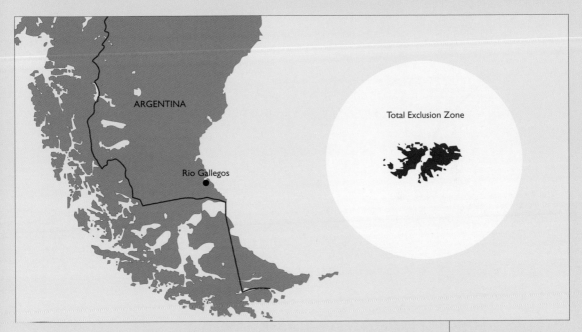

ARGENTINA

Rio Gallegos

Total Exclusion Zone

amphibious ships, and a supply fleet of 40 vessels from the Royal Fleet Auxiliary and the Merchant Navy, was soon on its way. The task force comprised some 15,000 personnel, including a landing force of 7,000 marines and soldiers.

On April 12 Britain declared a 200-mile (320-km) Total Exclusion Zone around the Falklands Islands, to hamper the movement of troops and supplies from Argentina, and this was enforced by three nuclear-powered attack submarines that had already reached the area. The US had, in the meantime, put forward peace proposals but these were rejected by Argentina, and by the end of April the US was giving both diplomatic and military support to Britain.

On April 25 British marines, under cover of naval gunfire, retook South Georgia from the occupying Argentine garrison, and by the end of April several British aircraft carriers (with Sea Harriers and Sea King helicopters on board), as well as several frigates, had reached the Falklands. With no diplomatic solution in sight and the South Atlantic winter approaching, British military operations began on May 1 with bombing raids on the runway at Stanley to prevent Argentine planes from using it.

EXCLUSION ZONE
The British declaration of a no-go area around the Falklands succeeded in preventing the Argentine Navy from operating in the area.

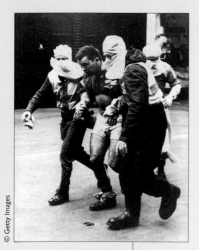

© Getty Images

SURVIVORS
When HMS *Sheffield* was struck by a sea-skimming Exocet missile on May 4, 1982, the resulting fires caused serious injuries to many of the crew. The ship sank six days later.

The following day, the British nuclear submarine *Conqueror* fired three torpedoes at the Argentine Navy cruiser *General Belgrano*, sinking the ship with the loss of more than 300 lives. The event proved to be a contentious one, with critics pointing out that the ship was outside the Exclusion Zone and was possibly headed toward the South American coast rather than toward the islands. The British navy maintained that neither the ship's position nor its bearing was relevant, only the potential threat that it posed, and senior figures in the Argentine military agreed that the sinking was legal in the context of the hostilities. In any case, the Argentine navy retired to coastal waters for the rest of the conflict and efforts were focused on airborne attacks launched from mainland bases.

Two days later, on May 4, HMS *Sheffield* was struck just above the waterline by a missile fired from an Argentine Super Etendard strike fighter, causing a major fire, killing 20 crew members and seriously injuring 24 others. The ship sank several days later. The Argentine Air Force continued to inflict considerable damage on the British vessels that now surrounded the islands, but also suffered significant losses. On May 21 British commandoes landed on the island by helicopter and amphibious craft, and in the course of the following three weeks the troops advanced across the difficult terrain, taking successive Argentine positions while aircraft from both sides engaged overhead and British ships and Harriers shelled and bombed strategic targets. The British suffered a major setback on May 25 when an Exocet missile sank the vessel carrying most of the task force's troop-carrying Chinook helicopters, killing 12 seamen and forcing soldiers to make a 60-mile (100-km) march across East Falkland Island, and on June 4 Argentine bombs struck two British landing craft, killing 50 soldiers and injuring many more. Nonetheless, by early morning on June 14 the Argentines had lost all the high ground and the commandoes were on the outskirts of Stanley, where some 8,000 Argentine troops were effectively trapped on the peninsula. The British advance was halted and at 9.30 that evening, after several hours of negotiations, the Argentine forces formally surrendered.

The outcome had been by no means a foregone conclusion. The logistical difficulties of conducting a British military operation so far from home were considerable, but the Argentine Air Force, who were widely praised for their bravery and professionalism, also had problems operating at the limit of their fuel range and lost more than half of their combat aircraft in the conflict. On the ground, the British troops—experienced career soldiers who had trained under conditions similar to those found on the islands—had an undeniable advantage. The Argentine troops were young and poorly trained conscripts led by an elitist officer class that did all it could to avoid the hardships of the battlefield. In the absence of adequate leadership, the Argentine soldiers were all too ready to fall back when British troops advanced on them. These, then, are some of the factors that made invading the Falklands a bad idea. Even if the territory could have been held by the Argentines, the level of casualties was unacceptably high, with Argentine losses put at 635 killed and 1,068 wounded, and British losses of 255 killed (including three Falkland Islanders) and 777 wounded.

For the Argentine military junta, the invasion was also a bad decision because the defeat ultimately led to its downfall. For the Argentine people, the silver lining was a gradual return to democratic rule, and in 1983 Margaret Thatcher reaped the reward of a second term in office.

MOTIVATION

Anger

Charity

Envy

Faith

Gluttony

Greed

Hope

Lust

Pride

Sloth

IRAQ INVADES KUWAIT

August 2, 1990

Main Culprit: President Saddam Hussein

Damage Done: Cost the lives of thousands of Kuwaiti civilians and Iraqi military, and devastated the oil fields of both countries

Why: Saddam Hussein mistakenly thought he could annex Kuwait without incurring a military response

Fight them with your faith in God. Fight them in defense of every free honorable woman and every innocent child, and in defense of the values of manhood and the military honor. Fight them because with their defeat you will be at the last entrance of the conquest of all conquests. The war will end with dignity, glory, and triumph for your people, army, and nation.

Saddam Hussein in a radio broadcast to the Iraqi people, January 19, 1991

When the Iran–Iraq War ended in August of 1988—a fruitless and costly war initiated in 1980 by Iraq under the leadership of President Saddam Hussein—Iraq found itself in a very serious economic situation. The war had brought economic growth within the country to a standstill, and oil production in the Basra oil fields—into which Iran had fired several million shells—had been seriously disrupted. The cost of the war had been astronomic and Iraq had borrowed heavily. It now had an international debt of more than $130 billion, $14 billion of which it owed to its neighbor Kuwait, whose financial support for Iraq had exposed it to Iranian reprisals and had led to Kuwaiti oil tankers being repeatedly attacked in the Persian Gulf. Now that the war was over, however, tensions between the two countries were mounting, for several reasons.

Unable to pay back the loans, Iraq requested Kuwait (among others) to waive its debt, which Kuwait refused to do. Kuwait also refused Iraq's request to reduce its oil production. Because Kuwait processes much of its own oil, the price per barrel was of less concern to it, whereas Iraq was desperate to get as high a price as possible for the limited amount of oil that it was producing. Kuwait's output, in excess of quotas set by OPEC, was having the effect of keeping oil prices down and was costing Iraq billions of dollars a year. While continuing high-level diplomatic talks and lobbying a divided OPEC for a solution to the problem, Iraq steadily built up the numbers of its troops along the border with Kuwait. When Iraq accused Kuwait, whose border with Iraq cut through the southern edge of the Rumaila oil field, of using slant drilling techniques to extract oil from beneath Iraqi territory, this was seen by outside observers as part of an Iraqi plan to further its territorial ambitions and gain control of the oil supplies.

SADDAM HUSSEIN
The oppressive ruler of Iraq invaded Kuwait as a means of gaining oil-rich territory for his country and avoiding the repayment of financial debts owed to Kuwait.

On July 25, 1990, OPEC announced that Kuwait had agreed to limit its oil production, but by this time Iraq had some 100,000 of its troops positioned along the border. That same day, in the presidential palace in Baghdad at a meeting requested by Saddam Hussein, the US Ambassador to Iraq, April Glaspie, asked the president for an explanation for the military build-up. Saddam replied that unless Iraq's dispute with Kuwait could be settled through negotiations then he would be willing to give up his goal of controlling the whole of the Shatt al-Arab waterway "to defend our claims on Kuwait to keep the whole of Iraq in the shape we wish it to be. What is the United States' opinion on this?"

According to one version of the transcript of this conversation, US Ambassador Glaspie replied, "We have no opinion on your Arab–Arab conflicts, such as your dispute with Kuwait. Secretary [of State James] Baker has directed me to emphasize the instruction, first given to Iraq in the 1960s, that the Kuwait issue is not associated with America." Opinions are divided over whether or not these words tacitly gave Iraq the "green light" to invade Kuwait. (When tackled by two British journalists a month later, Ambassador Glaspie said that neither she nor anyone else had imagined that Iraq intended to annex the whole of Kuwait, possibly implying that the US did think Iraq might attempt to push its border south to encompass the Rumaila oil field.) In any case, Saddam apparently smiled at this response. At a meeting between Iraq and Kuwait, held in Jeddah, Saudi Arabia, a few days later, the negotiations quickly degenerated into accusations and counter-accusations, and shortly after midnight the following day, August 2, Iraq invaded Kuwait. As events transpired, if Saddam thought that the US and the international community would respond with only verbal condemnation, he had badly misjudged the situation.

INVASION AND RESPONSE Despite worsening diplomatic relations over the preceding months and the large numbers of troops massed on the border, the invasion took the Kuwaiti military by surprise. As Iraqi armored divisions and mechanized infantry troops headed for Kuwait City, helicopter gunships and transport helicopters carrying commandoes began an assault on the city, as well as taking airbases and airports. Iraqi planes quickly gained supremacy in the air, and one fifth of the Kuwait Air Force's planes were lost before the remainder flew to bases across the border in Saudi Arabia. The deposed Emir of Kuwait and the royal family, along with senior government officials and many of the retreating military, also sought refuge there. Within 48 hours Iraq had control of the entire country, and Saddam soon installed a "Provisional Government of Free Kuwait," annexing the country as Iraq's 19th province.

Condemnation of the invasion by the international community—including countries formerly friendly toward Iraq—was instant and almost unanimous. The UN Security Council passed Resolution 660, calling for the unconditional withdrawal of all troops from Kuwait, even before the bullets had stopped flying, and at the same time the Arab League called for a solution to the crisis from within its own ranks and without the intervention of non-Arab nations. Arms embargoes and economic sanctions followed, and the UN authorized a naval blockade to achieve these. On August 7, in response to a request by King Fahd, the US sent troops to Saudi Arabia, a country with justifiable fears about Iraqi aggression—it shares a long border with Iraq, its oil fields were within easy reach of the Iraqi forces, and, like Kuwait,

MILITARY RESPONSE
With UN approval, a coalition of nations sent in troops to free Kuwait from Iraqi occupation. Operation Desert Storm lasted less than six weeks.

it was owed many billions of dollars by Iraq after the Iran–Iraq War. This was the start of Operation Desert Shield, ultimately leading to the stationing of more than half a million US troops in Saudi Arabia.

On August 12, Saddam Hussein sought a compromise solution, linking Iraq's withdrawal from Kuwait to the withdrawal—among others—of Israel from the occupied Palestinian territories, and calling for all US troops in Saudi Arabia to be replaced by Arab forces. The US, anxious that Iraq should in no way be rewarded for its actions, was opposed to any such linkage and remained adamant that the Iraqi withdrawal be unconditional. Various other compromise proposals by Saddam met with a similar response over the next few months, and on November 29 the UN passed Resolution 678, giving Iraq a deadline of January 15, 1991, after which force would be used to remove Iraqi troops from Kuwait.

By the time that date was reached, 34 countries had joined the US in a coalition, prompted not only by outrage at Iraq's initial act of aggression but also by the perceived threat to Saudi Arabia and other Middle East countries, by reports of human rights violations within Kuwait (some of which later turned out to be false), and by Iraq's use of chemical and biological weapons. Some of the participants were undoubtedly swayed by financial incentives or by threats to withdraw aid.

Operation Desert Storm began on January 16, 1991, with an air campaign that lasted 38 days and targeted the Iraqi air force, anti-aircraft defenses, missile launchers, and the Iraqi navy. The attacks — conducted in both Kuwait and Iraq — utterly disrupted Iraq's military infrastructure, as well as destroying morale. The ground campaign was launched on February 23, and within 100 hours Kuwait City

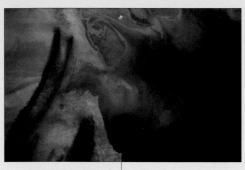

SEEN FROM SPACE
To force Kuwait to reduce oil production, Saddam ordered his retreating troops to set fire to the Kuwaiti oil wells and surround them with land mines. The fires burned out of control for months.

was in the hands of coalition and Kuwaiti forces as the Republican Guard retreated northward, setting fire to hundreds of Kuwaiti oil wells, and thousands of Iraqi troops surrendered. Coalition forces followed the retreating army into Iraq before declaring a ceasefire on February 28, opting not to continue on to Baghdad or attempt to overthrow Saddam, which would have been beyond the UN mandate and would have split the coalition. In April, Iraq agreed to UN terms for a permanent ceasefire, which included the destruction of all stockpiled weapons.

The occupation of Kuwait had lasted seven months, Iraq had suffered at least 20,000 military casualties and huge financial costs, thousands of Kuwaiti civilians had lost their lives, the oil fields of both countries had been devastated, and Saddam Hussein had made himself public enemy number one. He would not be forgiven.

MARGARET THATCHER INTRODUCES THE POLL TAX

1989–1990

MOTIVATION

Anger

Charity

Envy

Faith

Gluttony

Greed

Hope

Lust

Pride

Sloth

Main Culprit: Margaret Thatcher

Damage Done: Lost her the leadership of the Conservative Party

Why: Caused the people of Britain to rebel against an unfair government policy and made her party extremely unpopular

When Mrs. Thatcher says she has a nostalgia for Victorian values, I don't think she realizes that 90 percent of her nostalgia would be satisfied in the Soviet Union.

Peter Ustinov

When King Richard II of England introduced a head, or "poll," tax in 1377 it was, to say the least, unpopular. When he trebled the tax 14 years later and insisted that some poor people pay the same amount as the wealthy, it provided the spark that ignited the smoldering discontent that the peasants felt for the landowners and the governing classes. The outcome was the Peasants' Revolt. In June 1381, armed peasants from the counties of Kent and Essex converged on London, where they stormed the Tower of London and captured the Lord Chancellor, Simon Sudbury, and the Lord High Treasurer, Robert Hales. The two men, seen as the prime movers in the poll tax, were later beheaded at Tower Hill. Margaret Thatcher, British prime minister from 1979 to 1990, might not have championed the "Community Charge" had she studied history at Oxford instead of chemistry.

© Margaret Thatcher Foundation | Creative Commons

THE IRON LADY
Although she was renowned, and in some quarters admired, for her strength of will, Margaret Thatcher's refusal to give way on the Community Charge was politically inept.

Prior to the general election of 1987, local government services in the UK were funded by a property tax called rates, an annual sum payable by every house owner on the basis of an assessed rental value for the property. It may not have been perfect, but it had been in place for almost 400 years and it worked. To Margaret Thatcher, however, the tax was not in line with Conservative thinking—it meant that the wealthy paid more, the poorest paid nothing, and the middle class, who could be seen as the core of her popular support, were paying for the local government services being provided to those at the bottom of the social scale. It had to be changed. Indeed, it had been in her sights since 1974, five years before she became PM, and had been part of the Conservative Party manifesto since then.

In 1986, a government Green Paper proposed that the rates should be replaced by a community charge, a flat-rate tax levied on every adult regardless of their income—in other words, a poll tax. Margaret Thatcher was fully in support of this and the proposed change became part of the Conservative manifesto prior to the 1987 general election. It clearly did appeal to a majority of voters, as the Conservatives won the election and came to power for a third four-year term.

The Community Charge was introduced in Scotland in 1989, and in England and Wales in 1990, and it didn't take those same voters long to realize that the poll tax, even with reductions for students, the elderly, and the very poor, was outrageously unfair, as the opposition Labour Party quickly pointed out. While the wealthy in large and expensive homes would find themselves paying less, large families in small homes would pay more—sometimes far more, as it turned out.

Even before the tax was officially introduced, opposition to it was being voiced in Scotland and then throughout the UK, and anti-poll tax unions were formed to make those voices heard. In November 1989 the All Britain Anti-Poll Tax Federation was set up to coordinate the protest, and in the spring of 1990 a march was organized for Saturday March 31, a few days before the introduction of the Community Charge in England and Wales. The march, from Kennington on the South Bank of the Thames in London, was to end with a rally in Trafalgar Square. Trafalgar Square can hold about 60,000 people. Police estimates put the size of the crowd that marched at around 200,000. The result was chaos, as demonstrators crowded into the square and the length of Whitehall, which runs past Downing Street and the prime minister's residence. As police and mounted riot police attempted to control the crowd, violence broke out, and throughout the evening and the course of the night London saw its worst rioting in more than 100 years. More than 100 people (including police) were injured, some of them seriously, and there were several hundred arrests. As chance would have it, while the riots were in progress, the prime minister was attending a Conservative Party conference at which the Community Charge was the central topic. The evident unpopularity of the tax raised the first ripples of doubt about Margaret Thatcher's leadership.

In the following months, across the country, anti-poll tax unions urged people not to pay the Community Charge, a call that many hitherto law-abiding citizens heeded—up to 30 percent of them in some districts. Councils, police, and the courts were wholly unprepared and unable to deal with such a tidal wave of "criminals."

This was just one of the unforeseen hiccups in implementing the tax. Whereas the rates had been levied on homeowners, the poll tax applied to all adults, and tracking down the mobile—sometimes very mobile—portion of society that lived in rented accommodation proved to be a mammoth task and greatly increased the cost of collecting the tax.

THE BATTLE OF TRAFALGAR

Although, throughout her occupancy of 10 Downing Street, she attracted more than her fair share of criticism, even hatred, no one has ever doubted that Margaret Thatcher was a woman of principle. Far from caving in to pressure from the public, and even from her colleagues, to drop the tax, she made keeping it a matter of personal pride, nailing the Community Charge firmly to her own masthead as well as that of the Conservative Party and ignoring the question of whether, at a certain point, principle should perhaps give way to common sense or democracy.

As non-payment of the tax increased and polls showed that a vast majority of the British people (98 percent in one poll) were opposed to the Community Charge, the Conservatives' popularity plummeted in the opinion polls and Margaret Thatcher began to look more like a liability than an asset. In November of 1990, Michael Heseltine challenged her in a leadership election and received 40 percent of the vote, denying her a sufficient margin for an outright win. Rather than risk probable defeat in a second ballot, Margaret Thatcher resigned as Prime Minister and party leader.

The subsequent leadership election was won by John Major. Michael Heseltine was appointed as Environment Secretary and given responsibility for replacing the Community Charge. The following March, the introduction of the council tax—a tax based on the market value of a householder's property—was announced, and it came into force in 1993. It is not unlike the rates system.

© Newsfocus | Dreamstime.com

TRAFALGAR
In March 1990, a protest rally in central London turned nasty as police tried to control unexpectedly large numbers of people. Rioting continued through the night, vehicles were burned, and stores were looted.

THE INTERNATIONAL COMMUNITY FAILS TO PREVENT GENOCIDE IN RWANDA

1994

MOTIVATION

Anger

Charity

Envy

Faith

Gluttony

Greed

Hope

Lust

Pride

Sloth

Main Culprit: The countries of the United Nations Security Council

Damage Done: The brutal rape and slaughter of three-quarters of the Rwandan Tutsi population

Why: A failure to recognize the dreadful nature of what was happening, and a lack of political will to intervene

Jamie Owen: "In Rwanda, General Roméo Dallaire, head of the UN peacekeeping force, ended up attempting to stop the genocide with just two hundred men. He was ordered by the UN to leave on three occasions. He refused each time. Eyewitnesses report him driving into town at night and personally rescuing people."

General Roméo Dallaire: "Twelve years ago in a small African country a group of citizens met and decided the only way they could maintain power was to simply eliminate 1.2 million people by mutilation killing. A hundred days into the genocide they had slaughtered 800,000 and over 3 million had been displaced and refugeed of which not only the Tutsis but the moderate Hutus who supported them also suffered. And no one came."

Excerpts from speeches given at the national commemoration of Holocaust Memorial Day in Cardiff, Wales, on January 26, 2006

"The only thing necessary for the triumph of evil is for good men to do nothing." It's an oft-repeated phrase, but never was its truth more graphically demonstrated than in Rwanda in 1994. Despite abundant evidence that the majority Hutu people were carrying out an organized wholesale massacre of their Tutsi compatriots, the countries of the UN Security Council refused to take the necessary steps to prevent it, and the carnage that followed left a stain on the reputation and credibility of the United Nations.

When the territory of Rwanda fell under German colonial control at the end of the 1800s, the two largest ethnic groups in the country, the Hutus and the Tutsis, occupied different levels in the social hierarchy. In general the Hutus, who were by far the majority, were farmers. The Tutsis were cattle herders and of higher status, but there was some fluidity in the definitions and a Hutu that became a cattle owner effectively became a Tutsi. The Germans, and later the Belgians, nonetheless based their own system of rule on this distinction and gave greater political power to the Tutsis, whom they felt to be more "European-like" as they were lighter skinned and taller than the Hutus. The Belgians insisted that everyone must have an identity card stating whether they were Hutu or Tutsi, and this was done on the basis of how many cattle a person owned. In addition, Tutsis were generally more willing to convert to Catholicism, and were therefore given greater opportunities for education. The overall effect was to crystallize the ethnic division in the society.

COLONIAL DIVISIONS
Rwanda's tribal problems date back to at least the early period of colonization. Count Gustav Adolf Von Götzen, one of the first Germans to set foot on Rwandan soil, was governor of German East Africa in the early 1900s.

Throughout the 1950s, Hutu resentment against the ruling Tutsi minority grew, and, following assaults on Hutu political leaders in 1959, tens of thousands of Tutsis were killed by Hutus. Some 150,000 Tutsis were exiled to the neighboring countries of Burundi, Tanzania, and Uganda, and a policy of deliberate discrimination against the Tutsis in Rwanda was implemented. Democratic elections were held in 1960 in which the majority Hutu population elected a Hutu president and the Tutsi monarchy was ended. Over the next 30 years, through a series of major political upheavals, Tutsis were increasingly excluded from professional employment and positions of influence, until Rwanda became a one-party, Hutu-dominated society.

A similar Hutu/Tutsi conflict was raging in neighboring Burundi, which had a Hutu majority but a Tutsi-dominated military, and in 1972 the Burundi army killed an estimated 200,000 Hutus. Many Hutus fled to Rwanda. Meanwhile, Tutsi refugees from Rwanda, many of whom had fought with the Ugandan rebels, formed themselves into the Rwandan Patriotic Front. In 1990 the RPF began a series of incursions into Rwanda seeking democratic reforms and the reintegration of the nearly half a million Tutsis that had been excluded from their homeland. This was seen as an attempt by the Tutsis to retake power, and it led to three years of war during which both sides committed numerous human rights violations, but eventually a peace agreement—the Arusha Accords—was signed in August 1993. The agreement called for the establishment of a transitional government in Rwanda, for the reunification of the army, and for a UN peacekeeping force to oversee the process.

Many Hutus, however, were opposed to the agreement, and as ethnic tensions rose, the Hutu-led government deliberately fueled the rising animosity, using print media and state radio stations to spread anti-Tutsi propaganda and incite racial hatred, referring to the Tutsis as "cockroaches," claiming that they intended to enslave the Hutus, and blaming them for the country's economic woes.

Aware that the situation was likely to become violent, in October 1993 the UN Security Council established the United Nations Assistance Mission for Rwanda (UNAMIR) under the leadership of Canadian General Roméo Dallaire. It took contributing nations five months to supply the 2,500 troops needed. In December 1993, General Dallaire was warned that the powerful Hutu elite had formulated a plan to hold on to power by eliminating the Tutsis. The Rwandan Armed Forces and 1,700 militia in organized civilian "killing groups" had been armed with rifles and grenades, and more than half a million machetes had been imported. Dallaire was told where the arms were cached, but was told by the UN that he did not have a mandate to interfere in the internal affairs of the country unless an act of genocide was being perpetrated. The anti-Tutsi media statements, as well as propaganda inciting the rape of Tutsi women, increased in scale in the next few months.

HEADING FOR CIVIL WAR

On April 6, 1994, an event took place that lit the fuse. As a plane carrying the Rwandan president and the president of Burundi, both Hutus, prepared to land at the airport in Kigali, the capital of Rwanda, it was hit by two missiles and crashed, killing them both. According to the Arusha Accords, the task of leadership now fell to the prime minister, Agathe Uwilingiyimana, but her authority was disputed by

RWANDAN PRESIDENT

The assassination of pro-Hutu Juvénal Habyarimana (seen here on a visit to the US), sparked the violence that escalated into genocide.

the army and especially by Colonel Bagosora, who was the prime mover behind setting up and arming the "killing groups" and who may have engineered the missile attack on the president's plane. General Dallaire sent 10 Belgian peacekeepers to guard Uwilingiyimana's home and to escort her the following morning to the state radio station so that she could make a public announcement to ease the growing tension, but during the night of April 7, members of the army and the presidential guard disarmed the Belgians and then shot Uwilingiyimana and her husband. The Belgian soldiers were murdered later that day.

Then the killing began in earnest, an organized country-wide effort to eliminate as many Tutsis as possible from Rwanda. As mass violence broke out on an unprecedented scale, the UN directed Dallaire and UNAMIR to help in the evacuation of foreign nationals. When a peacekeeping force was removed from a school in which 2,000 Tutsis, including many children, were seeking refuge, the Hutus waiting outside rushed in and murdered every one of the refugees. Shortly afterward, the UN ordered the withdrawal of all but 270 of the peacekeepers, despite Dallaire's reports on what was happening and his requests for an additional 5,500 peacekeepers to prevent the slaughter. The US actually called for all UNAMIR troops to be withdrawn and refused to use its technology to block the radio stations broadcasting racial hatred.

In the course of the next 100 days, an estimated 800,000 people — mainly Tutsis, but also moderate Hutus who tried to help them or refused to participate in the killing — were shot or literally hacked to pieces by the army, the killing groups, and by Hutu civilians forced at gunpoint to murder their neighbors. Tutsi women and girls, as many as 500,000 of them, were brutally and systematically raped.

General Roméo Dallaire and his utterly inadequate force of peacekeepers did their best to create safe areas in which they could protect would-be victims of what was now quite clearly an act of genocide, and succeeded in saving tens of thousands of Tutsis, but Dallaire's reports and pleas for additional support went largely unheeded by the UN. The constituent countries were unwilling to become embroiled in what they preferred to see as the internal affairs of the country, and refused to accept that what was happening was indeed genocide, as such an acknowledgment would have required them to respond with money and manpower. Finally, after five weeks of indescribable violence, the UN did vote to send in the requested 5,500 extra peacekeepers but by the time they had been mobilized it was too late.

Fanny Schertzer | Creative Commons

LEST WE FORGET
The Nyamata Genocide Memorial, on the site of the Nyamata Parish Catholic Church near Kigali, houses the remains of more than 45,000 victims. Ten thousand of them died in the church itself.

In parallel with the genocidal war against the Tutsis, another war was taking place throughout the country, a civil war between the Rwandan Armed Forces and the Rwandan Patriotic Front. By mid-July the RPF had succeeded in taking control of the country and only then did the genocide abate, to be replaced by a mass exodus of some 2,000,000 Hutus into Zaire and other neighboring countries, creating overcrowded and disease-ridden refugee camps.

The UN commissioned its own inquiry into its response to the events of 1994, and its results were made public in December 1999. The report concluded that responsibility for the failure to halt the 1994 genocide in Rwanda lay with the UN system, members of the UN Security Council—the US and UK in particular—and other UN member states, and that the UN mission had not been planned, deployed, or instructed in a way that would have enabled it to stop the genocide. UNAMIR, it said, was the victim of a lack of political will in the Security Council and by other member states. In the report's words, "This international responsibility is one which warrants a clear apology by the organization and by the member states concerned to the Rwandese people."

MOTIVATION

Anger

Charity

Envy

Faith

Gluttony

Greed

Hope

Lust

Pride

Sloth

CLINTON DENIES SEXUAL RELATIONS WITH MONICA LEWINSKY

January 1998

Main Culprit: President Clinton

Damage Done: Focused the attention of the world on his bedroom behavior, cost the American taxpayer millions of dollars, and led to his impeachment

Why: Having failed to keep his pants zipped up, he thought he could cover it up and get away with perjury

But I want to say one thing to the American people. I want you to listen to me. I'm going to say this again. I did not have sexual relations with that woman—Miss Lewinsky. I never told anybody to lie, not a single time; never. These allegations are false....

President Clinton, January 26, 1998

President Clinton's problems began when a newspaper article, published in January 1994 and based on the accounts of two Arkansas State Troopers, claimed that they had arranged sexual encounters for Governor Clinton in 1991. The article referred to a woman called Paula, and in May 1994, as the "Troopergate" scandal grew, Paula Jones came forward and sued Clinton for sexual harassment. In late 1997, a judge ruled that, in putting her case together, she was entitled to information about any other state or federal employees with whom Bill Clinton had had, or had tried to have, sexual relations in the same period, in order to establish whether Clinton had a pattern of such behavior. It was in this context that the name of Monica Lewinsky came up.

In December 1997 Miss Lewinsky was subpoenaed by lawyers for Paula Jones, and on January 7, 1998, she filed an affidavit denying that she had had sexual relations with Bill Clinton. On January 17, having been given the court's very detailed definition of what constituted sexual relations—"a person engages in sexual relations when the person knowingly engages in or causes contact with the genitalia, anus, groin, breast, inner thigh, or buttocks of any person with an intent to arouse or gratify the sexual desire of any person"—President Clinton stated most emphatically under oath that he had not had sexual relations with Monica Lewinsky. In the light of what transpired afterward, these denials were a bad decision on both their parts.

I DID NOT . . .
Bill Clinton's attempt to deny his relationship with Miss Lewinsky led to months of very public investigations and embarrassment.

Miss Jones's case was later dismissed, but she appealed, and in November 1998 President Clinton, without admitting anything or offering an apology, settled out of court and paid her $850,000, the full amount she was claiming, on condition that she drop her appeal. And that, you would think, was that. Not quite.

Back in November 1995, when 22-year-old Monica Lewinsky was working as an intern at the White House, she had begun a physical affair with President Clinton that lasted, on and off, until March 1997 — or at least that is what she confided to her friend Linda Tripp, with whom she worked in the White House public affairs office. Tripp, of course, did what any good friend would. She discussed the matter with

Lucianne Goldberg, a literary agent and a vocal critic of Bill Clinton, who advised her to start secretly recording her telephone conversations with Monica. In the fall of 1997 that's precisely what she did, recording Lewinsky's account of the sexual liaison and her allegation that Clinton had asked her to lie about the affair under oath. Linda Tripp also told Monica to keep any gifts that Bill had given her, and to hang on to a blue dress that, despite having had some biological stains on it for many months, hadn't yet made it to the dry-cleaner.

When Linda Tripp learned in January 1998 that Monica had denied having had any sexual relations with Clinton, she felt it her duty to bring the tapes—20 hours of them, now deposited with Miss Tripp's lawyer—to the attention of Kenneth Starr, the Independent Counsel investigating the Whitewater property investments in which the Clintons had been involved. A meeting between Lewinsky and Tripp was then arranged at which Miss Tripp was wired by FBI agents to record the conversation. Three days later Starr was given permission, through the Attorney General, to investigate the possibility that Monica had been induced to commit perjury and obstruct justice in the Jones case. That same day Tripp asked Lewinsky to meet her again, and this time FBI agents and US attorneys turned up to question her and discuss the possibility of immunity from prosecution, presumably in return for her cooperation.

THREE DAYS LATER STARR WAS GIVEN PERMISSION, THROUGH THE ATTORNEY GENERAL, TO INVESTIGATE THE POSSIBILITY THAT MONICA HAD BEEN INDUCED TO COMMIT PERJURY.

The following day was January 17, the day on which President Clinton gave his deposition in the Jones lawsuit expressly denying that he had had sexual relations with Monica Lewinsky.

A report of the alleged sexual relationship between Monica Lewinsky and President Bill Clinton immediately appeared on the Drudge Report website, followed a few days later by a story in *The Washington Post*, and on January 26 Bill Clinton held a press conference, with Hillary at his side, in which he gave a forthright denial of any sexual relations with Monica and of the allegations that he had asked her to lie under oath. The following day, Hillary Clinton appeared on TV and suggested that the whole scandal could be blamed on an ongoing "vast right-wing conspiracy." What followed was one of the most literal examples of airing dirty laundry in public.

In late July 1998, having been given immunity from any prosecution in connection with any crimes related to her testimony, Monica Lewinsky gave details of her sexual relations with Clinton to a grand jury and handed over a semen-stained blue dress. DNA tests showed conclusively that her interactions with the president had been of a sexual nature, and Ken Starr concluded that Clinton's statement under oath had been false. Clinton was subpoenaed. In testimony before a grand jury, on August 17, he admitted to having had "an improper relationship" with Miss Lewinsky, and in a statement on national television he acknowledged that their relationship was "not appropriate" and "wrong."

When it came to charges of having committed perjury, however, Clinton had a cast-iron defense. Given the court's very precise definition of sexual relations, he believed that, although Monica had had sexual relations with him when she gave him oral sex, he—not having engaged in, or caused, contact with any of her naughty parts—had not had sexual relations with her. It was an easy mistake to make, but not everyone swallowed it. In Congress some Democrats and most Republicans felt that his testimony and alleged attempts to influence Lewinsky constituted perjury and obstruction of justice. He was impeached on these charges by the House of Representatives on December 19, 1998, but although the Republicans controlled the Senate they were unable to rally the necessary two-thirds majority to convict him. He was acquitted on all charges and he remained in office.

Surprisingly, he also retained the approval of the American public, although many had grown tired of having Clinton's peccadillo rammed down their throats for months on end. The Lewinsky affair not only dominated Bill Clinton's last year in office, but it also cost the taxpayer a small fortune. Independent Counsel Ken Starr's office had spent $6.2 million on its six-month investigation into the case against President Clinton. It was a high price to pay for his failure to 'fess up to what would probably have been seen as a relatively minor indiscretion.

COMING CLEAN

ON THE RECORD
The *Congressional Record* of February 12, 1999, carries an account of the "Trial of William Jefferson Clinton, President of the United States." The prisoner walked free.

MOTIVATION

Anger

Charity

Envy

Faith

Gluttony

Greed

Hope

Lust

Pride

Sloth

MASSACRE AT SREBRENICA

July 1995

Main Culprits: Bosnian Serb soldiers, paramilitary, and police

Damage Done: Mass murder of thousands of Bosnian Muslim men and boys, forced deportation of women and children, and widespread rape

Why: The horrific and unjustifiable crimes perpetrated by the Serbian troops made no sense on military grounds, and can only be interpreted as acts of ethnic hatred

... during several days of carnage after the fall of Srebrenica, more than 8,000 Muslim men and boys, who had sought safety in this area under the protection of the United Nations Protection Force (UNPROFOR), were summarily executed by Bosnian Serb forces commanded by General Mladi and by paramilitary units, including Serbian irregular police units which had entered Bosnian territory from Serbia.

... nearly 25,000 women, children and elderly people were forcibly deported, making this event the biggest war crime to take place in Europe since the end of the Second World War.

Excerpts from the European Parliament Resolution of January 15, 2009, on Srebrenica

In 1991, the Republic of Bosnia and Herzegovina was part of the Socialist Federal Republic of Yugoslavia, which had been formed at the end of World War II, and its population was composed principally of 43 percent Muslim Bosnians (later known as Bosniaks), 31 percent Orthodox Christian Serbs, and 17 percent Croats, who are mainly Catholic. These three groups were represented by three parties in the democratically elected coalition government. In the fall of 1991, the parliament passed a resolution as a first step toward declaring its independence from Yugoslavia, despite opposition from all the Serbian delegates, who then formed their own "Assembly of the Serb People in Bosnia and Herzegovina." The following January the Serb assembly proclaimed the Republic of the Serb People of Bosnia and Herzegovina, creating four separate autonomous administrative districts in areas of Bosnia Herzegovina where Serbs were in the majority. In these Serbian oblasts, an overwhelming majority voted to remain within the Yugoslavian Federation, but in a referendum held by the Bosnian parliament, the rest of the country voted equally vehemently for independence, which was declared in March 1992. The Serbs then proclaimed their separation from Bosnia and Herzegovina and the creation of the Serb Republic (Republika Srpska), a separate state within the territory of Bosnia and Herzegovina.

The army of the former Socialist Federal Republic of Yugoslavia, together with all its weaponry and vehicles, became the Army of the Serb Republic or Vojska Republike Srpske (VRS). The 80,000-strong VRS force soon began a war against the (principally Bosniak) Army of the Republic of Bosnia and Herzegovina (ARBiH) for territorial control, and not just for those areas proclaimed as the Serb Republic. Lasting for three years, it was a vicious war in which terrible war crimes were committed, mainly by the VRS, against the civilian population. The massacre at Srebrenica was the worst of these, made all the more noteworthy by the international community's culpable failure to prevent it.

As the Bosnian-Serb forces took control of ever larger areas of Bosnia Herzegovina, they attempted to "ethnically cleanse" those areas by removing or killing the Bosnian Muslims. In the extreme east of the country, close to the border with Serbia, the predominantly Muslim

THE BREAK-UP OF YUGOSLAVIA

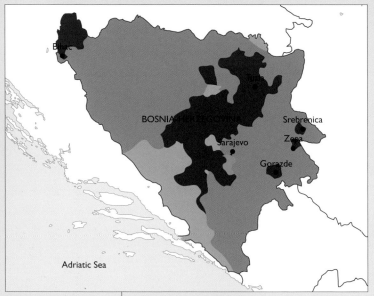

- ▮ VRS-controlled area
- ▮ HVO-controlled area
- ▮ ARBiH-controlled area
- ▮ UN-patrolled area

AREAS OF CONTROL
With a few areas under Croatian control (HVO), the majority of the country was held by the Bosnian Serbs (VRS). Although the central portion was controlled by the Army of the Republic of Bosnia and Herzegovina (ARBiH), the Muslim Bosnians in the east of the country found themselves surrounded in small enclaves.

town of Srebrenica and the surrounding region, comprising some 300 small villages, found itself isolated in VRS-held territory and under attack from Serb forces. For a period of 12 months from the spring of 1992 the town and villages were systematically shelled and bombed. As villages were destroyed, many of their inhabitants made their way to Srebrenica, and by the spring of 1993 the town was surrounded, hugely overcrowded and effectively under siege, without adequate electricity, medical supplies, food, or water. The commander of the United Nations Protection Force (UNPROFOR) visited the town and declared that the UN would protect it, and several thousands residents were evacuated to the main government-held region of central Bosnia, although the government was ambivalent about the evacuations because they could be seen as helping the Serbs to achieve the ethnic cleansing they desired.

The Serbian troops then issued an ultimatum saying that they would attack the town unless all the Bosniaks surrendered and agreed to be evacuated. The Bosniaks refused. Within days, an area of less than 1 square mile incorporating Srebrenica was declared a "safe area which should be free from any armed attack or any other hostile act" by the UN Security Council, and 600 Dutch UNPROFOR soldiers were brought in to protect the people there. It was also declared a demilitarized zone, which made little difference to the poorly equipped soldiers of the Bosnian Muslim troops of the 28th Division within the town, and no difference at all to the 1,500 or so Serbian troops surrounding the town, who refused to remove their heavy armaments. The situation remained at a stalemate for the next year, but the Serbian troops kept up their pressure on the town and allowed access to fewer and fewer relief convoys. Conditions for the trapped Bosniaks and UN peacekeepers steadily deteriorated, and in June 1995 people started dying of starvation.

In March 1995, the president of the Serb Republic, Radovan Karadžic, had issued a directive to the VRS to "create an unbearable situation of total insecurity with no hope of further survival or life for the inhabitants of Srebrenica." In early July, the Serb troops under the leadership of General Ratko Mladic began advancing into the "safe zone" from the south. The remaining 400 men of the UN Protection Force did little to prevent them. Their commanding officer urgently requested help from NATO, which ran air strikes against VRS gun positions and the advancing tanks until the Serbs threatened to kill the UN hostages that they were holding and to shell the UN compound at Potocari, a village outside the town.

In the meantime, the Bosniaks in Srebrenica fled to Potocari, a few miles away, and by the evening of July 11 there were more than 20,000 refugees in the compound and in the surrounding fields and outbuildings. The Bosnian-Serb troops followed, and in the following days they carried out tens (some reports say hundreds) of killings, taking away young men—and even children—and then shooting them or slitting their throats. Women and young girls were tortured and raped; mothers were forced to watch their children being killed. The details of what happened to countless individuals are horrific. The Dutch UNPROFOR soldiers could only look on, helpless.

As the evacuation got underway, women, children, and the elderly were herded onto buses to take them to the Bosniak-controlled central region of the country, but some of those buses went in other directions, and their passengers were almost certainly massacred. The men and boys were held separately, and by night the Serb army carried out mass executions behind industrial buildings in the village, the bodies being bulldozed into communal graves dug with heavy equipment. Members of UNPROFOR who tried to investigate were prevented by Serb soldiers. Thousands of men, captured within Potocari or on the roads leading away from Srebrenica, were marched or bussed to collection points to the northwest, outside the so-called safety zone.

THE FALL OF SREBRENICA

© Getty Images

RATKO MLADIC
Accused of committing war crimes, the Bosnian Serb leader was arrested in northern Serbia in May 2011 and was extradited to The Hague. His trial before the International Criminal Tribunal for the former Yugoslavia began on June 3, 2011.

Some were killed individually or in small groups, but the vast majority were gathered in warehouses and a football field and, beginning on July 13, they were taken to isolated fields in the area and systematically slaughtered, lined up and shot in well-organized mass executions. (In one instance, more than a thousand men in a farm warehouse were killed when Serb soldiers threw in hand grenades and opened up with gunfire.) Heavy earth-moving equipment was used to bury the thousands of bodies in gigantic mass graves, and in some cases the corpses were thrown into rivers.

THE MARCH TO SARAJEVO

On the night of July 11, while most of the Bosniaks were retreating to Potocari, the poorly armed soldiers of the Bosniak 28th Division, together with several thousand civilian men and a few women, took to the woods and started the 35-mile (60-km) march northwest toward Tuzla, in Bosniak government-held territory. They saw this as their only chance of survival. When the VRS realized what had happened, orders were issued to prevent the refugees from reaching safety. Some were captured soon after setting off, and they were taken to be held, and later executed, with the other male prisoners from Potocari. Others made it into the countryside, but over the next three days the column of some 12,000 people was bombed, shelled, and ambushed as they made their way, without food or water at the height of the summer, through mountainous terrain. At one point more than 200 were captured and then mown down by machine-gun fire.

As they approached Tuzla, the remains of the column broke through the VRS troops that were blocking the way, with help from the Bosniak 2nd Division that attacked the Serb army from the Bosnian side. After negotiations, a corridor was opened for them to make their way through to Tuzla, but it is estimated that more than 8,000 people died on the march. Certainly less than half of those who had left Srebrenica completed the journey. Emaciated and delirious with hunger, many of them barefoot and wounded, the survivors were seething with anger at the UN for its failure to protect them and at their own army for refusing to send reinforcements to help the 28th Division.

The war was finally brought to a close after a UN bombing campaign to crush the Army of the Serb Republic in the first three weeks of

September 1995. The Dayton Peace Agreement was signed by all parties in November 1995. That same month, Radovan Karadžic and Ratko Mladic were indicted for their roles in the atrocities. It was established that more than 8,000 Bosnian Muslims who had sought, and been guaranteed, refuge in the "safe area" of Srebrenica were massacred.

© Adam Jones | Creative Commons

Karadžic was arrested in 2008 and charged with genocide, war crimes, and crimes against humanity. In 2012 he was still being held by the International Criminal Tribunal for the former Yugoslavia (ICTY), which has ruled that the Srebrenica massacre was indeed an act of genocide. Ratko Mladic was arrested in Serbia in 2011 and is expected to be extradited to the ICTY to face charges. Since the end of the Bosnian War, there has been an international effort to locate the mass graves in the area, and to disinter and identify the thousands of bodies they contain using DNA analysis. So far more than 6,500 have been identified and given proper burials. To this day there are Serbs who deny that the massacre ever happened, and former soldiers of the Army of the Serb Republic who express pride in what they achieved.

IN MEMORIAM
On July 11 every year in Potocari, Bosnia and Herzegovina, a memorial ceremony is held at the monument for victims of the July 1995 Srebrenica Massacre.

MOTIVATION

Anger

Charity

Envy

Faith

Gluttony

Greed

Hope

Lust

Pride

Sloth

REPEALING THE GLASS–STEAGALL ACT

November 1999

Main Culprits: The financial industry and the US government

Damage Done: Shattered the US economy and forced millions of Americans to lose their homes and their jobs

Why: Created a culture of corporate greed, personal profit, and public risk

Although the Act grants financial services firms greater latitude to innovate, it also contains important safety and soundness protections. While the Act allows common ownership of banking, securities, and insurance firms, it still requires those activities to be conducted separately within an organization, subject to functional regulation and funding limitations.

President Bill Clinton, from his statement on signing the Gramm–Leach–Bliley Act, November 12, 1999

In November 1999, the Glass–Steagall Act, which placed limitations on the banking industry in the US, was repealed. In its place, the Gramm–Leach–Bliley Act ushered in a new era of less stringent regulation, mergers, and new possibilities for huge profits. The repeal of Glass–Steagall was a major contributing factor in the sub-prime mortgage debacle and the subsequent credit crisis that sent shock waves around the world.

After the Wall Street Crash of 1929 and the Great Depression that followed it, part of the blame was laid at the doors of the commercial banks for having been deeply involved in stock market investments. This not only placed their depositors' savings at risk but also led the banks to make unsound loans to companies in which they had invested and then encourage clients to buy those stocks. To prevent a repeat performance, the Glass–Steagall Act (GSA) was passed in 1933 to separate banking from investment activities, the combination of which was seen as creating a conflict of interests. Banks were required to choose between the two. Banks were also prevented from underwriting insurance, which was felt to pose too great a risk. (In 1956, the Bank Holding Company Act extended these rules to bank holding companies.) The GSA also led to the creation of bank deposit insurance, protecting depositors from a bank's inability to pay out.

WEAKENING RESTRICTIONS

From the 1960s on, the banks were lobbying to have the restrictions of the GSA loosened so they could broaden the range of their financial activities, and in 1986 the Federal Reserve "reinterpreted" the GSA to allow banks to derive 5 per cent of their gross revenue from investment banking, and later to deal in municipal bonds and mortgage-backed securities. Further weakening of the GSA followed, especially under the pro-deregulation Federal Reserve Chairman Alan Greenspan, who allowed banks to deal in a wider range of securities and in 1996 permitted bank holding companies to own investment banks. These changes were not unrelated to the level of lobbying by the major banks, who invested millions of dollars to persuade the government of the need to give them greater freedom.

Throughout the 1990s, the erosion of the regulations led to the steady consolidation of the banks into a smaller number of much larger institutions, and in 1998 the chairmen of Travelers Insurance

Group (Sandy Weill) and Citicorp (John Reed) announced plans to merge. The merger was technically in violation of the GSA and would require the newly formed Citigroup, Inc. to cease its involvement in the insurance business within two years, but—having spoken to Alan Greenspan, Treasury Secretary Robert Rubin, and President Clinton— Sandy Weill was confident that the GSA would be repealed before that became necessary. He was quite right. (Incidentally, Robin Rubin left the Treasury in 1999 and joined the board of Citigroup.)

In November 1999, after spending 20 years and $300 million lobbying for the repeal of the GSA, the financial companies got their payback plus interest. It was accomplished with the passing of the Gramm–Leach– Bliley Act, otherwise known as the Financial Services Modernization Act, which, in the words of Bill Clinton:

> . . . makes the most important legislative changes to the structure of the US financial system since the 1930s. Financial services firms will be authorized to conduct a wide range of financial activities, allowing them freedom to innovate in the new economy. The Act repeals provisions of the GSA that, since the Great Depression, have restricted affiliations between banks and securities firms. It also amends the Bank Holding Company Act to remove restrictions on affiliations between banks and insurance companies. It grants banks significant new authority to conduct most newly authorized activities through financial subsidiaries.

The legislation cleared the way for the creation of huge banking conglomerates that combined a large array of financial services and transactions, while at the same time reducing external regulation and supervision.

THE SUB-PRIME BOOM

The newly liberated mega-banks now had the go-ahead to deal in a whole range of different financial "instruments" and to create innovative new ones, and one of the new areas into which they moved was home mortgages. New kinds of mortgage were developed, such as adjustable rate mortgages (that homeowners would expect to refinance out of before the rate rose), interest-only mortgages, and even negative-amortization mortgages whereby the homeowner paid less than the necessary amount each month and the debt kept increasing. Wall Street began to bundle these mortgages together and sell them as mortgage-backed securities. The government-sponsored Federal

National Mortgage Association (Fannie Mae) and Federal Home Loan Mortgage Corp (Freddie Mac) had been selling these to pension funds, insurance companies, and foreign governments for years, but now Wall Street was able to get a piece of the action. The revenue was used to provide further mortgages to bundle and sell etc. As the lucrative cycle continued, both the private banks and Fannie and Freddie gave mortgages to borrowers with lower and lower credit ratings, creating a boom in sub-prime (read "high-risk") mortgage lending. Interest rates were low, house prices were rising at record rates, and even a mortgage for more than a property's value wasn't that big a risk for the lender, as the property would be worth that in a few months' time anyway. The greater a homeowner's equity, the less likelihood there is that they will default, and equity was increasing all the time. Moreover, the fact that in the mortgage-backed securities the sub-prime mortgages were bundled up with other, higher-quality mortgages meant that it was difficult to assess the actual risk. Homeowners kept borrowing (increasing their level of debt significantly), the banks kept lending and selling, and the hedge funds and insurance companies kept buying. And then, in mid-2006, it all went sour.

© Creative Commons

FANNIE & FREDDIE
Fannie Mae (with its headquarters, seen here, in Washington, D.C.) and Freddie Mac had combined losses of almost $15 billion and required a bailout by the US government that could end up costing more than $200 billion.

House prices started to fall, interest rates began to rise, adjustable-rate mortgages were reset at higher rates, and homeowners who had been sold mortgages that they couldn't, in the long run, afford started to default on repayments. Some who found themselves with negative equity simply handed back the keys to the house. Others found the banks foreclosing on them. The mortgage-backed securities, held by just about every financial institution, lost their value dramatically, causing some institutions to become insolvent, as investors withdrew their money, and others to find themselves unable to borrow funds.

Of the five largest investment banks, one went bankrupt, two were taken over, and two received massive bailouts from the government. Fannie Mae and Freddie Mac went into receivership. The total debt of these seven institutions amounted to $9 trillion—the equivalent of two-thirds of the US GDP. The credit squeeze that followed stifled economic growth, and not just in the US, where the auto industry suffered a major crash, but around the globe.

The repeal of the Glass–Steagall Act was by no means the only factor that brought about the financial crisis, but it was certainly a major one. For anyone still under the illusion that the USA is a democracy, the process by which deregulation of the financial sector took place amply demonstrated the unhealthy relationship that exists between big business and political power—a state of affairs that has become known as corporatocracy. It wasn't a surprise to most people.

AL-QAEDA ATTACKS THE USA

September 11, 2001

MOTIVATION

Anger

Charity

Envy

Faith

Gluttony

Greed

Hope

Lust

Pride

Sloth

Main Culprits: Al-Qaeda Islamic terrorists

Damage Done: Killed 2,753 people, provoked a tide of unjustified anti-Islamic feeling, and began an era of fear and suspicion

Why: In retribution for America's economic, political, and military involvement in the Middle East

How do I respond when I see that in some Islamic countries there is vitriolic hatred for America? I'll tell you how I respond: I'm amazed. I'm amazed that there is such misunderstanding of what our country is about, that people would hate us. I am, I am—like most Americans, I just can't believe it. Because I know how good we are, and we've got to do a better job of making our case. We've got to do a better job of explaining to the people in the Middle East, for example, that we don't fight a war against Islam or Muslims. We don't hold any religion accountable. We're fighting evil. And these murderers have hijacked a great religion in order to justify their evil deeds. And we cannot let it stand.

George W. Bush

SECOND STRIKE
As smoke poured from the North Tower, and photographers and film crews trained their cameras on the disaster, the South Tower was hit by a second plane, to the horror of millions who were watching.

No one who has seen the televised footage of the collapse of the Twin Towers—and who hasn't?—can fail to have been struck by a sense of awe and horror at the enormity of the tragedy. Even those who orchestrated the world's most deadly act of terrorism must have been staggered by the sheer scale of the devastation. It was an event that reshaped the political landscape and engendered fear, suspicion, and insecurity on a global scale, but did it further the aims of Al-Qaeda or was it just a pointless act of venomous hatred?

When they were completed in December 1970 and July 1971 respectively, towers 1 and 2 of the World Trade Center were the tallest buildings in the world, dominating New York City's Lower Manhattan skyline. Each standing 110 stories high, the "Twin Towers" were largely composed of offices, many of them leased by companies involved in the financial sector. Some 50,000 people came to work in the towers every day, and more than 100,000 members of the public passed through the doors each day to visit the public spaces such as the rooftop observatories and the famous Windows On The World Restaurant on the 106th and 107th floors of the North Tower, 1 WTC. As emblems of America's economic influence in the world they were instantly recognizable icons.

At 8:46am on the clear, bright morning of Tuesday, September 11, 2001, Boeing 767 American Airlines Flight 11 from Boston to Los Angeles carrying 92 people crashed through the north face of the North Tower between the 94th and 98th floors, severing the stairwells. The fuel in the jet's wings exploded into a giant fireball that roared through the elevator shafts up and down the building and started a huge fire that engulfed the upper floors in thick, toxic smoke. People in the floors below the impact zone immediately began to evacuate the building, but those above it were trapped. Within minutes, news of the plane crash and fire were being broadcast on radio and TV, the assumption being that this was a terrible accident. Emergency vehicles were soon rushing through the streets of Manhattan toward the World Trade Center, some arriving within minutes of the collision.

At 9:03, 17 minutes after the North Tower was hit, a second Boeing 767, United Airlines Flight 175, also flying from Boston to Los Angeles, crashed into the south face of the South Tower. The plane, traveling at almost 600 mph (950 kph) and carrying 65 people, was banking hard when it struck the building, slicing into floors 77 through 85. As in 1WTC, the floors of the South Tower burst into flame. Television film crews were by now covering the incident in the North Tower, and the approach and impact of the second plane were broadcast live to a horrified audience. There was now no doubt that this was a coordinated terrorist attack.

DEATH AND DESTRUCTION

All 157 people in the two planes died instantly as the planes hit the buildings, as did people working on the floors that were struck directly. In the North Tower, the few floors above the impact zone were rapidly affected by the fire encroaching from below. Soon after the impact, people in these upper floors found themselves unable to breathe and sought fresh air at the windows, but as the fire, heat, and smoke became overwhelming, some chose to jump from the building, plunging more than 1,000 feet (300 m) to the ground below. At least 100, and probably 200, died in this way.

In the South Tower, one stairwell remained open after the impact, but rather than face the choking smoke that filled it, people on the upper floors made their way upward, hoping to be rescued from the roof of the building. However, the only doors providing access to the roof were locked, and in any case no helicopter could have landed on the roof, which was engulfed in thick smoke. Only four people chose to descend through the smoke and debris and succeeded in making their way to safety. No one on the floors above the impact zone in the North Tower would survive.

Just before 10am, less than an hour after being struck, the South Tower collapsed down on itself, its steel structure weakened by the impact of the plane and by the raging fire. Half an hour later, the North Tower crumpled. Although the lower floors in both buildings had largely been evacuated, many rescue workers had entered the towers in an attempt to save those trapped. Only 20 people who were in the buildings at the time survived the collapse of the towers. The total death toll was 2,753 individuals, including 343 New York Fire Department firefighters and 23 officers of the New York Police Department. More than 1,300 vehicles were crushed beneath the collapsed buildings, including 91 FDNY fire and emergency vehicles. The fires at "Ground Zero," as the site of the collapsed towers became known, burned for the next 99 days, and the cleanup of the site was to take eight months.

THE TERROR SPREADS

In addition to the two passenger planes that were flown into the Twin Towers on September 11, 2001, two others had been hijacked at about the same time. All four were scheduled to fly to California, and the hijackers had chosen these long-distance flights because they would be carrying the maximum amount of fuel.

American Airlines Flight 77, a Boeing 757 bound for Los Angeles, took off from Dulles, North Virginia, at 8:20am carrying six crew, and 58 passengers, including five hijackers. Half an hour into the flight the hijackers took control, forced the passengers to the back of the cabin, and turned the plane back toward Virginia. Passengers had time to call their families on cell phones and tell them what was happening. At 9:37 the plane crashed into the side of the Pentagon, killing 125 people in the building as well as everyone on the plane.

MILITARY ACTION
In response to known connections between the Taliban and Al-Qaeda, and the Taliban's refusal to hand over Osama bin Laden, the US launched Operation Enduring Freedom in Afghanistan in October 2001.

United Airlines Flight 93, a Boeing 757 bound for San Francisco, was the last of the four to take off. Carrying seven crew and 37 passengers, including four hijackers, it was scheduled to leave Newark International Airport at 8am but was delayed on the tarmac and did not take off until 8:42, just minutes before American Airlines Flight 11 struck the WTC South Tower. Three-quarters of an hour into the flight the hijackers took control. The terrorist pilot announced to the passengers that there was a bomb on board and that the flight would be returning to Newark. Over the next half hour, using cell phones, the passengers learned what had happened in New York and realized that the bomb story was a hoax and that this was a suicide mission. At 10am they bravely stormed the cockpit and the hijackers were forced to abandon their target—probably the United States Capitol or the White House, in Washington, D.C. The plane crashed instead in a field in Pennsylvania, killing everyone on board.

As it became clear that the horrific events of the morning were the result of a concerted attack by 19 hijackers (some of whom had received flying lessons in the US), suspicion immediately fell on the extremist Islamic terrorist group Al-Qaeda and the militant group's leader, Osama bin Laden, but he denied having been involved. Not until three years later did he admit responsibility, writing an open letter to the US and citing America's support for Israel and US military and political involvement in the Middle East as the reasons for the attack. The murder of almost 3,000 civilians, he said, was justified because the US is a democracy and the actions of its government are therefore approved by its people.

The attack can hardly have been expected to induce a change of policy in the US, and it certainly didn't. As evidence against Al-Qaeda and Bin Laden mounted, the US demanded that the Taliban hand over Bin Laden, which they refused to do. In response, as part of its War on Terror, the US invaded Afghanistan. The war against Iraq was also, in part, provoked by the attack on the World Trade Center. The US devoted considerable resources to tracking down Osama bin Laden, and a CIA-led military attack on his compound in Pakistan in May 2011 resulted in his death.

THE CONSEQUENCES OF 9/11

In the US and many other countries new legislation was introduced to stamp out terrorism by increasing governments' powers of intelligence gathering and sharing, arrest and detention, and monitoring and surveillance. Some of this legislation has been criticized as eroding civil rights and personal privacy, and there is no doubt that cross-border travel, especially into the US, has been made far more difficult and far more intrusive, with everyone being treated as a potential terrorist.

One of the most insidious after-effects of 9/11 has been the misguided equation of Islam with terrorism, resulting in widespread prejudice against Arabs and Muslims in many countries and leading to an increasing polarization of ideologies. Whether Al-Qaeda achieved anything that served its aims or whether the West took the time to even reflect upon the contents of Osama bin Laden's "Letter to America," the world seems a more frightening and less tolerant place as a result of that terrible day in September 2001.

MOTIVATION

Anger

Charity

Envy

Faith

Gluttony

Greed

Hope

Lust

Pride

Sloth

FAILING TO PREVENT A BLOWOUT ON THE DEEPWATER HORIZON

April 20, 2010

Main Culprits: BP, Transocean, Halliburton

Damage Done: Killed 11 men, injured 17, and released almost five million barrels of oil into the Gulf of Mexico

Why: A corporate culture that places profitability above safety

The technology, laws and regulations, and practices for containing, responding to, and cleaning up spills lag behind the real risks associated with deepwater drilling into large, high-pressure reservoirs of oil and gas located far offshore and thousands of feet below the ocean's surface. Government must close the existing gap and industry must support rather than resist that effort.

From "Report to the President" by the National Commission on the BP Deepwater Horizon Oil Spill and Offshore Drilling, January 2011

There are some disasters that result from one single and supremely bad decision, and we have seen many examples of those, but others are the consequence of a series of small acts of poor judgment that have a cumulative effect and a terrible outcome. The explosion that took place on the Deepwater Horizon oil rig in the Gulf of Mexico and the subsequent oil spill—the largest in US history—are an example of this.

The drilling of the Macondo well by BP (formerly British Petroleum), in an area of the Gulf known as Mississippi Canyon Block 252, was always going to be a challenge. To begin with, the seabed was 5,000 feet (1,500 m) below the surface of the ocean. Furthermore, it was expected that the rig would have to drill more than 20,000 feet (6,000 m) below sea level to reach the hydrocarbon-bearing rock.

The 33,000-ton Deepwater Horizon was a gigantic, semi-submersible, "dynamically positioned," mobile offshore drilling unit (MODU) that used GPS technology and thrusters to remain positioned exactly over the well no matter what the sea or weather conditions. Owned and operated by Transocean, and leased to BP at a cost of almost half a million dollars a day, it took over from another rig (which had been damaged in Hurricane Katrina) in January 2010, and its first task was to put in place a blowout preventer, or BOP, on the seabed. This is a gigantic valve that is seated on top of the well and comprises several methods of closing off the well in the event of an emergency. The BOP also provides a means of monitoring what is happening in the drill bore. Above the BOP, a large diameter tube called a well-riser extends the well up through the ocean to the rig and carries power and control lines to the BOP.

© Sculpied | Dreamstime.com

MEGA-RIG
Built at a cost of $560 million, the Deepwater Horizon caught fire after a blowout and explosion on April 20, 2010. The rig sank two days later and caused the largest US oil spill ever.

By early April of 2010, the rig had drilled to a depth of more than 18,000 feet (5,500 m) and had reached hydrocarbon-bearing rock. Drilling at these depths is a delicate balancing act. Such deep reserves of hydrocarbons, trapped in porous rock beneath an impermeable layer, are under enormous pressure and the well has to be kept at a sufficiently high pressure to prevent the gases and liquids from flowing upward through the well bore and causing an uncontrolled

MOUNTING PRESSURE

discharge, or blowout. This is done by pumping in a complex and expensive mixture, known casually as mud, that circulates down through the drill, cooling and lubricating the drill bit, and back up to the rig carrying with it the debris from the drilling operation. Further protection is afforded by the tubular metal casing that is put in place as the well is extended down through the rock. Cement is pumped into the space between the casing and the walls of the bore, and this keeps the hydrocarbons out of the well. It also protects the surrounding rock from the pressure of the drilling mud, which can cause the rock to fracture. In this event the mud is forced into the rock and less mud returns to the rig than is being pumped down, a situation known as "lost circulation." On April 9, this is precisely what happened. It is not an uncommon occurrence, and the drilling crew responded by pumping down a special liquid to seal the fracture, but it prompted BP to stop drilling and to complete the well at that depth. The next step was to install the last section of casing (the "production casing" that would allow the oil and gas to be extracted when a production rig was brought in to replace the Deepwater Horizon) and then pump down a cement foam that would be forced out of the bottom of the casing and up into the space between the casing and the surrounding rock to seal off the hydrocarbon reserves from the well. This is when the problems and the sequence of bad decisions began.

SHORT CUTS | Installing the production casing was a long job, with sections being assembled and then slowly lowered the 18,000 feet (5,500 m) to the bottom of the well. As they were assembled, centralizers had to be fitted to the casing at intervals to keep it in the center of the bore. Without these, the cement can end up "channeling" as it comes up around the casing, producing thin patches and even allowing blocks of drilling mud to remain between the rock and the casing. Now it was found that there were only six centralizers on the rig and running a computer modeling program revealed that this would be insufficient. A further 15 centralizers were ordered for immediate delivery by helicopter, but when they arrived they were found to be of the wrong type. Rather than waiting for the correct ones to be sent, the decision was taken to go with just the six that were on hand, despite the potential risk of channeling that this posed.

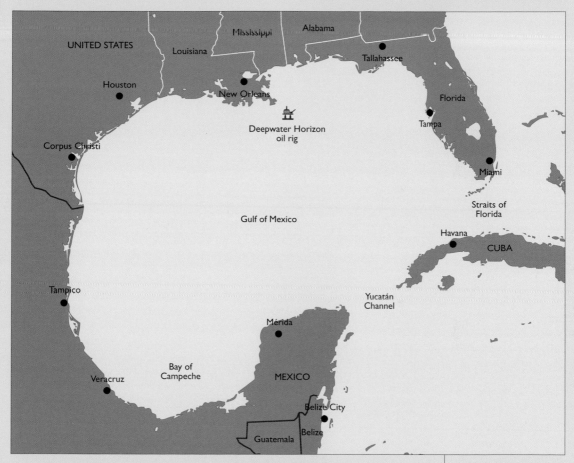

Sections continued to be added and lowered, and finally the top end of the 180-foot (55-m) length of casing was fitted with a pair of valves held open by a perforated tube that allowed the drilling mud to flow up through the casing as it was lowered. By April 19 it was in position at the well bottom.

Before the cement foam could be pumped down the casing, the tube holding the valves open had to be pushed down, allowing them to close and converting them into one-way valves that would prevent the cement from rising up the well. This was to be achieved by pumping mud down through the casing to push the perforated tube down, but despite pumping at high pressure the crew could not establish a flow of mud. After several attempts, and having raised the pressure to more

MACONDO PROSPECT

The Deepwater Horizon was drilling in some 5,000 feet (1,500 m) of water in the United States' sector of the Gulf of Mexico, about 40 miles (65 km) off the coast of Louisiana, when the explosion occurred.

than 3,000 pounds per square inch, the pressure suddenly dropped and the mud began to flow, but at a lower rate and a lower pressure than predicted. Rather than investigating these anomalies and finding the cause, the team put the low pressure reading down to a faulty gauge and concluded that the valves had successfully been converted.

Next came the cementing, the most critical part of the process in terms of preventing a blowout. Given the fragile nature of the rock structure, BP were anxious to keep pressure at the bottom of the well to a minimum, and this led to several questionable instructions being given to Halliburton, the company conducting the cementing. The first of these was not to follow the normal procedure of pumping mud through the system until material from the bottom reaches the top of the well. This practice ensures that the space between the casing and the rock is cleaned through and also allows technicians to check mud from the bottom for signs that hydrocarbons are leaking into the well. BP elected to pump down only about an eighth of the quantity of mud that would have been needed to complete the "bottom up" procedure. They also decided to pump down less cement than would have been ideal, meaning that the cement seal around the casing would extend upward far less than their own guidelines dictated, and to pump at a lower rate than normal. To compound the risk, laboratory tests conducted by Halliburton had already indicated that the particular cement/nitrogen foam that was to be used might be unstable, but this had not been brought to the attention of BP. The pumping of the cement was completed shortly after midnight on the morning of April 20, and technicians checked to see how much fluid flowed up from the casing when a valve was opened. The flow was slightly more than predicted but it then stopped and they concluded that the valves were holding and no cement was migrating back up the casing. The procedure was declared a success and, as there had been no "lost circulation" during the pumping, BP sent home a team of Schlumberger technicians who were waiting to run a series of tests to ascertain the integrity of the cement seal. Confidence was running high.

WARNING SIGNS

The crew of the Deepwater Horizon then set about completing the procedures to seal the well and remove the riser, and began by running two standard tests. The first was a "positive pressure test" that involved raising the pressure in the well to 2,500 psi and seeing whether the pressure held. It did, indicating that there was no leak from the well into the surrounding rock. They then ran a "negative pressure test," reducing the pressure in the well to zero and seeing whether it remained at zero. This is designed to check both the casing and the cement seal at the bottom of the well. If the pressure rises then hydrocarbons are leaking into the drill pipe, and only the pressure of the mud in the well bore and the riser are keeping it out. In this case, the crew were unable to even get the pressure down to zero in the first place. The lowest they could achieve was 266 psi, and the pressure jumped above 1,200 psi each time the drill pipe was closed. The team then conducted the test on another pipe, got a satisfactory result, and declared the test successful, but failed to explain why the pressure in the drill pipe was so high. The only explanation was that there was a leak at the bottom of the well, and this was ignored.

In the course of the evening the crew pumped seawater down the drill pipe and steadily forced up the mud in the well bore and the riser, retrieving it into tanks on the rig, and the pressure in the drill pipe gradually fell as the water replaced the heavier mud above it. However, just after 9pm the pressure in the drill pipe began to rise and continued to do so for the next 15 minutes. This is clear from the data logged by the monitoring systems and relayed to shore, but no one on the rig appears to have noticed what was happening. All the signs indicated that there had been a "kick," an intrusion of oil and/or gas into the well. A recorded drop in pressure at 9.39pm shows that a bubble of gas was rocketing up the casing, expanding as it rose, and a couple of minutes later workers on the rig saw drilling mud shooting out onto the rig floor. Valves in the BOP were quickly deployed but it was too late. They failed to contain the pressure, and in any case the gas was already above the BOP and coming up the riser. It blasted out of the top of the well and ignited, causing a massive explosion. Several of the rig's crew probably died in that first fireball.

One of the supervisors ran to the main control panel and activated the emergency disconnect system (EDS), which should have sheared off the drill pipe, sealed the well, and uncoupled the rig from the BOP, but none of this happened, probably because the explosion had damaged the cables from the rig to the BOP. An automatic cut-off system also failed to deploy, possibly due to poor maintenance.

A series of explosions ensued as the rig burned uncontrollably and the men and women on board scrambled to escape on lifeboats or by leaping from the decks into the ocean, being picked up by the rig's own ship, *Bankston*.

TROUBLED WATERS
The progress of the oil slick from the Deepwater Horizon was tracked using satellite imagery. The total amount of oil that leaked from the well was almost 20 times greater than the spill from the *Exxon Valdez* in 1989, and it contaminated more than 650 miles (1,000 km) of coastline.

Of the 126-person crew, 11 died that night and 16 were seriously injured. The Deepwater Horizon burned for the next 36 hours before finally sinking, ripping away the riser and starting an oil spill that released an estimated five million barrels of oil into the Gulf of Mexico and took three months to cap. The cost to BP—and potentially to Halliburton and Transocean—runs into the tens of billions. The cost to the environment and to the livelihoods of the people of the US Gulf coast is incalculable. And the blame? In its "Report to the President," the National Commission on the BP Deepwater Horizon Oil Spill and Offshore Drilling spotlights poor management and a culture of risk taking in the oil industry, as well as a lack of adequate regulation.

In the words of commission co-chair William K. Reilly:

> Our investigation shows that a series of specific and preventable human and engineering failures were the immediate causes of the disaster, but, in fact, this disaster was almost the inevitable result of years of industry and government complacency and lack of attention to safety. This was indisputably the case with BP, Transocean, and Halliburton, as well as the government agency charged with regulating offshore drilling—the former Minerals Management Service. As drilling pushes into ever deeper and riskier waters where more of America's oil lies, only systemic reforms of both government and industry will prevent a similar, future disaster.

Perhaps we should all shoulder some of the blame for humankind's unconscious "decision" to rely on an energy source whose extraction and use poses an unacceptable risk to the planet.

BUILDING NUCLEAR REACTORS ON THE COAST OF JAPAN

March 11, 2011

MOTIVATION

Anger

Charity

Envy

Faith

Gluttony

Greed

Hope

Lust

Pride

Sloth

Main Culprit: Tokyo Electric Power Company

Damage Done: Leaked significant amounts of radioactive material into the atmosphere and the ocean

Why: The Fukushima Daiichi nuclear power plant was built on the coast in an earthquake zone where it was known a major tsunami was possible

Every time we build and operate a nuclear reactor, we do so with the implicit assumption that we shall forever be able to contain the radioactive poisons we create in the reactor. In doing so, we presume that we can predict the future for centuries and millennia to come, that we can isolate and protect nuclear reactors and nuclear waste from every single catastrophe that nature and man can inflict, including earthquakes, tsunamis, volcanic eruptions, asteroids, human error, terrorism and war. History has already shown us that such assumptions are indeed both foolish and futile.

Steven Starr, "Nuclear Reactor Accidents," in "Lessons from Fukushima and Chernobyl for US Public Health, Physicians for Social Responsibility," Spring 2011

So when is hope a criminal offense? When it leads to an over-optimistic underestimate of a potentially lethal risk. The earthquake and tsunami that struck the east coast of Japan in 2011 damaged the Fukushima Daiichi nuclear reactors and their systems so badly that several explosions occurred and they released large quantities of radioactive material. Why? Well, given that a seismic event of that magnitude was a realistic possibility, the decision to build a nuclear power plant of that design in that location was clearly a bad one. Unfortunately, Fukushima is not alone.

TSUNAMI WARNING

In 2008, concerns were raised in Japan and by the International Atomic Energy Agency (IAEA) about the ability of Japan's nuclear installations to withstand a significant tsunami caused by an offshore earthquake of magnitude 7 or greater. In the same year, the Tokyo Electric Power Company (TEPCO), the owner and operator of the Fukushima Daiichi nuclear power plant, carried out a study that showed that a tsunami could reach a height of 33 feet (10.2 m), that the plant could be flooded by a tsunami greater than 28 feet (8.4 m) high, and that steps should be taken to improve protection at the site in case of such an event. Company officials regarded the probability of such a large earthquake or tsunami as insignificant and no action was taken. The report landed on the desk of the Japanese Nuclear and Industrial Safety Agency (NISA) on March 7, 2011.

On March 11, 2011, at 2:46pm, a magnitude 9 earthquake occurred 15 miles (24 km) beneath the Earth's crust, 80 miles (128 km) off the east coast of Honshu Island and 230 miles (370 km) northeast of Tokyo. The shock waves from the Great East Japan Earthquake caused 11 nuclear reactors at four sites on Japan's northeast coast to shut down automatically.

The Fukushima Daiichi power plant has six nuclear reactors. Units 4, 5, and 6 had been shut down for routine maintenance, and the fuel rods in Unit 4 had been removed and placed in the spent fuel pool. Units 1, 2, and 3, which were in operation at the time, shut down automatically, inserting the control rods into the core to slow the nuclear reaction. The earthquake cut off the external electrical power supply to the facility, but the backup diesel generators (two for each of five reactors and three for Unit 6) started up as they should and power was restored to all six units. So far, so good.

About 50 minutes after the earthquake, the first of a series of tsunamis struck the coast. It was 46 feet (14 m) high, more than twice the height of wave that the plant had been designed to withstand, and it crashed over the nuclear power plant, flooding the facility and knocking out the diesel generators in all but Unit 6. Operators managed to connect the Unit 6 generator to run Unit 5 as well, and both were now safe, but the other four were in a state known as "station blackout."

HEADING FOR MELTDOWN

Although Units 1, 2, and 3 had been shut down, each of the reactor cores contained extremely hot fuel rods and still needed to be cooled, as did the fuel rods in the spent fuel pool in Unit 4. With various safety features inoperable without an electricity supply, the temperatures in the reactor cores began to rise and the water level in each of them fell as the water evaporated, and possibly also because of fractures caused by the earthquake. Despite their courage and diligence, there was little that operatives could do to remedy the situation.

Within hours of the tsunami, the water level in Unit 1 fell below the top of the fuel rods, allowing them to heat up rapidly and damaging the core. The following day, March 12, the pressure in the reactor vessel rose and could not be vented remotely without electricity. Workers entered the reactor to vent it manually, taking an enormous risk, but an hour later there was an explosion that tore the top off the building, caused by hydrogen escaping into the reactor building from the "primary containment" around the reactor core.

BEFORE THE BLAST
When hydrogen gas that had accumulated in Unit 1 (nearest) exploded on March 12, 2011, the top half of the building was blown off. The Unit 3 building exploded two days later, followed by Unit 2 on the 15th.

At 7 in the evening the decision was taken to inject seawater into the reactor, using fire department pumping trucks, in order to cool it, despite the fact that this would do irreparable damage. Although it was not realized at the time, the core of the Unit 1 reactor had already completely melted and slumped to the bottom of the reactor vessel.

The following day, March 13, the water levels in Units 2 and 3 were causing concern, falling to the level of the top of the fuel rods. The pressure in Unit 2 was high, and it was thought that in Unit 3 there might be a partial meltdown. At 11 the next morning, the Unit 3 reactor building exploded violently, killing six workers. The explosion was heard 25 miles (40 km) away. Within hours, a large proportion of the fuel had fallen to the bottom of the reactor vessel. Meanwhile, the water level in Unit 2 had fallen further, damaging the core, and on March 15 it, too, suffered an explosion, followed shortly by a fire in Unit 4 where it was thought the water in the spent fuel pool may be boiling, raising the possibility that a nuclear chain reaction could begin.

On March 16, radiation levels at the plant rose to a dangerous level and the majority of the workers were evacuated temporarily. A range of measures was taken to try to keep the reactor cores and the spent fuel pools cool by spraying water into the reactors from fire trucks and dropping water onto the pools from helicopters, which succeeded in refilling the Unit 4 pool.

Over the next two days, high radiation levels were detected almost 20 miles (32 km) northwest of Fukushima, and the following week high levels of radioactivity were found in Tokyo's drinking water. At the plant it was discovered that water in the reactor buildings was contaminated with radioactive material, and that this contaminated water was leaking into the ocean. Over the following months, calculations of the total release of radiation showed that Fukushima Daiichi was the second most serious nuclear power plant accident after Chernobyl.

Throughout the rest of 2011, the work to render the plant safe continued, but it was not until December 16 that TEPCO and the Japanese government were able to announce that the reactors had achieved a state of cold shutdown, and in January 2012, hundreds of tons of highly radioactive water were still being discovered beneath the plant. So what had gone so horribly wrong?

FAILING TO PLAN FOR THE WORST The US Nuclear Regulatory Commission (NRC), in its earthquake engineering criteria for nuclear plants, uses the concept of the Safe Shutdown Earthquake (SSE), the vibratory ground motion for which certain structures, systems, and components must be designed to remain functional. These "structures, systems, and components" are those necessary to assure:

The integrity of the reactor coolant pressure boundary;

The capability to shut down the reactor and maintain it in a safe-shutdown condition; or

The capability to prevent or mitigate the consequences of accidents that could result in potential offsite exposures [above a specified dose].

In other words, a reactor must be designed so that, in the event of an earthquake, it doesn't lose reactor coolant, it can be shut down safely and kept that way, and it doesn't leak radioactive material into the surrounding area. Sounds reasonable enough, but the seismic events that struck in March 2011 were so far beyond the SSE that the Fukushima reactors failed on all three counts. Clearly the SSE was set too low.

The NRC regulations also state, "Seismically induced floods and water waves from either locally or distantly generated seismic activity . . . must be taken into account in the design of the nuclear power plant so as to prevent undue risk to the health and safety of the public."

The disaster has fueled the anti-nuclear debate in Japan, and in other countries around the world, and has stimulated research into other forms of renewable energy, including plans to build a wind farm off the coast of Japan.

Japanese prime minister Naoto Kan ordered one of the country's oldest reactors to be closed down, and the building of new reactors has been put on hold. He has been quoted as saying, "Japan should reduce and eventually eliminate its dependence on nuclear energy," and "If there is a risk of accidents that could make half the land mass of our country uninhabitable, then we cannot afford to take that risk."

MOTIVATION

Anger

Charity

Envy

Faith

Gluttony

Greed

Hope

Lust

Pride

Sloth

MR. WEINER'S WEINER

May–June 2011

Main Culprit: US Democratic Congressman Anthony Weiner

Damage Done: Steered his political career onto the rocks by sending lewd picture messages to women he met on Twitter—and getting caught

Why: Hard one to answer; perhaps there just wasn't enough risk in his life

Bret Baier: Is this Twitter picture in question a picture of you?

Anthony Weiner: Well, let's remember this Twitter picture in question is a hack or a prank that someone posted on my Twitter page with someone else's name in it who says she never got it and doesn't know me and I don't know her.

Interview for Fox News, June 1, 2011

To be clear, the picture was of me and I sent it. . . . In addition, over the past few years I have engaged in several inappropriate conversations conducted over Twitter, Facebook, email, and occasionally on the phone with women I have met online.

Anthony Weiner, press conference, June 6, 2011

Most of the bad decisions we've looked at have had a negative impact on people other than the decision maker—often on thousands or even millions of other people—but occasionally a bad decision is primarily self-harming. That was true in the case of Anthony Weiner, who chose to use social networking media to live a vicarious sex life with women he had never met. An accidental slip while "sexting" put a dent in his political career.

The public's gaze was first drawn to Mr. Weiner on May 28, 2011, when a message and linked photo, apparently sent from Republican Congressman Anthony Weiner's public Twitter account, were published on the Big Journalism website, run by Andrew Breitbart. The message and the link to a photo on Mr. Weiner's yfrog account (which were quickly removed, along with all the photos on his yfrog account) had been spotted by a Twitter user who took screen shots and sent them to Breibart. The photo was of a bulging pair of gray boxer briefs concealing a tumescent penis, and it had been sent to a 21-year-old female college student in Seattle. Her Twitter account had also disappeared by the time the media got hold of the story.

In the meantime, Anthony Weiner had Tweeted "Tivo shot. FB hacked. Is my blender gonna attack me next?" to let everyone know that his Facebook account (presumably he meant Twitter account) had been hacked and that an unknown someone had sent the message and the photo of an unknown person's boxer-clad erection to a woman he didn't know. To the media it was at least confirmation that the story on Big Journalism had a foundation and that the message and photo had been sent from his account.

GOING PUBLIC
Anthony Weiner, seen here using a megaphone to get his political message out to the people on the street, proved to be more reticent when it came to admitting his internet foibles.

Over the next few days, a spokesman for Mr. Weiner and Mr. Weiner himself repeatedly told the press that the account had been hacked, that there wasn't a story, and that he would like to move on, but the media doesn't work like that.

In an interview with Fox News on June 1, Weiner reiterated that his account had been hacked and that he had not sent the photo, but he was unable to say with certainty that the erection was not his, which raised the question in some minds of how an unknown person got hold of a picture of Weiner's namesake. He also told the interviewer, Bret Baier, that he had called in a lawyer and an internet security company, which begged the question of why a congressman whose social networking account had been hacked hadn't called in the FBI. The answer was not long in coming.

On June 6, Big Journalism published another picture, this time of Weiner shirtless, that had apparently been sent to another woman via Twitter, along with many other intimate photos, chats, and messages. According to Big Journalism blogger Andrew Breitbart, some of the photos sent were sexually explicit.

ACCEPTING DEFEAT

Denials really weren't going to work any more. Later that day Anthony Weiner spoke to a press conference in Manhattan and made a public apology for lying to everyone, especially his wife. He had sent the original underpants photo, it was of him, and he was very sorry. Forestalling further media revelations, he went on to admit that, "I have engaged in several inappropriate conversations conducted over Twitter, Facebook, email, and occasionally on the phone with women I have met online. I have exchanged messages and photos of an explicit nature with about six women over the last three years." Some of these inappropriate communications had taken place since his marriage less than a year earlier, but he had never met or had a physical relationship with any of the women. As Weiner saw it, he had done nothing that was illegal or that would harm the government or his role as a congressman, and he had no intention of resigning. His party saw things slightly differently.

Wednesday June 8 was a busy day for Weiner. To start with, a sexually graphic image of him appeared on a website and he was unable to deny that it was him. Then news broke that his wife was pregnant, and before the day was over a Democrat was calling for him to resign. The rest of the week just got worse, as it came to light that he had been communicating with a 17-year-old girl in Delaware, more Democrats called for his resignation, and a website published semi-nude photos of Weiner that had clearly been taken by him in the congressional gym. President Obama made Weiner's position even less tenable when, on Monday June 13, he said in an interview, "I can tell you that if it was me, I'd resign," but Weiner still didn't jump. Only after former porn star Ginger Lee gave a televised press conference in which she spoke of the messages that had passed between them, in some of which he boasted about the size of his "package," did Anthony Weiner announce, at a press conference in his New York district, that he would resign from his post. His resignation took effect on June 21—three weeks, as they say, is a very long time in politics.

In September 2011, a Republican was elected to replace him.

The "sexting" that brought his private life into the public eye and led to "Weinergate" was an accident—thinking he was using his private Twitter account, he had sent the message and link on his public account instead—but the risk that his strange internet relationships with unknown women would eventually come out was always there, potentially jeopardizing his political integrity, if not his marriage. What stands out, though, is his televised denial of any wrongdoing, in which he revealed himself to be a gifted liar, so he may yet have a glittering career in politics ahead of him.

FURTHER READING

In general, the most useful single book for any earnest student of history is a good historical atlas. The *Times Atlas of World History* is probably the best. For general reference and fact checking without expense or inconvenience, the internet is a remarkable source, and Wikipedia (www.wikipedia.org) in particular is a great starting point, although its nature as an open-source encyclopedia to which almost anyone can contribute means you should pay close attention to the references and footnotes if you want to make the most of it. You will also find some excellent links and information at www.bbc.co.uk/history.

Please note that the listings below for specific chapters are intended to be resources that will add to your understanding, rather than sources.

These listings include website addresses that may change due to the constantly evolving environment of the internet. If you find a web address that doesn't work, try using a keyword search, as the information will probably still be available online but will have moved to a different page.

Humankind Domesticates Plants and Animals

Diamond, Jared. *Guns, Germs, and Steel*. London: Penguin Books, 1999.

O'Connell, Sanjida. "Is Farming the Root of All Evil?" *The Daily Telegraph*, June 23, 2009.

Standage, Tom. *An Edible History of Humanity*. New York: Bloomsbury US, 2009.

Failing to Let God's People Go

The Holy Bible, Old Testament, The Book of Exodus, Chapters 1–14.

Greece, Persia, and Rome

For the history of these ancient civilizations, there is a wealth of information to be found at the internet Classics Archive (http://classics.mit.edu/), which contains English translations of "441 works of classical literature by 59 different authors." It is an absolute treasure trove for the works of Greek and Roman historians such as a Plutarch and Cicero, but you will also find the writings of philosophers such as Aristotle and Plato, and the great epic poets such as Homer and Virgil, as well as translations of Chinese and Persian works, including the Tao-te-Ching of Lao-tzu and the Rubaiyat of Omar Khayyam.

Another excellent site that has articles and essays on these topics is ancienthistory.about.com.

Persia Invades Greece

http://classics.mit.edu/Herodotus3history.html

Alexander the Great Pushes Too Far

http://classics.mit.edu/Plutarch/alexandr.html

Pyrrhus of Epirus Achieves Costly Victories

http://classics.mit.edu/Plutarch/pyrrhus.html

http://classics.mit.edu/Herodotus/history.html

Conspirators Murder Julius Caesar

http://classics.mit.edu/Plutarch/caesar.html

Choosing Caligula as Emperor

http://ancienthistory.about.com/

Julian "The Apostate" Rejects Christianity and Monophysitism Is Declared Heretical
The Great East–West Schism

A Short History of Byzantium, by John Julius Norwich (Penguin Books, 1998), is a wonderfully readable account of the Byzantine Empire, from its foundation in 330 CE to its conquest by the Ottoman Empire 1,123 years later. These three topics are covered in some detail and are placed in their complex historical context.

Harold Hurries to Meet William at Hastings

Bradbury, Jim. *The Battle of Hastings*. Stroud: Sutton Publishing, 2006.

The website http://www.battle1066.com traces the history of Britain from the Romans through to the Battle of Hastings.

The French Underestimate the English Archers at Agincourt

www.britishbattles.com has extensive entries on many battles in which the British have fought, including the Battles of Agincourt and Hastings.

www.eyewitnesstohistory.com/agincourt.htm includes a first-hand account of the battle by Jehan de Wavrin, who was the son of a Flemish knight fighting on the side of the French.

The Ming Dynasty Turns Its Back on the World

Sachs, Jeffrey. *The End of Poverty*. London: Penguin, 2005.

The Pope Excommunicates Martin Luther

See www.newadvent.org/cathen/07783a.htm for a fascinating explanation of what the Catholic Church believes indulgences are and are not.

The Inca Atahualpa Meets Pizarro the Conquistador

Hemming, John. *Conquest of the Inca*. London: Pan, 2004.

Robertson, William. *A General History of North and South America*. London: Mayhew, Isaac, and Co., 1834.

Henry VIII Wants a Son

http://historymedren.about.com/ has extensive articles on Henry VIII, the history of the period, and each of his wives.

Philip II of Spain Launches the Armada

www.britishbattles.com/spanish-war/spanish-armada.htm contains a wealth of detail.

Charles I's Cavalier Attitude Toward Parliament

Gregg, Pauline. *King Charles I*. Washington, D.C.: Phoenix Press, 2001.

Hibbard, Caroline M. *Charles I and the Popish Plot*. Chapel Hill: University of North Carolina Press, 1983.

Napoleon and the Louisiana Bargain-Basement Purchase

Brinkley, Alan. *The Unfinished Nation: A Concise History of the American People*. New York: McGraw-Hill Companies, Inc., 1997.

Napoleon's Second Bite at the Apple

For a very detailed account of the events that led to Napoleon's final downfall, go to http://napoleonistyka. atspace.com/Imperial_Guard_at_Waterloo.htm

British Troops Massacre Workers at "Peterloo"

Read, Donald. *Peterloo: The Massacre and its Background*. Manchester: Manchester University Press ND, 1958.

For a detailed account of the injuries sustained, see "The Tragedy at St. Peter's Field," Manchester, August 16, 1819, by J. Marrow, published in the *Journal of Accident and Emergency Medicine* 1994, vol. 11, pp. 97–100 (Google jaccidem00002-0034.pdf to find online)

Santa Anna Attacks the Alamo

Hardin, Stephen: *The Alamo 1836: Santa Anna's Texas Campaign*. Oxford: Osprey Publishing, 2001.

Britain Invades Afghanistan

Hopkirk, Peter. *The Great Game: The Struggle for Empire in Central Asia*. Kodansha International, 1992.

The Families in British India Society (FIBIS) website has links to excellent interactive maps relating to the First Afghan War: go to http://wiki.fibis.org/index. php?title=1st_Afghan_War and click on the Battle Maps Google Maps links.

Tragedy in the Valley of Death

www.britishbattles.com/crimean-war/balaclava.htm covers the Battle of Balaclava in detail, including maps and uniforms.

The Assassination of Tsar Alexander II

Mosse, W. E. *Alexander II and the Modernization of Russia*. London: English Universities Press, 1958.

Mazour, Anatole G. Princeton: *Russia: Tsarist and Communist*. D. Van Nostrand, 1962.

Austria's Mayerling Incident

Taylor, A. J. P. *The Hubsburg Monarchy, 1809–1918: A History of the Austrian Empire and Austria-Hungary*. London: Hamish Hamilton, 1948.

For the events that followed the assassination of Archduke Franz Ferdinand, see www.firstworldwar.com/origins/causes.htm

The German Navy Sinks the *Lusitania*

Many key documents are collected in the New York Times Current History; The European War, Vol 2, No. 4, July, 1915 April-September, 1915, which is available as an e-book at www.gutenberg.org/files/26377/26377-0.txt

The Treaty of Versailles

For complete details of the contents of the Treaty of Versailles, go to www.firstworldwar.com/source/versailles.htm

Stalin's First Five-Year Plan

Conquest, Robert. *The Harvest of Sorrow: Soviet Collectivization and the Terror-Famine*. Edmonton: University of Alberta Press, 1986.

Hitler Invades the Soviet Union

Rees, Laurence. *War of the Century: When Hitler Fought Stalin*. New York: The New Press, 2000.

Japan Attacks Pearl Harbor

Gillon, Steven M. *Pearl Harbor: FDR Leads the Nation Into War*. New York: Basic Books, 2011.

Britain Partitions India

James, Lawrence. *Raj: The Making and Unmaking of British India*. London: Little, Brown and Company, 1997.

France Tries to Hold on to Algeria

Aussaresses, General Paul. *The Battle of the Casbah: Terrorism and Counter-Terrorism in Algeria, 1955–1957*. New York: Enigma Books, 2003.

Evans, Martin, and John Phillips. *Algeria: anger of the dispossessed*. New Haven: Yale University Press, 2008

www.onwar.com/aced/data/alpha/algeria1954.htm

The USA and the Bay of Pigs

Kornbluh, Peter (Editor). *Bay of Pigs Declassified: The Secret CIA Report on the Invasion of Cuba*. New York: The New Press, 1998.

The website of the John F. Kennedy Presidential Library and Museum has a wealth of material, including declassified Top Secret documents concerning Cuba, Fidel Castro, and a proposal for a Cuban Freedom Brigade. Go to http://www.jfklibrary.org/JFK/JFK-in-History/The-Bay-of-Pigs.aspx

Vietnam

Herr, Michael. *Dispatches*. London: Vintage, 1991.

Baritz, Loren. *Backfire: A History of How American Culture Led Us into Vietnam and Made Us Fight the Way We Did*. Baltimore: The Johns Hopkins University Press, 1998.

Appleman, William, Thomas McCormick, Lloyd C. Gardner, and Walter LaFeber (Editors). *America in Vietnam: A Documentary History*. New York: W. Norton & Company, 1989.

Mao Zedong's Great Proletarian Cultural Revolution

Chang, Jung. *Wild Swans: Three Daughters of China*. London: Harper Perennial, 1992.

Esherick, Joseph, Paul Pickowic, Andrew Walder (Editors). *The Chinese Cultural Revolution as History*. Palo Alto: Stanford University Press, 2006.

Charles de Gaulle Faces Down the Students

Singer, Daniel. *Prelude to Revolution: France in May 1968*. Cambridge: South End Press, 2002.

Idi Amin Expels the Asian Population from Uganda

Dicklitch, Susan. "Idi Amin Dada Oumee," in *Encyclopedia of Human Rights, Volume 1*. Editor in Chief, David P. Forsythe. Oxford University Press, 2009.

For a biography of Idi Amin, see http://africanhistory. about.com/od/biography/a/bio_amin.htm

President Nixon and the Watergate Affair

Sussman, Barry. *The Great Coverup: Nixon and the Scandal of Watergate*. Market Harborough: Seven Locks, 1992. (Sussman was the city editor on *The Washington Post* at the time of Watergate.)

Argentina Invades the Falkland Islands

Smith, Gordon. *Battle Atlas of the Falklands War 1982 by Land, Sea and Air*. Cardiff: Naval-History, 2009.

Iraq Invades Kuwait

Bin, Alberto, Richard Hill, and Archer Jones. *Desert Storm: A Forgotten War*. Westport: Praeger Publishers, 1998.

Margaret Thatcher Introduces the Poll Tax

Evans, Eric J. *Thatcher and Thatcherism*. London: Routledge, 2004.

The International Community Fails to Prevent Genocide in Rwanda

Melvern, Linda. *Conspiracy to Murder: The Rwanda Genocide and the International Community*. New York: Verso, 2004.

Prunier, Gérard. *The Rwanda Crisis: History of a Genocide*. New York: Columbia University Press, 1995.

Clinton Denies Sexual Relations with Monica Lewinsky

Kuntz, Phil, and Kenneth Starr. *The Starr Report: The Starr Evidence: Complete Testimony from President Clinton and Monica Lewinsky, and Other Documents from the Independent Counsel's Investigation* (if you really want the whole story)

Massacre at Srebrenica

Burg, Steven L., and Paul S. Shoup. *The War in Bosnia-Herzegovina: Ethnic Conflict and International Intervention*. Armonk: M. E. Sharpe, 1999.

Repealing the Glass–Steagall Act

Stiglitz, Joseph E. *Freefall: America, Free Markets and the Sinking of the World Economy*. New York: W. W. Norton, 2010.

Al-Qaeda Attacks the USA

Wright, Lawrence. *The Looming Tower: Al-Qaeda's Road to 9/11*. New York: Penguin Books, 2007.

Failing to Prevent a Blowout on the Deepwater Horizon

The key document on this topic is the Report to the President by the National Commission on the BP Deepwater Horizon Oil Spill and Offshore Drilling (January 2011) entitled "Deep Water: The Gulf Oil Disaster and the Future of Offshore Drilling." It can be found online at www.oilspillcommission.gov/final-report

The *Guardian* newspaper has some very good articles, including one to be found at http://www.guardian.co.uk/environment/2011/apr/20/deepwater-horizon-key-questions-answered3

Building Nuclear Reactors on the Coast of Japan

Wikipedia is an excellent first port of call on almost any subject but in the case of the Fukushima Daiichi incident there is an exceptionally detailed timeline of the events that took place throughout 2011, together with a comprehensive list of references and links to many of the crucial reports. Take a look at http://en.wikipedia.org/wiki/Timeline_of_the_Fukushima_Daiichi_nuclear_disaster

http://enformable.com is another interesting site, with the mission of " . . . providing critical information about energy related topics for readers around the world."

Mr. Weiner's Weiner

http://bigjournalism.com

Follow links on www.tmz.com/person/anthony-weiner/